T5-CAI-048

3 2109 00850 3337

WITHDRAWN

Memphis State University Libraries
Memphis, Tennessee 38152

WITHDRAWN

CCCC

Bibliography of Composition and Rhetoric

1989

Erika Lindemann
Editor

Sandra Monroe Fleming
Associate Editor

Conference on College Composition and Communication

Southern Illinois University Press
Carbondale and Edwardsville

Copyright © 1991 by the Conference on College Composition and Communication
All rights reserved
Printed in the United States of America
Production supervised by Natalia Nadraga

ISSN 1046–0675
ISBN 0-8093-1712-5
ISBN 0-8093-1713-3 (pbk.)

The paper used in this publication meets the minimum requirements of
American National Standard for Information Sciences—Permanence
of Paper for Printed Library Materials, ANSI Z39.48-1984. ∞

Ref.
PE
1404
L 49x
1989

In memory of
Gordon T. R. Anderson,
who initiated this project

Contents

Entries that discuss concepts or hypotheses, that explain how people learn, that describe fields or
general methodologies, that examine historical developments, that review previous explanations
of a subject, or that advance conclusions drawn from empirical evidence.

Preface

Erika Lindemann

The *CCCC Bibliography of Composition and Rhetoric,* published by the Conference on College Composition and Communication, offers teachers and researchers an annual classified listing of scholarship on written English and its teaching. This volume cites 1857 titles that, with few exceptions, were published during the 1989 calendar year. The bibliography lists each work only once, but it descriptively annotates all citations, cross-references them when appropriate, and indexes all authors and editors. A group of 127 contributing bibliographers, listed on pages xiii to xiv, prepared the citations and annotations for all entries appearing in this volume.

SCOPE OF THE BIBLIOGRAPHY

The *CCCC Bibliography* includes works that treat written communication (whether the writing people do is in English or some other language), the processes whereby human beings compose and understand written messages, and methods of teaching people to communicate effectively in writing. The bibliography lists entries in five major categories (see the Contents for a fuller description of these categories):

Section 1. Bibliographies and Checklists
Section 2. Theory and Research
Section 3. Teacher Education, Administration, and Social Roles
Section 4. Curriculum
Section 5. Testing, Measurement, and Evaluation

The bibliography makes few restrictions on the format, medium, or purpose of the works it includes, so long as the subject of the work falls into one of the five categories described in the preceding list. It lists only published works: books, articles, monographs, published collections (of essays, conference presentations, or working papers), bibliographies and other reference works, films, microforms, videotapes, and sound recordings. It includes citations for unpublished doctoral dissertations appearing in *Dissertation Abstracts International.* It also includes review articles that discuss several works, define movements or trends, or survey an individual's contribution to the discipline. It excludes masters theses, textbooks, computer software, book reviews, and works written in a language other than English.

SOURCES

The *CCCC Bibliography* cites works from four major sources.

Periodicals. Journals publishing articles on composition and its teaching are the source for approximately 1000 entries. Each journal is identified by an abbreviation; an alphabetical list of Journal Abbreviations begins on page xv. With few exceptions, the contributing bibliographers preparing entries for journal articles examined the material firsthand.

Publishers. A second source of materials are commercial publishers and university presses. These publishers, whose participation in the bibliography project is voluntary, provided contributing bibliographers with written information for approximately 160 books listed in this volume. By and large, contributing bibliographers were unable to examine these materials firsthand.

This volume also includes scholarly essay collections, books that bring together essays, articles, or papers by several authors. The bibliography annotates these collections, but does not annotate each essay. Unless the annotation for a collection says otherwise, all authors contributing to the collection are listed in the Name Index.

Dissertation Abstracts International (DAI). *DAI* represents a third source for approximately 500 citations. Not all degree-granting institutions list their unpublished doctoral dissertations in *DAI*, and as a rule, the contributing bibliographers have not examined these dissertations firsthand. The citations in this volume serve only to direct readers to abstracts in *DAI*. Users will want to consult the *DAI* abstracts for additional information, including who supervised the degree candidate's work and which institution granted the degree.

Resources in Education (RIE). A fourth source of materials in the *CCCC Bibliography* is the Educational Resources Information Center

(ERIC), a federally funded document retrieval system coordinated by sixteen clearinghouses.

ERIC indexes its materials in two reference works. Journal articles appear in *Cumulative Index to Journals in Education (CIJE)*. *Resources in Education (RIE)*, on the other hand, indexes documents in the ERIC microfiche collection, which is available in 2600 regional libraries or directly from ERIC. These documents, frequently published elsewhere, include government documents, research and project reports, bibliographies, and conference papers. Documents indexed in *RIE* receive a six-digit "ED" number (e.g., ERIC ED 305 701) and are cross-referenced under various subject headings or "descriptors."

Some documents may be listed in *RIE* and may become available through ERIC several years after they were written. For convenience and to ensure comprehensiveness, the *CCCC Bibliography* reports ERIC documents cited in *RIE* during the years covered in the current volume; that is, this volume cites over 150 ERIC documents listed in *RIE* in 1989, even though the works themselves may have an earlier "date of publication." Also as a convenience, each ERIC entry includes the six-digit "ED" number.

Contributing bibliographers working with ERIC materials have developed the following criteria for determining what documents to include in this volume:

Substantiveness. Substantive documents of general value to college composition teachers and researchers are included. Representative publications are curriculum guides, federal government final reports, and technical reports from various publication series, such as those published, for example, by the Center for the Study of Writing and the University of Illinois Center for the Study of Reading.

Relevance. Documents that seem to represent concerns of high interest to researchers are included. The topics of functional literacy, computer-assisted instruction, and revision, for example, represent concerns of greater relevance than the teaching of handwriting.

Inclusiveness. All papers on composition and rhetoric available in ERIC and delivered at the annual meetings of the Conference on College

Composition and Communication (CCCC) and the National Council of Teachers of English (NCTE—Fall and Spring conventions) are included. Papers delivered at other regional and national meetings—for example, meetings of the American Educational Research Association (AERA), the International Reading Association (IRA), and the Modern Language Association (MLA)—are selected for inclusion on the basis of their substantiveness and relevance.

Reference value. Items for which the ERIC microfiche system might provide unique access are included. Representative of entries meeting this criterion would be books or collections of articles no longer available from their original publishers.

Alternate access. Many professional organizations regularly make copies of book and monograph publications available as ERIC microfiche. And many papers presented as reports or conference talks and available in ERIC are later published as monographs or as articles in journals. When such information is available, the entry in this volume will include ERIC ED numbers to indicate an alternate source of access to the document. However, users of this volume should keep in mind that, although a book in ERIC reflects the exact contents of the published work, an article in ERIC is a manuscript that may see substantial revision before it is published.

The following criteria determine which items cited in *RIE* are excluded from this volume:

Communication theory. ERIC documents broadly concerned with human communication or with language study in general, rather than with college composition and rhetoric, are routinely excluded.

Local interest. ERIC documents concerned with composition and rhetoric but judged to be primarily of local interest are excluded. For example, this volume omits annual evaluation reports of writing programs in local schools.

Availability. Publications of commercial publishers and other organizations that are listed in *RIE* and assigned an ERIC ED number but are not available through the ERIC microfiche system are omitted.

Users of the *CCCC Bibliography* may wish to supplement this resource by consulting *RIE*

or various computer-assisted retrieval systems that access ERIC documents. Copies of most documents indexed in *RIE* can be purchased in paper or microform from the ERIC system. ERIC clearinghouses also make available free or inexpensive guides to special topics of interest to rhetoric and composition teachers and researchers. Order forms and current addresses for these clearinghouses appear at the back of each monthly issue of *RIE*.

A few entries in this volume show publication dates earlier than 1989. By and large, these materials have two sources. They represent articles published in 1989 but appearing in journals showing earlier volume numbers, or they represent materials accessioned by ERIC clearinghouses in 1989 but originally published earlier.

Authors, publishers, and editors may send offprints of articles, copies of books and journals, or microforms to me for possible inclusion in the *CCCC Bibliography;* however, I will be unable to return them.

The items listed in the annual bibliography are not housed in any single location or owned by any single individual. The *CCCC Bibliography* lists and describes these materials but does not provide users of the bibliography any additional means of retrieving them. However, users of this volume will find librarians extremely helpful in finding copies of particular works to examine firsthand. Some materials may be available through interlibrary loan, OCLC and on-line catalogues, ERIC and other information retrieval systems, or in state and university libraries. To locate materials cited in this volume, ask your librarian to help you.

CONTRIBUTING BIBLIOGRAPHERS

The reliability and usefulness of these annual volumes depend primarily on a large group of contributing bibliographers. Contributing bibliographers accept responsibility for compiling accurate entries in their areas of expertise, for preparing brief, descriptive annotations for each entry, for determining where each entry will appear within one of the five sections of the bibliography, for cross-referencing entries when appropriate, and for submitting completed entries by a specified deadline.

To ensure consistency, contributing bibliographers receive a *Handbook for Contributing Bibliographers* to guide them in their work and fill out a printed form for each entry. Contributing bibliographers agree to serve a three-year term and, thereafter, may request reappointment for another two-year term. In return for their valuable service to the profession, they receive a copy of each annual volume they have helped to prepare. Graduate students, teachers, researchers, or other individuals who wish to become contributing bibliographers may write to me.

ceives an "entry number" so that cross-references to other sections are possible. Cross-references are necessary because much scholarship in composition and rhetoric is interdisciplinary. Cross-references appear as a listing of entry numbers preceded by "See also," found at the end of each subsection of the bibliography.

The Subject Index lists most of the topics discussed in the works cited in this volume. Consulting the Subject Index may help users locate sections and subsections of the bibliography that contain large numbers of entries addressing the same topic.

The Name Index lists all authors, editors, and contributors to publications cited in this volume.

ANNOTATIONS

Annotations accompany all entries in this volume. They describe the document's contents and are intended to help users determine the document's usefulness. Annotations are brief and, insofar as the English language allows, are meant to be descriptive, not evaluative. They explain what the work is about but leave readers free to judge for themselves the work's merits. Most annotations fall into one of three categories: they present the document's thesis, main argument, or major research finding; they describe the work's major organizational divisions; or they indicate the purpose or scope of the work.

CROSS-REFERENCES AND INDEXES

This volume cites and annotates each document only once, in one of the five major sections of the bibliography. Every entry, however, re-

ACKNOWLEDGMENTS

A publication of this scope depends on many people, especially the contributing bibliographers, whose conscientious work represents a significant contribution to the profession. I am also grateful to the CCCC officers, CCCC Executive Committee members, and colleagues in the profession whose support have made this project possible. The Department of English at the University of North Carolina—Chapel Hill offered generous and welcome financial support. Larry Mason provided important technical help in computer programming. Sandra Monroe Fleming, an invaluable associate editor, devoted an important summer of her life to preparing this volume. Finally, my thanks to Kenney Withers, Susan Wilson, and Robyn Laur Clark of Southern Illinois University Press for their sound editorial advice and their extraordinary commitment to publishing books important to the profession.

Contributing Bibliographers

Jim Addison
Clara Alexander
J. D. Applen
Ken Autry
Brenda Barrett
Richard Behm
Laurel Black
Virginia A. Book
Robert Broad
Jody Brown
Lady Falls Brown
Stuart Brown
Mary Louise Buley-Meissner
Barbara Cambridge
Lee Campbell
Gary Caret
Cora Castaldi
Gregory Clark
John Clifford
Joseph Colavito
Rick Cypert
Donald A. Daiker
Thomas E. Dasher
Kenneth W. Davis
Bonnie Devet

Judith Dobler
William M. Dodd
Robert Donahoo
Suellynn Duffey
Chuck Etheridge
Timothy J. Evans
Marisa Farnum
Janis Forman
Richard Fulkerson
Patricia Goubil Gambrell
Roger Gilles
Beate Gilliar
Joan I. Glazer
Judith Goleman
Gwendolyn Gong
Alice Goodwin
Barbara Griffin
C. W. Griffin
Evonne Kay Halasek
Kathy Haney
Jim Hanlon
Kristine Hansen
Jeanette Harris
Sarah E. Harrold
Patrick Hartwell

Karen Hayes
Malcolm Hayward
Cozette Heller
John F. Heyda
Dona Hickey
Dixie Elise Hickman
Betsy Hilbert
JaneE Hindman
Deborah H. Holdstein
Sylvia A. Holladay
Stacy Hooks
Elizabeth Huettman
Jack Jobst
Johndan Johnson-Eilola
Patricia Kedzerski
Joyce Kinkead
James Kinney
Alexandra R. Krapels
Elizabeth Larsen
Janice M. Lauer
Naton Leslie
Maggy Lindgren
Steven Lynn
Kate Mangelsdorf
Stefan E. Martin

Judy Massey
Matt Matcuk
Donald A. McAndrew
Geraldine McNenny
Stephen Merrill
Vincent P. Mikkelsen
Corinne L. Miller
Max Morenberg
Kathleen V. Murphy
Neil Nakadate
Terence Odlin
Peggy Parris
Michael A. Pemberton
Elizabeth F. Penfield
Pamela Pittman
Virginia G. Polanski
Deborah L. Pope
James Postema

John W. Presley
Paul W. Ranieri
Diane Rawlings
Rebecca Rickly
Duane Roen
Audrey J. Roth
Judith Scheffler
Cynthia L. Selfe
Yolan Shetty
Barbara M. Sitko
Betsy Smith
Penelope Smith
Susan R. Smith
Barbara Stedman
Gail Stygall
Patricia Sullivan
Dan J. Tannacito
Josephine K. Tarvers

Nathaniel Teich
Myron Tuman
Rex Veeder
Billie J. Wahlstrom
Keith Walters
Sarah Watke
Robert H. Weiss
James D. Williams
David E. Wilson
Steven Wolfel
J. Randal Woodland
Mindy Wright
William Wright
George Xu
Janet Ziegler
Valerie Zimbaro

Journal
Abbreviations

Contributing bibliographers reviewed the journals listed below in preparing entries for this volume. Entries for journal articles cited in this volume will include an abbreviation identifying the journal or serial in which it was published.

A&E	Anthropology and Education Quarterly	CAC	Computer-Assisted Composition Journal
AdEd	Adult Education	CalE	California English
AdLBEd	Adult Literacy and Basic Education	CC	Computers and Composition
		CCC	College Composition and Communication
AERJ	American Educational Research Journal	CCR	Community College Review
AM	Academic Medicine	CCrit	Cultural Critique
AmA	American Anthropologist	CE	College English
AmE	American Ethnologist	CEAC	CEA Critic
AmP	American Psychologist	CEAF	CEA Forum
ArEB	Arizona English Bulletin	CHE	Chronicle of Higher Education
AS	American Speech	CHum	Computers and the Humanities
ASch	The American Scholar	CI	Cognition and Instruction
		CJL	Canadian Journal of Linguistics
BABC	Bulletin of the Association for Business Communication	CLAJ	College Language Association Journal
BADE	Bulletin of the Association of Departments of English	Cognition	Cognition
		CollL	College Literature
BL	Brain and Language	CollM	Collegiate Microcomputer
Boundary	Boundary 2	CollT	College Teaching
BRMMLA	Rocky Mountain Review of Language and Literature	ComEd	Communication Education
		ComM	Communication Monographs

CompC	Composition Chronicle		Management
CompEd	Computers and Education	IRAL	International Review of Applied
ComQ	Communication Quarterly		Linguistics in Language
ComR	Communication Research		Teaching
ComS	Communication Studies	Issues	Issues in Writing
CPsy	Cognitive Psychology		
CritI	Critical Inquiry	JAC	Journal of Advanced
CSc	Cognitive Science		Composition
CSWQ	Center for the Study of Writing	JAF	Journal of American Folklore
	Quarterly	JBC	Journal of Business
			Communication
Daedalus	Daedalus: Journal of the	JBS	Journal of Black Studies
	American Academy of Arts and	JBTC	Iowa State Journal of Business
	Sciences		and Technical Communication
DAI	Dissertation Abstracts	JBW	Journal of Basic Writing
	International	JC	Journal of Communication
DP	Developmental Psychology	JCBI	Journal of Computer-Based
DPr	Discourse Processes		Instruction
EdM	Educational Measurement: Issues	JCS	Journal of Curriculum Studies
	and Practice	JCST	Journal of College Science
EdPsy	Educational Psychologist		Teaching
EEd	English Education	JDEd	Journal of Developmental
ELT	English Language Teaching		Education
	Journal	JEdM	Journal of Educational
EnEd	Engineering Education		Measurement
EngR	English Record	JEdP	Journal of Educational
EngT	English Today		Psychology
EQ	English Quarterly	JEdR	Journal of Educational Research
ESP	English for Specific Purposes	JEngL	Journal of English Linguistics
ET	English in Texas	JEPG	Journal of Experimental
ETC	ETC: A Review of General		Psychology: General
	Semantics	JEPH	Journal of Experimental
ExES	Explorations in Ethnic Studies		Psychology: Human Perception
ExEx	Exercise Exchange		and Performance
		JEPL	Journal of Experimental
FEN	Freshman English News		Psychology: Learning, Memory,
FLA	Foreign Language Annals		Cognition
Focuses	Focuses	JFR	Journal of Folklore Research
FS	Feminist Studies	JGE	JGE: The Journal of General
			Education
GR	Georgia Review	JL	Journal of Linguistics
HCR	Human Communication Research	JLD	Journal of Learning Disabilities
HD	Human Development	JML	Journal of Memory and
HER	Harvard Educational Review		Language
HT	History Teacher	JNT	Journal of Narrative Technique
IE	Indiana English	JourEd	Journalism Educator
IL	Informal Logic	JPsy	Journal of Psychology
IlEB	Illinois English Bulletin	JPsyR	Journal of Psycholinguistic
Intell	Intelligence		Research
IPM	Information Processing and	JR	Journal of Reading

JT	Journal of Thought	Raritan	Raritan
JTEd	Journal of Teacher Education	Reader	Reader
JTW	Journal of Teaching Writing	RER	Review of Educational
JTWC	Journal of Technical Writing and Communication		Research
		Rhetorica	Rhetorica
		RIE	Resources in Education
L&M	Literature and Medicine	RR	Rhetoric Review
L&S	Language and Speech	RRQ	Reading Research Quarterly
Lang	Language	RSQ	Rhetoric Society Quarterly
Lang&S	Language and Style	RTE	Research in the Teaching of
LangS	Language Sciences		English
Leaflet	The Leaflet	RW	Reading and Writing: An
Learning	Learning		Interdisciplinary Journal
Ling	Linguistics		
LSoc	Language in Society	SAF	Studies in American Fiction
		SAm	Scientific American
M&C	Memory and Cognition	SCJ	Southern Communication
MCQ	Management Communication Quarterly		Journal
		SCL	Studies in Canadian Literature
MEd	Medical Education	SFS	Science Fiction Studies
MissQ	Mississippi Quarterly	SHum	Studies in the Humanities
MLJ	The Modern Language Journal	SLang	Studies in Language
MLQ	Modern Language Quarterly	SNNTS	Studies in the Novel
MLS	Modern Language Studies	ST	Science Teacher
MM	Media and Methods	Style	Style
MSE	Massachusetts Studies in English	SubStance	SubStance
MT	Mathematics Teacher	TC	Technical Communication
		TESOLQ	Teachers of English to Speakers of Other Languages Quarterly
NYRB	The New York Review of Books	TETYC	Teaching English in the Two-Year College
OralH	Oral History Review	TWM	Teachers and Writers of Magazines
P&L	Philosophy and Literature	TWT	Technical Writing Teacher
P&R	Philosophy and Rhetoric		
PhiDK	Phi Delta Kappan	UEJ	Utah English Journal
PhS	Philosophical Studies		
PMLA	Publication of the Modern Language Association	V&R	Visions and Revisions
		VLang	Visible Language
PMS	Perceptual and Motor Skills	WC	Written Communication
PPR	Philosophy and Phenomenological Research	WCJ	Writing Center Journal
		WE	Writing on the Edge
PR	Partisan Reivew	WI	Writing Instructor
Pre/Text	Pre/Text	WJSC	Western Journal of Speech Communication
PsyR	Psychological Review		
PsyT	Psychology Today	WLN	Writing Lab Newsletter
PT	Poetics Today	WLWE	World Literature Written in English
		WPA	Journal of the Council of Writing Program Administrators
QJS	Quarterly Journal of Speech		
QRD	Quarterly Review of Doublespeak	Writer	The Writer
		WS	Women's Studies

Abbreviations in Entries

ABC	Association for Business Communication	ERIC/RCS	ERIC Clearinghouse on Reading and Communication Skills
ABE	Adult Basic Education	ESL	English as a Second Language
ACT	American College Test	ESP	English for Specific Purposes
ACTFL	American Council on the Teaching of Foreign Languages	EST	English for Science and Technology
ADE	Association of Departments of English	ETS	Educational Testing Service
		FIPSE	Fund for the Improvement of Postsecondary Education
AERA	American Educational Research Association	GED	General Education Development
AP	Advanced Placement	GPA	Grade Point Average
CAI	Computer-Assisted Instruction	GRE	Graduate Record Examination
CCCC	Conference on College Composition and Communication	IRA	International Reading Association
		LEP	Limited English Proficiency
CEE	Conference on English Education	LES	Limited English Speaking
CSW	Center for the Study of Writing	L1	First Language
EDRS	ERIC Document Reproduction Service	L2	Second Language
		MCAT	Medical College Admission Test
EFL	English as a Foreign Language		
ERIC	Educational Resources Information Center	MLA	Modern Language Association
		NAEP	National Assessment of Educational Progress
ERIC/AIR	ERIC Clearinghouse on Tests, Measurement, and Evaluation	NCTE	National Council of Teachers of English
ERIC/FLL	ERIC Clearinghouse on Language and Linguistics	NEA	National Education Association

NEH	National Endowment for the Humanities	TESOL	Teachers of English to Speakers of Other Languages
NIE	National Institute of Education	TOEFL	Test of English as a Foreign Language
NIH	National Institute of Health		
OCLC	Online Computer Library Center	TSWE	Test of Standard Written English
SAT	Scholastic Aptitude Test	WPA	Council of Writing Program Administrators
SCA	Speech Communication Association		
SLATE	Support for the Learning and Teaching of English		

1

Bibliographies and Checklists

1 BIBLIOGRAPHIES AND CHECKLISTS

1. *Bibliographic Guide to Education: 1988.* Boston: G. K. Hall, 1989.

   Lists material recorded on the OCLC tapes of Columbia University Teachers College during the year, supplemented by listings from the New York Public Library for selected publications. Covers all aspects of education, including composition pedagogy.

2. Bishop, Wendy, Steve Bailey, Scott Herzer, Carolyn Krammers, Tracie Melnick, Peg Pooples, Jill Robinson, and Terry Wike. *Teaching Creative Writing: A Selective, Annotated Bibliography.* Bloomington, Ind.: ERIC/RCS, 1989. ERIC ED 307 634. 32 pages

   Contains 147 annotated items, focusing on pedagogical issues.

3. Chapman, David W. "Checklist of Recent Writing Center Scholarship: April 1988– March 1989." *WCJ* 10 (Fall-Winter 1989): 53–58.

   Cites a year's scholarship on writing centers.

4. Davis, Ken. "Hypertext for Business Communication: An Introduction and Bibliography." *BABC* 52 (December 1989): 20–22.

   Defines hypertext, discusses its implications for business communicators, and presents an annotated bibliography of sources on hypertext.

5. Durst, Russel K., and James D. Marshall. "Bibliography of Research in the Teaching of English." *RTE* 23 (May 1989): 208–222.

   Abstracts of articles, papers, and dissertations from 1987 and 1988. Main headings include writing, language, literature, and teacher education.

6. Durst, Russel K., and James D. Marshall. "Bibliography of Research in the Teaching of English." *RTE* 23 (December 1989): 424–442.

Abstracts of articles, papers, and dissertations from 1987 through 1989. Main headings include writing, language, literature, and teacher education.

7. Eppele, Ruth. *Ethnography and Personal Narrative: Uses in Education*. Focused Access to Selected Topics Bibliography, no. 20. Bloomington, Ind.: ERIC/RCS, 1989. ERIC ED 307 569. 5 pages

Contains 27 items reflecting conflicting opinions on the appropriateness of using ethnography and personal narratives to describe classroom research.

8. Greene, Beth G. "A Brief Overview of the ERIC Clearinghouse on Reading and Communication Skills." *BABC* 52 (June 1989): 42–44.

Describes the scope, publications, and products of ERIC/RCS. Includes information on how users may become involved in ERIC/RCS.

9. Greene, Beth G. "ERIC: Computer Technology and Business Communication." *BABC* 52 (December 1989): 36–39.

A bibliography from the ERIC database on desktop publishing, computer-assisted writing instruction, and resources for teaching.

10. *Higher Order Thinking Skills: A Catalog of Products, Publications, and Services*. Research Triangle Park, N.C.: Southeastern Educational Improvement Laboratory, 1989. ERIC ED 303 784. 17 pages

Offers a bibliography of 31 products available from federal sources.

11. Horner, Winifred Bryan. "Nineteenth-Century Rhetoric at the University of Edinburgh with an Annotated Bibliography of Archival Materials." *RSQ* 19 (Fall 1989): 365–376.

Descriptively annotates archival students' notes of professors' lectures housed at Edinburgh University Library, Glasgow University Library, and the National Library of Scotland.

12. Houlette, Forrest. *Nineteenth-Century Rhetoric: An Enumerative Bibliography*. New York: Garland, 1988. 308 pages

Cites 3932 English-language articles, books, and chapters on rhetoric, composition, grammar, writing, and the teaching of English between 1800 and 1920.

13. Jensen, J. Vernon. "Bibliography of Argumentation." *RSQ* 19 (Winter 1989): 71–82.

An unannotated listing of books, chapters, articles, essays, and bibliographic aids.

14. Jobe, Linda G. "Office Machines in the Writing Class: A Bibliographical Essay." *TETYC* 16 (October 1989): 179–185.

Urges business and technical writing teachers to familiarize students with modern equipment. Includes bibliography.

15. Keeler, Heather E. "Portrait of a Technical Writer: An Annotated Bibliography." *JTWC* 19 (1989): 297–303.

Summarizes 16 current articles, each of which "describes and humanizes the technical writer—the skills they value, products they produce, roles they play, or industries they serve."

16. Kitao, Kenji, and S. Kathleen Kitao. *Intercultural Communication Bibliography, Part 4*. Washington, D.C.: ERIC/FLL, 1988. ERIC ED 304 001. 48 pages

Offers the fourth part of a continuing bibliography, citing 480 books, articles, and reports. See also ERIC ED 273 125 and ERIC ED 282 271.

17. McBride, Donald. "Rhetorical Studies of Television News: A Bibliography." *RSQ* 19 (Fall 1989): 389–392.

Lists 57 entries dealing with rhetorical issues in broadcasting.

18. McCleary, Bill. "Start-Up of Five New Professional Book Series in Composition a Sign of Growth in the Profession." *CompC* 2 (December 1989): 1–3.

Discusses the aims and gives the titles of series published by both academic and commercial publishers.

19. Moran, Michael G., and Debra Journet, eds. *Research in Technical Communication: A Bibliographic Sourcebook*. Westport, Conn.: Greenwood Press, 1985. 515 pages

A collection of 15 bibliographic essays arranged in four sections: A Theoretical Examination of Technical Communication; Technical Communication and Rhetorical Concerns; Specific Types of Technical Communication; and Related Concerns and Specialized Forms of Technical Communication. Appendixes survey textbooks, style manuals, and the technical writing profession.

20. "New Professional Books." *CompC* 2 (December 1989): 7, 12.

Annotates nine entries.

21. "1988 ATTW Bibliography." *TWT* 16 (Fall 1989): 251–277.

Lists citations in eight categories, including bibliographies, books, reviews, the profession, theory and philosophy, research, pedagogy, and communication in the profession.

22. Payne, Melinda A., Suzanne M. Ratchford, and Lillian N. Wooley. "Richard M. Weaver: A Bibliographical Essay." *RSQ* 19 (Fall 1989): 327–332.

Surveys primary and secondary works.

23. Peyton, Joy Kreeft. "Computer Networks for Real-Time Written Interaction in the Writing Classroom: An Annotated Bibliography." *CC* 6 (August 1989): 105–122.

Annotates entries for journals, articles, chapters of books, research reports, and resource guides.

24. "Professional Books for Writing Teachers: 1988–1989." *CompC* 2 (April 1989): 8–10.

An annotated, partially categorized list of 40 books.

25. Rasnak, Mary Ann, Carol A. Auer, Susan Davis, Mary R. Debates, Renee McDougall, Teresa Marie Serio, and Norman A. Stahl. *Comparative Reading: An Annotated Bibliography*. College Reading and Learning Assistance Technical Report, no. 88–05. Alexandria, Va.: EDRS, 1989. ERIC ED 307 586. 65 pages

Contains 188 annotated items on reading in various countries, addressed from various philosophical and pedagogical viewpoints.

26. Schack, Edna O., and Markham B. Schack. "Guide to On-Line Databases for Higher Education." *CollM* 7 (February 1989): 19–26.

Reviews hardware and software requirements, interactive search techniques, and costs for information searches. Abstracts eight information services of interest to colleges.

27. Shermis, Michael. *Adult Literacy: Instructional Strategies*. Focused Access to Selected Topics Bibliography, no. 32. Bloomington, Ind.: ERIC/RCS, 1989. ERIC ED 307 579. 6 pages

Annotates 36 items accessioned by ERIC from 1987 to 1989.

28. Shermis, Michael. *Adult Literacy: Overview, Programs, and Research*. Focused Access to Selected Topics Bibliography, no. 31. Bloomington, Ind.: ERIC/RCS, 1989. ERIC ED 307 578. 6 pages

Annotates 34 items accessioned by ERIC from 1987 to 1989.

29. Shermis, Michael. "Using Word Processing for Writing Instruction: Basic Writers and Learning-Disabled Students." *CompC* 2 (November 1989): 8–9.

Cites six sources with abstracts.

30. Sides, Charles H., ed. *Technical and Business Communication: Bibliographic Essays for Teachers and Corporate Trainers*. Urbana, Ill.: NCTE and Society for Technical Communication, 1989. 360 pages

Seventeen essays in two sections. "Issues and Abilities in Technical Communication" examines such areas as ethics, rhetoric, style, and theories of communication. Essays in the second section discuss several genres, including proposals, computer documentation, memos, and advertising.

31. Stahl, Norman A., Cynthia R. Hynd, and William G. Brozo. *The Development and Validation of a Comprehensive List of Primary Sources in College Reading Instruction*. College Reading and Learning Assistance Technical Report, no. 88-03. Bloomington, Ind.: ERIC/RCS, 1989. ERIC ED 307 597. 60 pages

    Lists 593 items. Covers material used in college reading and study skills instruction from 1896 to 1987.

32. *Technical and Business Communication: Bibliographic Essays for Teachers and Cor-*

porate Trainers. Washington, D.C.: Society for Technical Communication, 1989. 360 pages

    Collects essays about reading, ethics, visual representation, interpersonal communication, consulting, presentations, annual reports, brochures, newsletters, proposals, and computer documentation as they relate to technical and business communication. Authors are not indexed separately in this volume.

33. Wolff, William C. "Annotated Bibliography of Scholarship on Writing Centers and Related Topics, 1987–1988." *Focuses* 2 (Spring 1989): 27–55.

    Lists 176 entries, including books, collected essays, and journal entries.

See also 633, 880, 948, 1110, 1159, 1195, 1315

2
Theory and Research

2.1 RHETORICAL THEORY, DISCOURSE THEORY, AND COMPOSING

34. Agee, Anne S. "The Concept of Audience as a Tool for Composing and Interpreting Texts." *DAI* 50 (November 1989): 1307A.

Traces the development of audience theory in rhetoric and accounts for the absence of audience as a factor in contemporary composition classrooms.

35. Ahlstrom, Amber Dahlin. "Not So Easily Defined: Notes from a Natural-Process Expressionist Vitalist Process-Person Practitioner." Paper presented at the CCCC Convention, Seattle, March 1989. ERIC ED 304 687. 15 pages

Claims that the categories North, Berlin, and Hillocks use in recent books oversimplify and distort work in composition theory and research.

36. Anderson, Matthew Paul. "The Transfer and Declarative Representation of Procedural Knowledge." *DAI* 50 (July 1989): 361B.

Investigates the effect of expert procedural knowledge on the declarative representation of sentences that correspond to an expert's own or to another expert's cognitive procedure.

37. Antczak, Frederick J. "Teaching Rhetoric and Teaching Morality: Some Problems and Possibilities of Ethical Criticism." *RSQ* 19 (Winter 1989): 15–22.

Discusses ethical criticism and the teacher's role in developing a student's *ethos*.

38. Balester, Valerie M. "The Social Construction of *Ethos:* A Study of the Spoken and Written Discourse of Two Black College Students." *DAI* 49 (May 1989): 3348A.

Examines *ethos* in the spoken and written discourse of two black college students interacting with a white researcher and their black same-sex peers.

39. Banerjee, Abhijit Vinayak. "Essays on Information Economics." *DAI* 50 (August 1989): 514A.

Three essays on the theme of the macroeconomic implications of informational imperfections.

40. Baumlin, James S., and Tita French Baumlin. "*Psyche/Logos:* Mapping the Terrains of Mind and Rhetoric." *CE* 51 (March 1989): 245–261.

Argues that psychology "describes the workings of human rhetoric." Advocates expanding the current definition of rhetoric to include iatrology, thereby reincluding the feminine voice.

41. Bazerman, Charles. "What Are We Doing as a Research Community?" *RR* 7 (Spring 1989): 223–293.

Reports on a symposium held during the 1988 CCCC Annual Convention. Explains research methods used to study writing, contrasts their similarities and differences, and proposes further research.

42. Beach, Richard, and Mark Christensen. "Discourse Conventions in Academic Response Journals." Paper presented at the CCCC Convention, Seattle, March 1989. ERIC ED 304 691. 22 pages

Investigates the relationship between learning and academic journal writing, examining some features of journal entries and characteristics of students.

43. Beard, John D., David L. Williams, and Stephen Doheny-Farina. "Directions and Issues in Technical Communication Research." *TC* 36 (August 1989): 188–194.

Summarizes results of a survey conducted at a forum for practitioners and academicians interested in research.

44. Beauvais, Paul J. "A Speech-Act Theory of Metadiscourse." *WC* 6 (January 1989): 11–30.

Criticizes earlier discussions of metadiscourse by Harris, Crismore, Williams, and Vande Kopple. Offers definitions of metadiscourse and discusses its functions and forms in terms of speech-act theory.

45. Berger, Charles, Susan Karol, and Jerry Jordan. "When a Lot of Knowledge Is a Dangerous Thing: The Debilitating Effects of Plan Complexity on Verbal Fluency." *HCR* 16 (Fall 1989): 91–119.

Three experiments examine the relationships among plan complexity, access to planned actions, and verbal fluency while pursuing an oral persuasive goal with a dissenting partner.

46. Berkenkotter, Carol. "The Legacy of Positivism in Empirical Composition Research." *JAC* 9 (1989): 69–82.

Pleads for an understanding ecumenism about research paradigms. The fear of a positivist hegemony felt by many hermeneutically oriented scholars reveals an epistemological ethnocentricity.

47. Berthoff, Ann E. "Counter Response [to Harkin, Schilb, and Swearingen, *Pre/Text* 9 (Spring-Summer 1988)]." *Pre/Text* 9 (Spring-Summer 1988): 83–90.

Accepts Schilb's inclusion of politics, rejects Harkin's narratives, and elaborates on Swearingen's comparative reading of her early and current work.

48. Berthoff, Ann E. "How Philosophy Can Help Us." *Pre/Text* 9 (Spring-Summer 1988): 61–66.

Argues that philosophy allows composition scholars to "account for meaning" and to give "accounts of meaning," rejecting neopragmatism and neohistoricism as "gangster" theories.

49. Biesecker, Barbara A. "Rethinking the Rhetorical Situation from within the Thematic of Differance." *P&R* 22 (1989): 110–130.

Proposes a rethinking of the rhetorical situation, challenging notions circumscribing the power of rhetoric. Asks how insights of deconstruction can help in explaining and comprehending rhetorical events.

50. Biesecker, Barbara Ann. "Kenneth Burke's *A Grammar of Motives, A Rhetoric of Motives,* and *The Rhetoric of Religion:* Towards

an Ontology of Individual and Collective Action." *DAI* 50 (December 1989): 1481A.

Rereads Burke's work, seeing textual discrepancies as productive of supplementary readings and of deeper insights into the political aspects of Burke's dramatism and logology.

51. Bitner, Maria. "Canonical and Noncanonical Argument Expressions." *DAI* 49 (May 1989): 3348A.

Proposes a classification scheme to make predictions about default and scope in argument expressions of verbs.

52. Black, Kathleen. "Audience Analysis and Persuasive Writing at the College Level." *RTE* 23 (October 1989): 231–253.

A two-part study reports that three of four variables predicted over half the variance in the overall persuasiveness of essays. Audience awareness affected three outcome variables.

53. Bliese, John. "The Conservative Rhetoric of Richard Weaver: Theory and Practice." *SCJ* 54 (Summer 1989): 401–421.

Outlines Weaver's theory of arguments, contrasting his theory with the kinds of arguments he himself used.

54. Bliese, John. "Richard M. Weaver and the Rhetoric of a Lost Cause." *RSQ* 19 (Fall 1989): 313–326.

Explicates Weaver's theory for persuading a hostile audience.

55. Blyler, Nancy Roundy. "Purpose and Composition Theory: Issues in the Research." *JAC* 9 (1989): 97–111.

Surveys five areas of research on purpose: definition, influences, writers' awareness, process, and pedagogy. Concludes that the research is inadequate and fails to make connections.

56. Blyler, Nancy Roundy. "Purpose and Professional Writers." *TWT* 16 (Winter 1989): 52–67.

Concludes that professional writers have a multidimensional view of purpose and that purpose considerations are derived from situation, reader, and text.

57. Borgman, Christine L. "Bibliometrics and Scholarly Communication." *ComR* 16 (October 1989): 583–599.

Explores the application of bibliometrics, using mathematics and statistical methods to study the media of communication, as a research method in the field of communication.

58. Brave, Stephen E. "Composition Theory, Pedagogy, and Radical Change: The Ideology of Contemporary Writing Instruction." *DAI* 49 (April 1989): 2953A.

Argues that, despite a shift to process orientation, traditional ideology continues to inform composition pedagogy.

59. Breslow, Lori. "The Mediated I: The Consequences of Communications Technology for the Conceptualization of the Self." *DAI* 50 (November 1989): 1125A.

Traces how the phonetic alphabet and the printing press contributed to the development of the concept of individuality in the West.

60. Bridwell-Bowles, Lillian. "Designing Research on Computer-Assisted Writing." *CC* 7 (November 1989): 79–91.

Evaluates five kinds of research, defines the kinds of questions the work has answered, and makes recommendations for future research methodologies and topics.

61. Briggs, Lynn Craigue, Sharon Kane, and Patricia Spencer Soper. "Considerations, Complications, and Consequences on Practitioner Inquiry." *JTW* (Special Issue 1989): 151–164.

Describes two kinds of classroom research: a dialogue between a researcher and a teacher and an account by a teacher researcher.

62. Britton, James. "The Spectator as Theorist: A Reply [to Harris, *EEd* 20 (February 1989)]." *EEd* 21 (February 1989): 53–60.

Comments on Harris's critique of the spectator role by producing evidence indicating that poetic discourse can become the vehicle of deeper meaning.

63. Brooke, Robert. "Control in Writing: Flower, Derrida, and Images of the Writer." *CE* 51 (April 1989): 405–417.

Discusses Flower's reading of Derrida and explains how to help student writers accept "loss of control" as part of the learning process.

64. Burnham, Christopher C. "Expressive Writing: A Heretic's Confession." *Focuses* 2 (Spring 1989): 5–18.

Discusses expressive writing as a "framework for viewing writing both as process and product," citing Britton and Kinneavy.

65. Calendillo, Linda T. "The Art of Memory and Rhetoric." *DAI* 49 (April 1989): 3011A.

Suggests how modern rhetorical theory might benefit from classical mnemonic arts.

66. Campbell, Kathleen G. "Enactment as a Rhetorical Strategy/Form in Rhetorical Acts and Artifacts." *DAI* 49 (January 1989): 1620A.

Analyzes a film, a building, and nine television commercials to test the presence of enactment, "the physical embodiment of the rhetorical stance."

67. Carroll, Jeffrey G. "Disabling Fictions: Institutionalized Delimitations of Revision." *RR* 8 (Fall 1989): 62–72.

Argues that revision is "layered and organic." It needs "less naming of parts and more dialogue between and among the forces that stimulate, affect, and require writing."

68. Carroll, Jeffrey G. "Reception and Representation: A Theory of Composing." *DAI* 49 (January 1989): 1718A.

Theorizes that composing should be treated as an interrelated web of parameters of schooled and unschooled selves transcending pedagogical strategies.

69. Carroll, Regina M. "The Writing Processes of Three Deaf High School Students." *DAI* 49 (February 1989): 2169A.

Examines current theoretical models of writing processes as applied to learning-disabled students.

70. Carter, Michael. "Michael Carter Responds [to Scriven and Flower, *CE* 51 (November 1989)]." *CE* 51 (November 1989): 777–779.

Describes information processing as the theoretical foundation of cognitive psychology and defines *goal* as part of a problem-directed writing process.

71. Chappell, Virginia Anne. "Fitting Texts to Context: Student Writers and the Construction of Audience." *DAI* 49 (March 1989): 2567A.

A descriptive, empirical study examining the process by which the writer "creates a place . . . in the reader's world . . . ." Writing problems are more situational than cognitive.

72. Clark, Gregory. *Dialogue, Dialectic, and Conversation: A Social Perspective on Function of Writing*. Studies in Writing and Rhetoric. Carbondale, Ill.: Southern Illinois University Press, 1989. 120 pages

Articulates an ethics of reading that places primary responsibility for the social influences of a text on the responses of its readers.

73. "Composing Real-World Documents: A Conversation with Dr. Janice C. Redish." *Issues* 1 (Spring 1989): 82–98.

Interviews the Director of the Document Design Center, American Institutes for Research, Washington, D.C. Describes problems associated with writing in the bureaucratic contexts of large organizations.

74. Consigny, Scott. "Dialectical, Rhetorical, and Aristotelian Rhetoric." *P&R* 22 (1989): 281–287.

Asserts that Aristotelian rhetoric is neither dialectical, as Gaines argues, nor rhetorical, as Holmberg argues, but offers a third alternative that negotiates between these positions.

75. Conti, Diane C. "Word Processing and the Composing Process." *DAI* 50 (July 1989): 126A.

Concludes that word processing not only integrates some of the stages of writing but automates them as well.

76. Corbett, Edward P. J. *Selected Essays of Edward P. J. Corbett.* Edited by Robert J. Connors. SMU Studies in Rhetoric and Composition. Dallas: Southern Methodist University Press, 1989. 352 pages

Prints 20 addresses and essays written by Corbett between 1958 and 1986. Headnotes to each selection derive from a 1987 interview with Corbett.

77. Couture, Barbara, ed. *Functional Approaches to Writing Research.* Advances in Writing Research. Edited by Marcia Farr. Norwood, N.J.: Ablex, 1988. 288 pages

Sixteen essays describe the functions of written language, explore the processes of producing and interpreting written language, discuss how it is valued, and apply functional language theory to writing instruction.

78. Cowley, Nancy R. "Composing, Uniting, Transacting: Whys and Ways of Connecting Reading and Writing." *CE* 51 (February 1989): 192–200.

Reviews three books that treat the theory and practice of connecting reading and writing: Petersen's *Convergences,* Newkirks *Only Connect,* and Bartholomae and Petrosky's *Facts, Artifacts, and Counterfacts.*

79. Craven, Jacqueline Clark. "Creating a Persona: Theory and Examples." *DAI* 49 (June 1989): 3644A.

Analyzes essays to trace the evolution of the persona and to examine how this illu-

sion determines the style, content, and form of the final text.

80. Crosswhite, James. "Mood in Argumentation: Heidegger and the *Exordium*." *P&R* 22 (1989): 28–41.

Argues that mood is indispensable to argumentation, challenging the strict distinction between appeals to emotion and to reason. Treats *exordium*-initiated rhetoric as the purest form of argumentation.

81. Crosswhite, James. "Universality in Rhetoric: Perelman's Universal Audience." *P&R* 22 (1989): 157–173.

Uses Perelman's concept of a universal audience to explore what universality exists in rhetoric. Claims that this concept provides ways to distinguish valid from effective argumentation.

82. Crusius, Timothy W. *Discourse: A Critique and Synthesis of Major Theories.* New York: MLA, 1989. 150 pages

Analyzes the theories of Kinneavy, Moffett, Britton, and D'Angelo and synthesizes their work into a view of the composing process that unifies rhetoric with hermeneutics.

83. Dascal, Marcelo. "Hermeneutic Interpretation and Pragmatic Interpretation." *P&R* 22 (1989): 239–259.

Compares Gadamer's hermeneutic theory with pragmatic theories of content, production, and interpretation. Sees the disciplines as complementary, though differences exist in scope and thus in methodology.

84. Dearin, Ray D., ed. *The New Rhetoric of Chaim Perelman: Statement and Response.* Lanham, Md.: University Press of America, 1989. 266 pages

Eleven essays summarize Perelman's contributions to rhetoric and present representative responses to his new rhetoric. An appendix contains comments by Perelman.

85. Dobrin, David N. *Writing and Technique*. Urbana, Ill.: NCTE, 1989. ERIC ED 303 817. 216 pages

Examines how writing is taught in an age of technology, concluding that writing is rooted in meaning and human relations.

86. Dorff, Dianne Lee, and Ann Hill Duin. "Applying a Cognitive Model to Document Cycling." *TWT* 16 (Fall 1989): 234–249.

Reports on a study using Flower and Hayes's model to analyze the composing processes of a team of writers.

87. Douglas-Steele, Darleen K. "Everyday Troubles and Their Stories: A Study in the Practice of Commonsense Reasoning." *DAI* 49 (May 1989): 3505A.

Analyzes conversation, focusing on orderliness and categorization devices in talk with family and friends about difficulties.

88. Durst, Russel K. "Monitoring Processes in Analytic and Summary Writing." *WC* 6 (July 1989): 340–363.

Studies monitoring strategies used by 20 high school juniors during analytic and summary writing about reading passages.

89. Dyson, Anne Haas. "'Once upon a Time' Reconsidered: The Developmental Dialectic between Function and Form." *WC* 6 (October 1989): 436–462.

Considers literary language from the child's point of view. Assumes that stories are cultural discourse forms that serve multiple functions. Learning them requires children to transform them into tools that are functional within their own social world.

90. Ebbs, Gary Martin. "Meaning and Compositional Structure." *DAI* 49 (June 1989): 3751A.

Argues that the meanings of many natural language sentences are strongly compositionally dependent.

91. Ebert, P. K. "Cognitive Ergonomics in Information System Design." *DAI* 50 (July 1989): 196A.

Shows that information format makes a significant difference and that matched users perform at a higher level than unmatched users.

92. Elbow, Peter. "Toward a Phenomenology of Freewriting." *JBW* 8 (Fall 1989): 42–71.

Explains why freewriting is central to the author's work as a writer and teacher. It facilitates entering "more easily and fully" into writing and thinking.

93. Endres, Thomas G. "Rhetorical Visions of Unmarried Mothers." *ComQ* 37 (Spring 1989): 134–150.

Combines Bormann's fantasy theme analysis and Q-methodology to examine the symbolic reality of unmarried mothers. Dramatistic humanistic analysis yields three of these women's visions.

94. Evans, Joy D. "Effects of Guided Imagery on Written Occupational Narratives." *DAI* 50 (September 1989): 675A.

Investigates the influence of guided imagery on university students' written occupational narratives. Finds no significant effects.

95. Flottum, Kjersti. "The Formal Structure of School Summaries." Paper presented at the International Association of Applied Linguistics, Sydney, Australia, August 1987. ERIC ED 302 058. 10 pages

Compares and categorizes summaries written by students and experts.

96. Flower, Linda. "Cognition, Context, and Theory Building." *CCC* 40 (October 1989): 282–311.

Discusses principles of an interactive theory of cognition and context in the writing process. Examines the role of observational research in building such a theory.

97. Flower, Linda. *The Construction of Purpose in Writing and Reading*. Pittsburgh: CSW, 1988. ERIC ED 298 493. 25 pages

Calls for refining purpose in reading and writing and for seeing purpose as constructive, cognitive, and rhetorical, leading to a meaningful and coherent text.

98. Flynn, Dale, and Susan Palo. "An Interview with Oliver Sacks." *WE* 1 (Fall 1989): 99–106.

Sacks discusses his use of a writing journal, his style, and his revision process.

99. Ford, Leigh Arden. "Fetching Good out of Evil in AA: A Bormannean Fantasy Theme Analysis of *The Big Book* of Alcoholics Anonymous." *ComQ* 37 (Winter 1989): 1–15.

A fantasy theme analysis of Alcoholics Anonymous's basic text. Its rhetorical vision is a variation of Bormann's "Fetching Good out of Evil."

100. Fortune, Ron, and Janice Neuleib. "Manuscript Studies, Literature-Writing Connections, and the Teacher Researcher." *JTW* (Special Issue 1989): 227–238.

In analyzing all versions of a text, teachers identify manuscript materials of literary texts, articulate patterns in the texts, and apply patterns to student texts.

101. Gaines, Ernest. "Bloodline in Ink." *CEAC* 51 (Winter-Spring 1989): 2–12.

Narrates a writer's search for material and tools for writing, emphasizing the need to discover the stories of a community.

102. Gates, Rosemary L. "Applying Martin Greenman's Concept of Insight to Composition Theory." *JAC* 9 (1989): 59–68.

Philosopher Greenman used Wallas's model of problem-solving to develop a theory of insight that clarifies the writing process and writing to learn.

103. Gee, James Paul. "Self, Society, Mushfake, and Vygotsky: Meditations on Papers Redefining the Social in Composition Theory." *WI* 8 (Summer 1989): 177–183.

Argues that school can never teach language acquisition when language is defined as "situated discourse." Teaching changes the *status quo* and must inculcate a metaknowledge of language and discourse.

104. Gibson, Sharon Slaton. "Classroom Communities and Global Coherence: A Sociocognitive Model for Composition Theory, Pedagogy, and Research." *DAI* 49 (June 1989): 3645A.

Derives a sociocognitive model from theories of Piaget, Vygotsky, and Bruner to understand different mixes of knowledge constructs as an approach to writing across the curriculum.

105. Golden, Joanne M., and Carol Vukelich. "Coherence in Children's Written Narratives." *WC* 6 (January 1989): 45–65.

Uses de Beaugrande's concept analysis to study local and global coherence in 145 narratives written by 20 third graders.

106. Gordon, Eleanor R. "The Authority of the Essay: Philosophical, Rhetorical, and Cognitive Considerations of Person." *DAI* 50 (August 1989): 449A.

Draws from literary criticism, composition theory, rhetoric, and pedagogy to identify the use of person and describe its relationship to the essay's rhetoric and epistemology.

107. Grant-Davie, Keith. "Rereading in the Writing Process." *Reader* 19 (Spring 1989): 2–21.

Synthesizes research that examines how writers read and represent texts during composing. Classifies writers' purposes for rereading their texts and outlines areas for further research.

108. Green, Judith L., and Judith O. Harker, eds. *Multiple Perspective Analyses of Classroom Discourse*. Advances in Discourse Processes, vol. 28. Norwood, N.J.: Ablex, 1988. 356 pages

Fourteen essays explain how to study classroom discourse on a content level and on a theoretical or methodological level.

109. Greene, Brenda M. "Paths to Empowerment: Problem Identification and Resolution Strategies of Basic Writers." Paper presented

at the CCCC Convention, Seattle, March 1989. ERIC ED 307 620. 25 pages

Reports on a study using think-aloud protocols to examine the revision strategies of three basic writers.

110. Greene, John B. "A Phenomenological Analysis of Self-Descriptive Essays Written by West German and American Students." *DAI* 49 (June 1989): 5558B.

Analyzes, using protocols, the contents of self-descriptive essays written by German and American students, finding both culture-specific and common themes.

111. Grimshaw, Allen D., ed. *Collegial Discourse: Professional Conversation among Peers*. Advances in Discourse Processes, vol. 32. Norwood, N.J.: Ablex, 1989. 640 pages

Reports on three detailed studies of a doctoral dissertation defense. The analyses focus on the social accomplishment of evaluation, communicative nonsuccess in ongoing talk, and processes of conflict talk in a cross-status dispute.

112. Hall, Susan Marie J. "Rhetorical Influences on Writers in Academic and Nonacademic Settings." *DAI* 50 (September 1989): 613A.

Finds that graduate business students used more rhetorical rationales in nonacademic settings than in academic ones.

113. Harkin, Patricia. "Response to Berthoff [*Pre/Text* 9 (Spring-Summer 1988)]." *Pre/Text* 9 (Spring-Summer 1988): 69–77.

Rejects Berthoff's position on neopragmatist narratives and provides examples of its use in rhetorical history.

114. Harris, Jeanette. "Construction and Reconstructing the Self in the Writing Class." *JTW* 8 (Spring-Summer 1989): 21–30.

Contrasts the views of expressionists and social constructivists on conventions and on the roles of teachers and of students.

115. Harris, Jeanette. *Expressive Discourse*. SMU Studies in Rhetoric and Composition.

Dallas: Southern Methodist University Press, 1989. 192 pages

Presents a new model for analyzing expressive discourse by demonstrating the distinctness of four rhetorical phenomena: interior text, generative text, aesthetic discourse, and experience-based discourse.

116. Harris, Joseph. "The Idea of Community in the Study of Writing." *CCC* 40 (February 1989): 11–22.

Critiques contemporary notions of community in composition theory and argues for a view of community less lacking in conflict.

117. Harris, Muriel. "Composing Behaviors of One- and Multi-Draft Writers." *CE* 51 (February 1989): 174–191.

After analyzing students' composing behaviors, Harris recommends that teachers individualize advice and avoid imposing a single "ideal" composing style on students.

118. Haswell, Richard H. "Textual Research and Coherence: Findings, Intuition, Application." *CE* 51 (March 1989): 305–319.

Asserts the validity of previous and the necessity of future textual research despite many teachers' doubts about its usefulness.

119. Hatlen, Burton. "Burton Hatlen Responds [to Popkin, *CE* 51 (December 1989)]." *CE* 51 (December 1989): 883–884.

Clarifies his original intent as challenging the professionalization of literary studies at the expense of literacy.

120. Herrmann, Andrea W. "The Participant Observer as Insider: Researching Your Own Classroom." Paper presented at the CCCC Convention, Seattle, March 1989. ERIC ED 303 835. 17 pages

Discusses the role of ethnographic participant observation in writing classes.

121. Hershey, Lewis B. "Arguing Affect: The Rhetoric of Peripheral Persuasion." *DAI* 49 (February 1989): 2020A.

Examines the nature of persuasion from several perspectives, including cognition, narrative models, and advertising.

122. Holbrook, Paul Evans, Jr. "The Metaphoric Function: Myth, Metaphor, and the Achievement of Meaning." *DAI* 49 (May 1989): 3384A.

Examines the role of metaphor in human imagination and creativity, concluding that metaphor is essential to growth.

123. Hu, Li-tze. "The Effects of Group Composition on Persuasion: A Comparison of Self-Attention Theory and the Minority Influence Paradigm." *DAI* 50 (September 1989): 649A.

Finds no difference between majority and minority group members.

124. Hurlbert, C. Mark, Nancy Mack, and James Thomas Zebroski. "Different Words: Response to James Paul Gee [*WI* 8 (Summer 1989)]." *WI* 8 (Summer 1989): 184–190.

A dialogue among the authors about political pedagogies, language and institutional change, metaknowledge of language and discourse, and the role of composition teachers.

125. Jacquette, Dale. "The Hidden Logic of Slippery Slope Arguments." *P&R* 22 (1989): 59–70.

Concludes that all slippery slope arguments are reducible to a single category of argument. The analysis offers a framework for distinguishing unsound sophisms from legitimate arguments.

126. Janda, Mary Ann. "Talk into Writing: Writers in Collaboration." *DAI* 49 (April 1989): 3011A.

Finds evidence of shared writing processes among four collaborative groups—grade school children, college seniors, an interdisciplinary public health committee, and newspaper columnists.

127. Jensen, Deborah Ann. "College Students' Self-Concept of Learning as Revealed through

Dialogue Journals." *DAI* 50 (November 1989): 1200A.

Focuses on 10 college students' written reflections on their academic experiences.

128. Kantz, Margaret. *Written Rhetorical Syntheses: Processes and Products.* CSW Report, no. 17. Berkeley: CSW, 1989. ERIC ED 303 821. 30 pages

Studies college students who were asked to synthesize their reading. Based on three case studies and 17 text analyses. Notes the value of goal setting and of structured assignments.

129. Karis, Bill. "Conflict in Collaboration: A Burkean Perspective." *RR* 8 (Fall 1989): 113–126.

Since rhetoric is "agonistic and dialectical," collaborators (especially students) "need to be made more aware of the role and value of substantive conflict."

130. Karis, William M. "Collaborative Writing and 'Extra-Organizational' Technical Communication." *TC* 36 (August 1989): 268–270.

Argues for beginning research on collaborative writing that takes place in a context larger than that of a single organization.

131. Kastely, James L. "Complicating Sartre's Rhetoric of Generosity." *P&R* 22 (1989): 1–27.

Examines Sartre's contribution to rhetorical theory in light of deconstruction. Sees generosity as a rhetorical virtue necessary to creating conditions for genuine community.

132. Kaufer, David S., and Cheryl Geisler. "Novelty in Academic Writing." *WC* 6 (July 1989): 286–311.

Treats novelty in academic writing as a body of strategic knowledge. Seeks to specify its nature and parameters. Analyzes protocols from expert and novice publishers.

133. Kent, Carolyn E. "A Tagmemic Analysis of Coherence in the Writing of Descriptive

14   THEORY AND RESEARCH

Texts by College Students." *DAI* 50 (July 1989): 127A.

Shows that papers with high coherence locate texts in time and space, include purpose and reasons, and focus on human beings.

134. Kent, Thomas. "Beyond System: The Rhetoric of Paralogy." *CE* 51 (September 1989): 492–507.

Calls for a "reinventing" of rhetoric that accounts for the paralogic nature of language as set forth in Davidson and Derrida.

135. Kent, Thomas. "Paralogic Hermeneutics and the Possibilities of Rhetoric." *RR* 8 (Fall 1989): 24–42.

Builds on Davidson and Derrida to claim that reading and writing cannot be taught as a systematic process. Suggests instead "open-ended dialogic activities."

136. Kersten, Astrid Levina. "A Critical Theory of Organizational Communication: Foundations, Models, and Guidelines for Critical Research." *DAI* 50 (September 1989): 571A.

Explores philosophical issues in social science and communication, then develops a critical approach to the study of organizational communication.

137. Kirsch, Gesa. "Authority in Reader-Writer Relationships." *Reader* 19 (Spring 1989): 56–67.

Examines a writer's sense of audience and authority during composing. Uses theories of audience and protocol study to describe how writers establish authority and address readers.

138. Kostelnick, Charles. "Process Paradigms in Design and Composition: Affinities and Directions." *CCC* 40 (October 1989): 267–281.

Examining process theories of design can help composition theorists assess the writing process paradigm.

139. Kreuz, Roger J., and Sam Glucksberg. "How to Be Sarcastic: The Echoic Reminder

Theory of Verbal Irony." *JEPG* 118 (December 1989): 374–386.

Studies what statements people identify as being sarcastic. People see positive statements about negative events as more sarcastic than negative statements about positive events.

140. Lanham, Richard A. "Digitizing Some Keywords." *CC* 6 (August 1989): 123–128.

Speculates that the electronic presentation of classical rhetorical notions of mimesis, topic, and decorum implies deep changes for teaching composition.

141. Lee, Chingkwe A. "Information Structure in Planned Written and Unplanned Spoken Discourse." *DAI* 49 (April 1989): 3014A.

Presents a taxonomy of discourse entities and a quantitative measure of communication breakdown.

142. Leonardi, Susan J. "Recipes for Reading: Summer Pasta, Lobster a la Riseholme, and Key Lime Pie." *PMLA* 104 (May 1989): 340–347.

Uses recipes as models of written narratives that convey information as they engage writer and reader in a relationship of personal exchange.

143. Levi, Primo. "Reflections on Writing." *PR* 56 (1989): 21–33.

Describes the author's feelings while writing a novel, discusses reasons for writing, and gives advice to potential writers.

144. Lewis, Harry Will. "Text as Informant: Infant Sexuality in Key Cultural Texts." *DAI* 50 (September 1989): 722A.

An ethnomethodological content analysis of five editions of *Dr. Spock's Baby and Child Care* offers a means of locating texts that are the product of "common sense" concerns while at the same time draw on a body of specific "scientific data."

145. Lievrouw, Leah A. "The Invisible College Reconsidered: Bibliometrics and the Develop-

ment of Scientific Communication Theory." *ComR* 16 (October 1989): 615–628.

Examines the relationship of bibliometric techniques, especially citation analysis, to communication theory and research. Explores theory building in scientific communication.

146. Littlejohn, Stephen W. *Theories of Human Communication*. 3d ed. Belmont, Calif.: Wadsworth, 1989. 315 pages

Defines communication theory and discusses its purpose and evolution. Outlines general theories from a range of disciplinary perspectives as well as contextual theories of interpersonal, group, organizational, and mass communication.

147. Lloyd, Pamela. *How Writers Write*. Portsmouth, N.H.: Heinemann, 1989. 160 pages

Studies the composing processes of 23 writers of children's books, including authors of picture books, fantasy, humor, fiction, and poetry.

148. Lyons, Gregory T. "Theoretical Origins of Contemporary Expressive Writing Pedagogies in Classical Rhetoric, Romantic Poetry, and Humanist Therapy." *DAI* 50 (August 1989): 427A.

Expressive pedagogies, which derive from rhetoric, romantic criticism, and therapy, allow the individual to rationalize experience through confessional autobiography and to discover an authentic voice.

149. MacDonald, Susan Peck. "Data-Driven and Conceptually Driven Academic Discourse." *WC* 6 (October 1989): 411–435.

Contrasts data-driven writing in the humanities with conceptually driven writing in the social sciences. Discusses difficulties students have in shifting between the two types of discourse.

150. Mackin, James Andrew, Jr. "Towards an Ethics of Rhetoric: An Ecological Model for Assessing Public Moral Argument." *DAI* 50 (December 1989): 1482A.

Argues that a model using Aristotelian moral philosophy combined with the idea of a communicative ecosystem provides a means of assessing public moral argument.

151. Malachowski, Ann Marie. "An Examination of Written Products and Writing Processes of Two Brain-Damaged Adults." *DAI* 49 (June 1989): 3605A.

Explores disruptive writing competency, examining writing samples of two expert writers who were recovering writing skills after strokes that caused aphasia.

152. Maranhao, Tullio, ed. *The Interpretation of Dialogue*. Chicago: University of Chicago Press, 1989. 360 pages

Discusses different perspectives on dialogue and communication within the framework of postmodern debates in hermeneutic philosophy, phenomenology, neopragmatism, and deconstructionism.

153. Marcus, Maxine M. "Self-Regulation in Expository Writing." *DAI* 49 (February 1989): 2091A.

Examines the composing processes and behaviors among expository writers in several age groups.

154. Martin, James R. *Factual Writing: Exploring and Challenging Social Reality*. Language Education. Edited by Frances Christie. New York: Oxford University Press, 1989. 100 pages

Describes the types of writing used as tools of communication in the adult world, comparing them with the writing tasks that teachers set for their pupils and with the ways in which schools measure success.

155. Martin, Merthelle Loretta. "Speech Blocks and Gender: A Case Study." *DAI* 49 (March 1989): 2451A.

A study of seven men and women found performance anxiety to be a major factor in speech blocks. Analyzes the relationship of speech blocks to reading blocks, writing blocks, and gender.

156. Massey, M. Kathleen. "Poststructuralism, the New Rhetoric, and Composition." *DAI* 50 (November 1989): 1313A.

    Examines journals and textbooks to trace the effects of poststructuralist literary theory on composition pedagogy.

157. Matalene, Carolyn, ed. *Worlds of Writing: Teaching and Learning in Discourse Communities of Work*. New York: Random House, 1989. 288 pages

    A collection of 23 essays by academicians who are also professional writing consultants. Eight sections compare studies of academic and nonacademic writing, argue for integrating these worlds in undergraduate courses, discuss the role of writing in different writing cultures, treat writing constraints, and report on specific discourse communities such as journalism, finance, computer technology, and the law.

158. McCleary, Bill. "Influence of James L. Kinneavy and *A Theory of Discourse* Continues to Grow." *CompC* 2 (April 1989): 1–2.

    Traces the influence of Kinneavy's work in the field of composition.

159. McGinley, William, and Robert J. Tierney. "Traversing the Topical Landscape: Reading and Writing as Ways of Knowing." *WC* 6 (July 1989): 243–269.

    Proposes that "various forms of reading and writing" are "unique ways of thinking about and exploring a topic of study en route to acquiring knowledge."

160. McGuire, J. E., and Trevor Melia. "Some Cautionary Strictures on the Writing of Rhetoric of Science." *Rhetorica* 7 (Winter 1989): 87–100.

    Cautions against replacing an arrogant scientism with a rampant rhetoricism, arguing that scientific practice cannot be reduced to textuality.

161. McMahon, Robert. "Kenneth Burke's Divine Comedy: The Literary Form of *The Rhetoric of Religion*." *PMLA* 104 (January 1989): 53–61.

    Argues that Burke's book both explains and enacts the "comic" critical response that is his revision of the agonistic model dominating the rhetorical tradition.

162. Mebane, Dorothy L. "Letters of Recommendation: What Writers Do with Negative Information." *DAI* 49 (June 1989): 5508B.

    Studies letters of recommendation and determines that writers and readers differ greatly in their expectations of whether and how negative information is disclosed.

163. Meyer, Michel. "Toward a Rhetoric of Reason." *RSQ* 19 (Spring 1989): 131–140.

    Discusses the place of inference in problematological rhetoric.

164. Michener, Darlene. "Reading Aloud to Students and Written Composition Skills: Assessing Their Relationship." *EQ* 21 (1989): 212–223.

    Studies with third-grade students at two socioeconomic levels showed that reading aloud to students in the classroom contributed to the development of written syntactic maturity.

165. Middleton, Joyce I. "Confronting Lingering Questions in Plato's *Phaedrus:* How Textbook Authors Draw on Historical Speech Strategies to Teach Writing." *DAI* 49 (February 1989): 2134A.

    Applies Ong's concept of "residual orality" to the teaching of writing and then examines three composition textbooks from the perspective of Ong's contrastive features.

166. Miller, Lori Ann. "Thinking, Feeling, Intuiting, and Sensing: Using Four Psychological Functions as a Model to Empower Student Writers." Paper presented at the CCCC Convention, Seattle, March 1989. ERIC ED 303 823. 18 pages

    Considers writing an act of self-construction and discusses the usefulness of Jung's four functions and the Myers-Briggs Type Indicator in considering how students process information.

167. Morgan, Margaret Patricia. "Four Dimensions of the Collaborative Composing Processes of Student Writers." *DAI* 50 (September 1989): 640A.

Analyzes problem identification, group organizing patterns, drafting behaviors, and leadership.

168. Mortensen, Peter L. "Reading Authority, Writing Authority." *Reader* 19 (Spring 1989): 35–55.

Describes how writers' different reading strategies lead to different textual representations, how writers locate authority in readings, and what types of evidence they accept in arguments.

169. Mumby, Dennis K. "Ideology and the Social Construction of Meaning: A Communication Perspective." *ComQ* 37 (Fall 1989): 291–304.

Examines ideology's role in the social construction of meaning, focusing on how social relations of power affect the process of creating meaning.

170. Nakayama, Thomas Kazuo. "Rhetorical Dimensions of Translation: A Theoretical Inquiry." *DAI* 50 (October 1989): 828A.

Uses Cicero's perspective on translation to analyze a Karl Marx text and its translation. Translation creates "rhetorical resources hegemonically."

171. Neill, Catherine R. "Sources of Meaning in Thai Narrative Discourse: Grammar, Rhetoric, and Sociocultural Knowledge." *DAI* 50 (October 1989): 939A.

Shows that speakers and hearers make use of grammatical, rhetorical, and sociocultural aspects of meaning in the process of interpretation.

172. Newell, George E., and Peter Winograd. "The Effects of Writing on Learning from Expository Text." *WC* 6 (April 1989): 196–217.

Examines the effects of various writing tasks on learning. Measures the recall of text-specific knowledge and of the gist of expository text among eight eleventh graders.

173. Nilsen, Don L. F. "Discourse Tendency: A Study in Extended Tropes." *RSQ* 19 (Summer 1989): 263–272.

Discusses the function of tropes in discourse.

174. Nystrand, Martin. "A Social-Interactive Model of Writing." *WC* 6 (January 1989): 66–85.

Rejects the notion that meaning is in the text or the reader, arguing that "meaning is between writer and reader." Outlines social-interactive principles of text production.

175. Oller, John W., Jr., ed. *Language and Experience: Classic Pragmatism.* Lanham, Md.: University Press of America, 1989. 314 pages

Collects seven writings of "classic pragmatists," arguing that language use and acquisition largely depend on linking representations with the facts of experience. An appendix relates these writings to contemporary thought on language, language acquisition, and literacy.

176. Olsen, Leslie A. "Computer-Based Writing and Communication: Some Implications for Technical Communication Activities." *JTWC* 19 (1989): 97–118.

Argues that communication researchers should broaden their studies to include professional writing that is "collaborative, computer-based, not exclusively prose."

177. Olson, Gary A. "Social Construction and Composition Theory: A Conversation with Richard Rorty." *JAC* 9 (1989): 1–9.

Rorty disagrees with some composition applications of his theories. He opposes writing across the curriculum and does not know "social constructionism," but he supports cultural literacy.

178. Olson, Rex. "Derrida (f)or Us? Composition and the Taking of Text." *Pre/Text* 9 (Spring-Summer 1988): 28–60.

Describes the importance of Derridian deconstruction in defining the object of composition's study and in developing its theory.

179. Paisley, William. "Bibliometrics, Scholarly Communication, and Communication Research." *ComR* 16 (October 1989): 701–717.

Examines the uses of bibliometrics in research on scholarly and scientific communication as well as on political communication.

180. Palacas, Arthur L. "Parenthetics and Personal Voice." *WC* 6 (October 1989): 506–528.

Analyzes some uses of appositive and parenthetical structure in professional writers' texts to identify the role of these structures in creating a personal voice.

181. Penrose, Ann Marie. "Individual Differences in Writing Strategies: Effects on Learning through Writing." *DAI* 49 (March 1989): 2594A.

Uses think-aloud protocols and comprehension testing to examine the relative effects of writing and studying as learning aids.

182. Peyton, Joy Kreeft, Jana Staton, Leslee Reed, and Roger Shuy. *Dialogue Journal Communication: Classroom, Linguistic, Social, and Cognitive Views*. Advances in Writing Research. Edited by Marcia Farr. Norwood, N.J.: Ablex, 1988. 356 pages

Focuses on dialogue journals as a corpus for analyzing children's communicative competence.

183. Phillips, Donna Burns. "Persona, Voice, and Style: Their Place and Treatment in Current Composition Theory and Curriculum." *DAI* 49 (June 1989): 3647A.

Uses theories of Bakhtin, Barthes, Festinger, and Goffman to understand the self and language, persona, voice, and style in students' writing.

184. Pitts, Beverly. "Model Provides Descriptions of News Writing Process." *JourEd* 44 (Spring 1989): 12–18.

Analyzes the composing processes of eight professional writers and five journalism students, utilizing protocol analysis to construct a model of the writing process of journalists.

185. Popkin, Susan M. "A Comment on 'Michel Foucault and the Discourse(s) of English' [*CE* 50 (November 1988)]." *CE* 51 (December 1989): 882–883.

Comments on the lack of attention given to composition faculty within English departments. Emphasizes giving priority to teaching excellence.

186. Potts, Meta W. "Developing Critical Literacy: A Case Study of Small Reading-Writing Discussion Groups." *DAI* 49 (April 1989): 2917A.

Analyzes writing groups over a four-month period by using observation, interviews, protocol analyses, and surveys.

187. Proctor, Mersedeh. "Discourse Organization Patterns and Their Signals: A Clause Relational Approach to the Analysis of Written Discourse." *DAI* 49 (January 1989): 1788A.

Investigates the identification and description of organizational patterns in written texts and their explicit linguistic signals.

188. Rafoth, Bennett A. "Audience and Information." *RTE* 23 (October 1989): 273–290.

Finds that below-average and good first-year college writers defer audience considerations until the revision stage. Rationales for writers' decisions show similarities between groups.

189. Rafoth, Bennett A., and Donald L. Rubin, eds. *The Social Construction of Written Communication*. Advances in Writing Research. Edited by Marcia Farr. Norwood, N.J.: Ablex, 1988. 336 pages

Fourteen essays examine four interrelated perspectives on how people socially construct written communication: writers construct mental representations of social constructs; writing as a social process can create social constructs; writers create texts collectively; and writers assign consensual values to writing.

190. Ramsey, Shirley A. "Science Interviews: Asymmetric or Symmetric." *JTWC* 19 (1989): 181–197.

Interviews designed to produce articles of general interest differ from interviews leading to more technical articles according to the language principles emphasized.

191. Reber, Thomas Clark. "Modern Epideictic Discourse: The Commemorative Speech in Twentieth-Century America." *DAI* 50 (December 1989): 1484A.

Studies 81 commemorative speeches and argues that traditional conceptions of epideictic rhetoric have expanded to include nostalgic, didactic, and partisan aims.

192. Recchio, Thomas E. "A Dialogic Approach to the Essay." *Issues* 1 (Spring 1989): 99–119.

Offers a Bakhtinian reading of Montaigne's "Of Experience" to suggest how a dialogic approach to the essay can inform the teaching of writing.

193. Renner, Judith A. "Development of Temporality in Children's Narratives." *DAI* 50 (October 1989): 1665B.

Studies how children produce narratives and finds that age differences account for much variation in degrees of coherence and completeness.

194. Reynolds, John Frederick. "Concepts of Memory in Contemporary Composition." *RSQ* 19 (Summer 1989): 245–252.

Discusses treatments of the canon of memory in modern rhetorical theories.

195. Ronald, Kate. "Ann Berthoff's Dialectic: Theory and Applications." *Issues* 1 (Spring 1989): 150–164.

Examines connections between Berthoff's theory and the dialectical relationship between rhetoric and thought in Plato. Discusses how a first-year student uses dialectical methods to find the "uses of chaos" in her own writing.

196. Ronald, Kate, and Jon Volkmer. "Another Competing Theory of Process: The Student's Journal of Advanced Composition." *JAC* 9 (1989): 83–96.

Participant observation in advanced composition courses reveals that contextual pressures prevent students from enacting any major process theory. One-draft, last-minute writing is customary.

197. Rose, Holly K. "Problem-Solving Orientation: An Interaction of Problem Context and Source of Reference." *DAI* 50 (July 1989): 125A.

Concludes that there is some evidence to prefer a problem-solving model that addresses interactions between context and source of reference.

198. Rosebury, Ann S., Linda Flower, Beth Warren, Betsy Bowen, Bertram Bruce, Margaret Kantz, and Ann M. Penrose. *The Problem-Solving Processes of Writers and Readers*. CSW Occasional Paper, no. 7. Berkeley: CSW, January 1989. ERIC ED 303 822. 34 pages

Studies the reading and writing of college and high school students, noting the importance of flexible problem-solving strategies.

199. Rowland, Robert C. "On Limiting the Narrative Paradigm: Three Case Studies." *ComM* 56 (March 1989): 39–54.

Assesses the applicability of the narrative paradigm to all types of written and visual texts.

200. Rubin, David C., and Wanda T. Wallace. "Rhyme and Reason: Analyses of Dual Retrieval Cues." *JEPL* 15 (July 1989): 698–709.

Explains why rhyme does not aid recall significantly in laboratory research yet is a major mnemonic device in other situations.

201. Salgu, Deborah F. "Cohesion in Children's Fictional Stories: Transitivity and Goal-Directed Causal Analysis." *DAI* 49 (June 1989): 3708A.

Compares analyses of cohesion in children's stories and examines how the ability to construct coherent stories changes with age.

202. Schilb, John. "Composition and Poststructuralism: A Tale of Two Conferences." *CCC* 40 (December 1989): 422–443.

Discusses the relationship between composition and poststructuralism by examining contrasting notions of rhetoric at the 1963 CCCC and the 1966 Johns Hopkins conferences.

203. Schilb, John. "Response to Berthoff [*Pre/Text* 9 (Spring-Summer 1988)]." *Pre/Text* 9 (Spring-Summer 1988): 66–69.

Calls for the study of relations among politics, philosophy, and rhetoric, but rejects Berthoff's use of the terms *philosophy* and *misreading*.

204. Schultz, John. "Voice, Image, and Idea: The Use of Nonverbal Perception in the Development of Extended Discourse." Paper presented at the CCCC Convention, St. Louis, March 1988. ERIC ED 299 563. 20 pages

Calls attention to nonverbal thinking in classroom and conference practices, especially as they relate to the writing processes of rhetorical argumentation.

205. Schumacher, Gary M., Byron T. Scott, George R. Klare, Frank C. Cronin, and Donald A. Lambert. "Cognitive Processes in Journalistic Genres: Extending Writing Models." *WC* 6 (July 1989): 390–407.

Examines the composing processes of 24 journalism seniors writing a news story or an editorial under three conditions: pausal, pausal interview, or protocol.

206. Scott, DeWitt. "Writing That Works." *ETC* 46 (Winter 1989): 320–321.

Discusses reasons and strategies for eliminating "to be" verbs, for avoiding superlatives, for using *I* instead of *we*, and for writing in plain language.

207. Shotter, John, and Kenneth J. Gergen, eds. *Texts of Identity*. Inquiries in Social Construction. Newbury Park, Calif.: Sage, 1989. 244 pages

Fourteen essays explore how "culturally established texts furnish their 'inhabitants' with the resources which both enable and constrain their construction of their selves." Topics include "the motivations of terrorists, the indignity of a medical examination, the mystery story, lesbianism, and developmental theory."

208. Simons, Herbert W., ed. *Rhetoric in the Human Sciences*. Inquiries in Social Construction. Newbury Park, Calif.: Sage, 1989. 240 pages

Seventeen essays on "the rhetorical dimensions of scholarly discourse" bring rhetorical theory to bear on such subjects as "language acquisition, television viewing, ethnographic writing, psychotherapy, jurisprudence, and structuralist poetics."

209. Simons, Herbert W., and Trevor Melia, eds. *The Legacy of Kenneth Burke*. Madison: University of Wisconsin Press, 1989. 324 pages

Scholars define and assess Burke's contributions to several fields, rereading his work against recent developments in critical and social theory.

210. Simpson, Mark D. "Writing for Multiple Audiences: An Ethnographic Study." Paper presented at the CCCC Convention, Seattle, March 1989. ERIC ED 303 831. 10 pages

Reports on an observational study of professional writing, revising a computer manual. Concludes that audience constraints are more complicated than textbooks admit.

211. Smagorinsky, Peter. "The Reliability and Validity of Protocol Analysis." *WC* 6 (October 1989): 463–479.

Historically contextualizes protocol analysis as a method of data collection. Evaluates recent criticisms of protocol analysis, arguing that it is a useful tool in composition studies.

212. Smith, Douglas C. "Error Detection: A *Gestalt* Response." *BABC* 52 (December 1989): 29–36.

Reviews perceptual research in error detection, emphasizing conclusions concerning proofreading. The goal is to assist researchers who study proofreading.

213. Smith, Robert E., III. "Reconsidering Richard Rorty." *RSQ* 19 (Fall 1989): 349–364.

Provides a brief history of Rorty's life and works, placing his work in the modern canon and discussing its lasting importance.

214. Sternglass, Marilyn S. *The Presence of Thought: Introspective Accounts of Reading and Writing*. Advances in Discourse Processes, vol. 34. Norwood, N.J.: Ablex, 1988. 244 pages

Reports on a study of graduate students in English and language education involving a series of teacher- and self-designed reading and writing tasks over a semester's time.

215. Sternglass, Marilyn S. "School-Sponsored and Self-Sponsored at the Same Time." *JAC* 9 (1989): 162–173.

Case studies of two graduate students show that "when the context supports sustained writing, both assigned and self-designed tasks can foster learning and commitment."

216. Swearingen, C. Jan. "Response to Berthoff [*Pre/Text* 9 (Spring-Summer 1988)]." *Pre/Text* 9 (Spring-Summer 1988): 78–83.

Compares Berthoff's early work in "The Problem of Problem-Solving" to her current position.

217. Tappan, Mark B., and Lyn Mikel Brown. "Stories Told and Lessons Learned: Toward a Narrative Approach to Moral Development and Moral Education." *HER* 59 (May 1989): 182–205.

Argues for using storytelling and narrative to facilitate moral development.

218. Tirrell, Mary Kay. "A Study of Two Scholar-Practitioners in Composition: Developmental Themes in the Work of James Moffett and James Britton." *DAI* 49 (March 1989): 2673A.

Offers Moffett and Britton as models for composition researchers because they have done away with unproductive dichotomies by bridging the gap between theory and practice.

219. Waller, Preston L. "The Role of *Ethos* in the Writing of Proposals and Manuals." *DAI* 49 (May 1989): 3353A.

An ethnographic study of how proposal and manual writers project their personalities into technical writing.

220. Walzer, Arthur E. "The Meanings of Purpose." Paper presented at the CCCC Convention, Seattle, March 1989. ERIC ED 303 799. 10 pages

Explores the meaning of *purpose* within three rhetorical traditions: classical-poetic, romantic, and classical-rhetorical.

221. Webb, Sarah J. "Using Figurative Language in Epistemic Writing: The Purposes and Processes of First and Second Language Writers." *DAI* 49 (May 1989): 3353A.

Describes how the production and use of figurative language facilitates insight. Also examines how language background determines the type of figures that are used.

222. Weintraub, Robin Lynn. "Telling Is Being: Creating Meaning in Old Age." *DAI* 49 (February 1989): 2292A.

Shows that aging adults define, validate, and create meaning for their lives by choosing what to tell in their stories.

223. Whitson, Steve. "'Sanitized for Your Protection': On the Hygiene of Metaphors." *RSQ* 19 (Summer 1989): 253–262.

Discusses the role of metaphor and metonymic analysis in rhetoric.

224. Wilhoit, Stephen. "The Analytic Synthesis: Forming and Defending Positions in Writing." *DAI* 49 (April 1989): 2956A.

Uses protocols, interviews, drafts, and notes to analyze how students prepared for, drafted, and revised an assigned essay.

225. Winsor, Dorothy A. "An Engineer's Writing and the Corporate Construction of Knowledge." *WC* 6 (July 1989): 270–285.

A case study of a research engineer writing a monthly report and a conference paper. Focuses on the communal nature of the texts and the inscribing process.

226. Worsham, Lynn. "The Question of Writing Otherwise: A Critique of Composition Theory." *DAI* 49 (June 1989): 3756A.

Asserts that because composition is based in the Enlightenment—and is thus "modern"—the discipline is likely to "misread" writing as a "male" experience.

227. Yablick, Gary S. "A Genetic-Dramatistic Study of Narrative Rhetoric." *DAI* 50 (December 1989): 2674B.

Using a genetic-dramatistic perspective, analyzes the ways addressors organize rhetoric to gain their objectives. Concludes that audience determines narrative rhetoric.

228. Youngkin, Betty Rogers. "The Contributions of Walter J. Ong to the Study of Rhetoric: History and Metaphor." *DAI* 50 (December 1989): 1485A.

Explores the contributions Ong has made in his study of history and metaphor, arguing that they culminate in a paradigm of human history and consciousness.

229. Zappen, James P. "The Discourse Community in Scientific and Technical Communi-

cation: Institutional and Social Views." *JTWC* 19 (1989): 1–11.

Surveys the content and implications of theoretical studies of discourse communities as defined by Fish and Rorty.

230. Zebroski, James Thomas. "The Social Construction of Self in the Work of Lev Vygotsky." *WI* 8 (Summer 1989): 149–156.

Discusses the Vygotskian reclamation of self as a transformative entity in interactions with the social and with language. Questions the current popularity of the social, asserting that it is inadequately examined.

231. Zebroski, James Thomas. "Vygotsky's Ideas Gaining Favor among Compositionists." *CompC* 2 (March 1989): 4–5.

Vygotsky's concept of inner speech supports writing as process and as social act.

See also 13, 22, 239, 265, 290, 485, 655, 706, 717, 754, 756, 767, 795, 814, 847, 858, 903, 996, 1001, 1007, 1028, 1056, 1231, 1299, 1325, 1522, 1531, 1534, 1811

2.2 RHETORICAL HISTORY

232. Abbott, Don Paul. "The Influence of Blair's Lectures in Spain." *Rhetorica* 7 (Summer 1989): 275–290.

Discusses the wide influence of Blair's work on early nineteenth-century Spanish rhetoricians, resulting from its comprehensive belletristic approach, liberalism, and eclecticism.

233. Adams, John Charles. "Allegations of Antihumanism and John Milton's Ramist *Artis Logicae*." *WJSC* 53 (Winter 1989): 1–12.

Focuses on Sloane's analysis of Milton's concept of *ethos* and the allegation that Ramists are antihumanistic.

234. Addington, Thomas G. "A Rhetorical Study of Student Notes of Lectures on Compo-

sition Delivered by William Leechman." *DAI* 50 (August 1989): 300A.

A transcription and analysis of notes reveals four themes—natural law, reason, the speaker's integrity, and the ends of discourse—that establish a relationship between Leechman's rhetoric and that of other eighteenth-century rhetoricians.

235. Anderson, Wilda. "Scientific Nomenclature and Revolutionary Rhetoric." *Rhetorica* 7 (Winter 1989): 45–54.

Critiques the use of scientific nomenclature in creating the postrevolutionary school system in France to produce well-behaved citizens, showing how public science took over private science.

236. Barilli, Renato. *Rhetoric*. Translated by Giuliana Menozzi. Theory and History of Literature, vol. 63. Minneapolis: University of Minnesota Press, 1989. 192 pages

Presents a history of rhetoric from its origins in ancient Greece to the media technologies of the late twentieth century.

237. Bennett, Beth S. "The Function of Adaptation in Notker's *Rhetorica*." *Rhetorica* 7 (Summer 1989): 171–184.

Explains how Notker's medieval treatise adapted traditional rhetorical doctrine (cases, status) to fit the needs of monks.

238. Blackson, Thomas A. "Cause, Definition, and Explanation in Plato." *DAI* 49 (February 1989): 2251A.

Reexamines three central concepts and their development in Plato's thought.

239. Boerckel, Susan Denise. "Kenneth Burke's Rhetoric of the 1920s, 1930s, and 1940s." *DAI* 50 (December 1989): 1649A.

Argues that Burke's texts of this period are over-determined and historically specific productions. Points to their significance in developing a Marxist theory of rhetoric.

240. Branson, Mark K. "Whats it going to be, eh?: Tracing the English Paragraph into Its

Second Century." *DAI* 50 (September 1989): 678A.

Traces the history of paragraph theory from the 1860s.

241. Briggs, John C. *Francis Bacon and the Rhetoric of Nature*. Cambridge, Mass.: Harvard University Press, 1989. 336 pages

Examines the close relation between Bacon's reform of scientific method and his conceptions of rhetoric, nature, and religion. Argues that for Bacon rhetoric implied everything from gentle persuasion to "coercion and duplicity."

242. Broughton, Bradford B. *"The Art of Falconry:* A Surprising Manual of Rhetoric." *JTWC* 19 (1989).

This medieval manual "offers extended examples of definition, contrast, partition, causal analysis, classification, and description."

243. Burkett, Eva, and Joyce S. Steward. *Thoreau on Writing*. Lanham, Md.: University Press of America, 1989. 294 pages

Collects and classifies Thoreau's reflections on his way of writing, his goals for himself as a writer, and his comments on the craft of other writers.

244. Cahn, Michael. "Reading Rhetoric Rhetorically: Isocrates and the Marketing of Insight." *Rhetorica* 7 (Summer 1989): 121–144.

Analyzes the anti-rhetoric in Isocrates's *Against the Sophists,* which critiques rhetorical handbooks, emphasizes *kairos* and *prepon,* and proposes educating the *orator perfectus.*

245. Campbell, JoAnn Louise. "Gertrude Buck and the Celebration of Community: A History of Writing Instruction at Vassar College." *DAI* 50 (December 1989): 1579A.

Maintains that the writing curriculum at Vassar College under Buck reflected cooperative and democratic conceptions of writing unique to women's colleges.

246. Campbell, Karlyn Kohrs. *Man Cannot Speak for Her, Vol. I: A Critical Study of Early Feminist Rhetoric*. Contributions in Women's Studies, no. 101. Westport, Conn.: Greenwood Press, 1989. 220 pages

A critical analysis of the speeches and writings that set forth the platform and arguments of the early women's rights movement.

247. Campbell, Karlyn Kohrs. *Man Cannot Speak for Her, Vol. II: Key Texts of the Early Feminists*. Contributions in Women's Studies, no. 102. Westport, Conn.: Greenwood Press, 1989. 587 pages

A collection of speeches by national leaders documents the history of American women's rights and suffrage movements from the 1840s through 1920.

248. Campbell, Mary B. "The Rhetoric of Exotic Travel Literature, 400–1600." *DAI* 50 (December 1989): 1652A.

Traces patterns of rhetoric, narrative structure, and imagery in nine works.

249. Condon, Denis. "The Foundation of the Cornell School of Rhetoric." *DAI* 50 (December 1989): 1482A.

Traces the history of the school, focusing on seven men, particularly Edward Lee Hunt, and discussing their philosophical impact on rhetoric.

250. Congalton, Kathryn Jeanine. "Early Twentieth-Century American Origins of Argumentation." *DAI* 49 (March 1989): 2449A.

Examining early developments in argumentation and academic debate reveals a need to define the field of forensics, a shift from written to oral forms, and a continuity of values.

251. Cook, Albert. *History/Writing*. New York: Cambridge University Press, 1989. 275 pages

Argues that historical writing is shaped by two contradictory constraints: the "truth-claims" of texts and the rhetoric of historical discourse.

252. Crowley, Sharon. "A Plea for the Revival of Sophistry." *RR* 7 (Spring 1989): 318–334.

Cites Protagoras and Gorgias as appropriate models for a dynamic "skeptical epistemology" that sees rhetoric and teaching in a sociopolitical context.

253. Engstrom, Timothy M. "Philosophy's Anxiety of Rhetoric: Contemporary Revisions of a Politics of Separation." *Rhetorica* 7 (Summer 1989): 209–238.

Argues for aligning sophistic rhetoric—from Gorgias to Quintilian—with contemporary metaphilosophy and literary theory by remodeling the issue of genre and by appropriating rhetoric.

254. Erdmann, Edward E. "Rhetorical Imitation and English Renaissance Literacy." *DAI* 49 (February 1989): 2127A.

Examines classical rhetorical imitation exercises as used in sixteenth-century English education.

255. Farrell, James Michael, Jr. "John Adams and the Ciceronian Paradigm." *DAI* 49 (June 1989): 3549A.

Analyzes the influence of Cicero's rhetorical precepts on Adams, particularly after 1758, and on American public address in the eighteenth century.

256. Ferrario, Larry S. "The Pariah in the Marketplace: The Audience-Centered Rhetoric of Thomas De Quincy." *DAI* 50 (November 1989): 1311A.

Focuses on how De Quincy took rhetoric out of the classroom and into the marketplace by writing magazine articles aimed at a middle-class audience.

257. Forbis, Elizabeth Peyton. "The Language of Praise in Roman Honorary Inscriptions for Italian Municipals, A.D. 1–300." *DAI* 49 (June 1989): 3839A.

A collection of honorary inscriptions and an analysis of their language and purpose.

258. Fucso, Margaret A. "From Auditor to Actor: Cicero's Dramatic Use of *Personae*

in the *Exordium.*" *DAI* 49 (January 1989): 1792A.

Analyzes Cicero's use and efficacy of personae in the introduction, illuminating their significance for the overall persuasiveness in the rhetorical drama.

259. Glenn, Cheryl. "Women's Empowerment/ Women's Enslavement: Stories from the History of Literacy." *FEN* 17 (Spring 1989): 29–31.

Using examples of educated women through the Renaissance, suggests that literacy alone does not guarantee the power and ability to critique given assumptions.

260. Goodwin, David. "*Controversiae Meta-Asystatae* and the new Rhetoric." *RSQ* 19 (Summer 1989): 205–216.

Discusses the theory of *stasis,* its history, and its evolution into *meta-asystatae* of contemporary rhetoric.

261. Handlin, Oscar, and Lillian Handlin. "Who Reads John Locke? Words and Acts in the American Revolution." *ASch* (Autumn 1989): 545–556.

Discusses the influence of Locke's writings and "words" on the American Revolution, exploring his arguments and rhetorical legacy.

262. Hariman, Robert. "Political Style in Cicero's Letters to Atticus." *Rhetorica* 7 (Summer 1989): 145–158.

Sees Cicero's letters as outlining a style of political republican conduct through rhetorical technique, consensus, and the personal embodiment of public culture.

263. Harris, Roy. *The Origin of Writing*. Peru, Ill.: Open Court, 1986. 176 pages

Uses McLuhan and Derrida to address how human beings came to employ writing as a means of communication.

264. Heath, Robert L. "Kenneth Burke's Poetics and the Influence of I. A. Richards: A Cornerstone for Dramatism." *ComS* 40 (Spring 1989): 54–65.

Examines the development of Burke's view of the connections he believes exist between language, thought, and behavior.

265. Huber, Carole. "Hugh Blair and the Female Pen." Paper presented at the CCCC Convention, St. Louis, March 1988. ERIC ED 297 331. 20 pages

Argues that Blair's rhetoric is paternalistic. Composition teachers should liberate all writers, especially women writers, by valuing private discourse.

266. Hunter, Paul. "On a Covered Railway Platform: A Dialogue Impossible, Completely and Entirely." *CE* 51 (September 1989): 474–477.

An imaginary dialogue sets quotations from Cicero against lines from Heidegger.

267. Impson, Maribeth. "The Concept of *Ethos* in Classical and Modern Rhetoric." *DAI* 50 (November 1989): 1297A.

Argues that understanding the concept of *ethos* can help students use and evaluate persuasive discourse.

268. Jarratt, Susan C. "Walter Pater and the Sophistication of Rhetoric." *CE* 51 (January 1989): 73–87.

Examines rhetoric in *Marius the Epicurean* and in an unpublished manuscript, showing how both works inform late nineteenth-century histories of rhetoric and English studies.

269. Jolliffe, David A. "The Moral Subject in College Composition: A Conceptual Framework and the Case of Harvard, 1865–1900." *CE* 51 (February 1989): 163–173.

Takes the view that, despite the changes wrought by the process movement in the past two decades, composition remains a conservative field.

270. Jost, Walter. *Rhetorical Thought in John Henry Newman*. Columbia, S.C.: University of South Carolina Press, 1989. 278 pages

Asserts that Newman's intellectual stance—his theory and practice of inquiry, argument, interpretation, and judgment—is persistently and thoroughly rhetorical.

271. Langford, Paul B. "Horace's Protean Satire: Public Life, Ethics, and Literature in *Satires II*." *DAI* 50 (July 1989): 131A.

Examines the satirist's use of reported speakers as opposed to direct speech to explain the unity of the second book and its relationship to the first.

272. Lentz, Tony M. *Orality and Literacy in Hellenic Greece*. Carbondale, Ill.: Southern Illinois University Press, 1989. 221 pages

Argues that the key to many of the most exciting cultural developments of the Greek world was the competition between written and oral modes of thought and communication. Proposes that culture flourishes when competition among media emphasizes the strength of each.

273. McKerrow, Raymie E. "Antimasonic Rhetoric: The Strategy of Excommunication." *ComQ* 37 (Fall 1989): 276–290.

Applies to nineteenth-century antimasonic rhetoric Therborn's conception of people as constituted or reconstituted by discourse that articulates what exists, is good, and is possible.

274. Miller, Joyce Rausch. "Language during the Late Renaissance Years: Historical Survey of Issues and Circumstances Responsible for Changes in Attitudes toward Rhetoric during the Seventeenth Century." *DAI* 50 (September 1989): 692A.

Demonstrates Locke's influence on future rhetorics, especially those of Blair, Campbell, and Whately.

275. Miller, Susan. *Rescuing the Subject: A Critical Introduction to Rhetoric and the Writer*. Carbondale, Ill.: Southern Illinois University Press, 1989. 200 pages

Surveys the history of the discipline of composition, explaining how the contemporary study of writing is related to both written and oral rhetoric. Argues that the history of rhetoric is shaped by an aware-

ness that from the beginning oral and written discourse were related.

276. Moran, Michael G. "Joseph Priestley and the Psychology of Style." Paper presented at the CCCC Convention, Seattle, March 1989. ERIC ED 303 837. 13 pages

Examines the psychological theory of style developed in Priestley's *A Course of Lectures on Oratory and Criticism* (1788).

277. Moss, Jean Dietz. "The Interplay of Science and Rhetoric in Seventeenth-Century Italy." *Rhetorica* 7 (Winter 1989): 23–44.

Examines the increasing use of rhetorical arguments by the disputants in the Copernican revolution. Cites Galileo, Guiducci, and Grassi.

278. Murphy, James J. "The Modern Value of Ancient Roman Methods of Teaching Writing, with Answers to 12 Current Fallacies." *WE* 1 (Fall 1989): 28–37.

Quintilian's account of Roman education usefully discusses peer review, sequencing, and integrated language arts. It offers a perspective from which to reevaluate American education.

279. Natali, Carlo. "*Paradeigma:* The Problems of Human Acting and the Use of Examples in Some Greek Authors of the Fourth Century B.C." *RSQ* 19 (Spring 1989): 141–152.

Discusses the use of "model lives" in arguments.

280. Ochs, Donovan J. "Cicero and Philosophic *Inventio*." *RSQ* 19 (Summer 1989): 217–228.

Investigates the connection between philosophy and rhetoric in the construction of philosophic discourse.

281. Poulakos, Takis. "The Cultural Specification of Isocrates's Epideictic Works at the Political, Social, and Economic Levels." *DAI* 49 (January 1989): 1793A.

Examines the historicist conditions of Isocrates's times to see how the public sphere was shaped in his epideictic works.

282. Poulakos, Takis. "Towards a Cultural Understanding of Classical Epideictic Oratory." *Pre/Text* 9 (Fall-Winter 1988): 146–166.

Using Isocrates's *Evagoras* as an example, argues that epideictic rhetoric is a site of cultural critique rather than a means of transmitting timeless, stable values.

283. Quandahl, Ellen. "What Is Plato? Indeference and Allusion in Plato's *Sophist*." *RR* 7 (Spring 1989): 338–348.

Reads this dialogue as undercutting the traditional view of Plato as being opposed to "sophistic relativism." It demonstrates instead "the power of contextual and contigent."

284. Rosetti, Livio. "The Rhetoric of Socrates." *P&R* 22 (1989): 225–238.

Argues that Socrates employed macrorhetorical devices to prepare a situational context. A tendency toward concealment systematically marks Socrates's way of shaping dialogues.

285. Russo, John Paul. *I. A. Richards: His Life and Works*. Baltimore: The Johns Hopkins University Press, 1989. 843 pages

A biography that examines Richards's theories and methods and traces their development through his major critical works.

286. Schriver, Karen A. "Document Design from 1980 to 1989: Challenges That Remain." *TC* 36 (November 1989): 316–331.

Describes the evolution of document design over the past 10 years and proposes a research agenda for the 1990s.

287. Secor, Marie J. "Bentham's *Book of Fallacies:* Rhetorician in Spite of Himself." *P&R* 22 (1989): 83–94.

Explores Bentham's treatment of fallacy from a rhetorical standpoint, suggesting that boundaries between logic and rhetoric

be withdrawn so that the study of fallacy might belong to rhetoric.

288. Shinozaki, Michio Tomonobu. "Rethinking *Ethos* in the Age of Subjectivism." *DAI* 49 (February 1989): 2272A.

Examines Heidegger's perceptions of *ethos*.

289. Short, Bryan C. "The Temporality of Rhetoric." *RR* 7 (Spring 1989): 367–379.

Explores philosophical connections between Aristotle's *Rhetoric* and the ideas of Lacan, Derrida, and Rorty.

290. Sullivan, Dale. "Attitudes toward Imitation: Classical Culture and the Modern Temper." *RR* 8 (Fall 1989): 5–21.

Since modern culture values progress, genius, and technique, "imitation seems antiquarian, tedious, and unscientific." Suggests, however, that it can be valuable.

291. Waggenspack, Beth M. *The Search for Self-Sovereignty: The Oratory of Elizabeth Cady Stanton*. Westport, Conn.: Greenwood Press, 1989. 216 pages

Collects several of Stanton's speeches and analyzes the rhetoric of one of America's earliest and most outspoken advocates of women's rights.

292. Walker, Jeffrey. "Aristotle's Lyric: Re-Imagining the Rhetoric of Epideictic Song." *CE* 51 (January 1989): 5–28.

Examines the Aristotelian paradigm for lyric. Concludes that the prose-lyric antithesis still dominates modern thinking about poetry, but it should not.

293. Wallace, William A. "Aristotelian Science and Rhetoric in Transition: The Middle Ages and the Renaissance." *Rhetorica* 7 (Winter 1989): 7–22.

Evaluates condemnations of medieval distinctions among rhetoric, dialectic, and science. Treats the rise of nominalism and probabalism and Galileo's use of rhetoric in the new science.

294. Whitson, Steve. "The Phaedrus Complex." *Pre/Text* 9 (Spring-Summer 1988): 9–25.

> Argues that rhetoric is subordinated to philosophy by comparing rhetoric in the *Phaedrus* to the position of women in the Oedipus complex.

295. Whittenberger-Keith, Kari Elise. "Paradox and Communication: The Case of Etiquette Manuals." *DAI* 50 (December 1989): 1485A.

> Analyzes the rhetoric of 50 American etiquette manuals published between 1876 and 1985.

296. Wildermuth, Mark E. "The Rhetoric of Wilson's *Arte:* Reclaiming the Classical Heritage for English Protestants." *P&R* 22 (1989): 43–58.

> Examines an overlooked feature of Wilson's *Arte of Rhetorique* (1553), his conviction that a fully developed Ciceronian communication system is the most appropriate method of advancing Christian faith.

297. Yates, JoAnne. "The Emergence of the Memo as a Managerial Genre." *MCQ* 2 (May 1989): 485–510.

> Traces the evolution of the memo as a genre of written communication in American business during the late nineteenth and early twentieth centuries.

See also 11, 12, 50, 65, 76, 113, 140, 148, 191, 194, 226, 299, 303, 308, 329, 391, 397, 553, 587, 595, 720, 939, 977, 988, 994, 997, 1020, 1158, 1286, 1474, 1475, 1481

2.3 POLITICAL, RELIGIOUS, AND JUDICIAL RHETORIC

---

298. Aden, Roger C. "Entrapment and Escape: Inventional Metaphors in Ronald Reagan's Economic Rhetoric." *SCJ* 54 (Summer 1989): 384–400.

> Analyzes the use of inventional metaphors as a rhetorical strategy. Stresses the importance of context and whether metaphors are textual or inventional.

299. Akers, Stanley W. "The Role of Rhetoric in American Cinema in the U.S. Interventionist Movement, 1936–1945." *DAI* 50 (December 1989): 1481A.

> Uses theories of classical rhetoric, social movements, and propaganda to analyze the role of cinema in social policy.

300. Arnold, Thomas Clay. "Political Theory and Language." *DAI* 49 (June 1989): 3855A.

> Argues that language is central to the discipline of political science.

301. Barendse, Nancy Roberta. "My Word Shall Not Return to Me Void: The Rhetoric of Three Television Evangelists." *DAI* 50 (August 1989): 300A.

> Analyzes the rhetoric of three evangelists—Robertson, Copeland, and Angley—on the word, sentence, and discourse levels. Finds that each appeals to a separate audience.

302. Benkendorf, Ray Robert. "Ralph Nader: A Rhetorical Criticism of Epideictic Performative Discourse." *DAI* 50 (August 1989): 301A.

> Demonstrates that Nader's public rhetoric is a fusion of deliberative and epideictic forms.

303. Benson, Thomas W., ed. *American Rhetoric: Context and Criticism.* Carbondale, Ill.: Southern Illinois University Press, 1989. 427 pages

> Nine scholars examine American public discourse through close readings of documents, concepts, and symbols. Each essayist establishes the historical context of a work and explains the methods used to interpret it.

304. Bhardwaj, Umesh Chandra. "Rhetorical Life of Gandhi: His Message of Non-Violence to the Universal Audience." *DAI* 50 (August 1989): 301A.

Uses Burke and Perelman to analyze 11 speeches. Finds that Gandhi's persuasion was based on *logos,* not *ethos.*

305. Blake, Richard Dudley. "The Rhetoric of Malachi." *DAI* 49 (May 1989): 3395A.

Focuses on the rhetorical structure of Malachi, using Ricoeur's categories of understanding.

306. Bruner, Michael S. "The Symbolic Dynamics of German Nationalism: An Analysis of Public Discourse in the Federal Republic of Germany, 1985–1987." *DAI* 49 (January 1989): 1619A.

This discourse study of newspapers and political speeches finds a correlation between the rhetorical processes in texts and speeches and the sense of nationalism.

307. Bruner, Michael S. "Symbolic Uses of the Berlin Wall, 1961–1989." *ComQ* 37 (Fall 1989): 319–328.

A rhetorical analysis of public discourse from 1961–1989 reveals symbolic uses of the Berlin Wall. These uses are part of East-West "constitutive rhetoric."

308. Cali, Dennis D. "A History and Analysis of Selected National Urban League Discourse, 1910–1985." *DAI* 49 (January 1989): 1620A.

Uses Weaver's hierarchy of argument to analyze conference addresses of National Urban League directors.

309. Cohn, Carol E. "Nuclear Discourse in a Community of Defense Intellectuals: The Effects of Techno-Strategic Language and Rationality and Their Role in American Public Culture." *DAI* 49 (February 1989): 2374A.

Examines the discourse of nuclear defense intellectuals, exploring its effects within the professional community and in American political culture.

310. Cox, Erwin Samuel. "An Assessment of Jimmy Swaggart's Responses to ABC's WBRZ Documentary from the Perspective of the Rhetorical Situation." *DAI* 49 (June 1989): 3549A.

Uses Bitzer's criteria to analyze Swaggart's rhetoric, thereby critiquing the theory and suggesting new areas for research.

311. Czernis, Loretta Maria. "The Report of the Task Force on Canadian Unity: Reading a (Re)Writing of Canada." *DAI* 49 (June 1989): 3893A.

Performs a contextual analysis and examines the discursive style of *The Report of the Task Force on Canadian Unity.*

312. Dow, Bonnie J. "The Function of Epideictic and Deliberative Strategies in Presidential Crisis Rhetoric." *WJSC* 53 (Summer 1989): 294–310.

Concludes that crisis rhetoric is not a homogeneous type of discourse. It should be analyzed in relation to different exigencies and functions.

313. Durlesser, James A. "The Rhetoric of Allegory in the Book of Ezekiel." *DAI* 49 (January 1989): 1829A.

Rhetorically examines the allegory of 10 oracles in Ezekiel, concluding that expansive metaphor characterizes the prophecy.

314. Erickson, Keith V. "Presidential Leaks: Rhetoric and Mediated Political Knowledge." *ComM* 56 (September 1989): 199–214.

Argues that presidential leaks constitute rhetorical acts that can initiate public policy, defame opponents, divert public attention, and construct political realities.

315. Feldman, Allen. "Formations of Violence: The Body, Narrativity, and Political Terror in Northern Ireland." *DAI* 49 (March 1989): 2706A.

Concerned with the structural reproduction of political violence as a performative, narrative, symbolic, and hegemonic system.

316. Ferri, Joseph Michael. "Pedro Albizu Campos, 'El Maestro': Translation and Rhetorical Analysis of Selected Speeches." *DAI* 50 (October 1989): 827A.

Presents English translations of three speeches and analyzes their rhetorical features.

317. Foster, David Ruel. "A Study and Critique of Thomas Aquinas's Arguments for the Immateriality of the Intellect." *DAI* 49 (May 1989): 3384A.

Categorizes, clarifies, and assesses arguments in five principal texts. Studies the generation and sustaining of Aquinas's argument throughout the texts.

318. Ganer, Patricia Marian. "An Analysis of the Role of Values in the Argumentation of the 1980 Presidential Campaign." *DAI* 50 (July 1989): 21A.

Compares and contrasts the values, conflicts, and resolutions expressed in the campaigns of Anderson, Reagan, and Carter.

319. Gilder, Eric. "The Process of Political *Praxis:* Efforts of the Gay Community to Transform the Social Signification of AIDS." *ComQ* 37 (Winter 1989): 27–38.

Using Foucault's concepts, this study analyzes how gay people see themselves in relation to the social construction of AIDS discourse.

320. Goldzwig, Steven R., and George N. Dionisopoulos. "John F. Kennedy's Civil Rights Discourse: The Evolution from Principled Bystander to Public Advocate." *ComM* 56 (September 1989): 179–198.

Discusses the shift in President Kennedy's civil rights discourse and the rhetorical constraints that account for this shift.

321. Graves, Michael Clayton. "A Study of Kenneth Burke's Model of Persuasion by Identification and the Concept of Indirect Communication and Their Implications for Sermon Structure." *DAI* 50 (July 1989): 168A.

Advocates biductive preaching, suggesting that Burke's model of persuasion by identification leads to the production of such sermons.

322. Gunnarsson, Britt-Louise. "Text Comprehensibility and the Writing Process: The Case of Laws and Lawmaking." *WC* 6 (January 1989): 86–107.

Discusses the relationship between law text comprehensibility and the legislative writing process. Analyzes sections of Sweden's consumer legislation using rhetorical and sociolinguistic models of writing.

323. Hardy-Short, Dayle Christina. "Defeat and Renewal in the Women's Movement: A Rhetorical Analysis of the Response to the Failure of the Equal Rights Amendment." *DAI* 49 (March 1989): 2450A.

Examines the rhetorical paradoxes that both shaped and hindered leading spokespersons for the Equal Rights Amendment after its defeat in 1982.

324. Heller, Michael A. "Soft Persuasion: A Rhetorical Analysis of John Woolman's Essays and 'Journal.' " *DAI* 50 (December 1989): 1657A.

In establishing a context and describing diction, syntax, and larger patterns, this study explores how Woolman expressed his deep faith and compassion.

325. Hinck, Edward Alan. "Enacting the Presidency: A Rhetorical Analysis of Twentieth-Century Presidential Debates." *DAI* 49 (May 1989): 3200A.

Uses the Aristotelian concept of character in rhetorical persuasion to analyze four presidential debates.

326. Hitchens, Christopher. "Terrorism: A Cliche in Search of a Meaning." *ETC* 46 (Summer 1989): 147–152.

Analyzes the political use of the term *terrorism*. Concludes that it takes on various colorations as it is applied indiscriminately to disparate situations.

327. Huxman, Susan Schultz. "In the World, but Not of It: Mennonite Rhetoric in World War I as an Enactment of Paradox." *DAI* 49 (May 1989): 3201A.

Analyzes from several perspectives the rhetorical postures used by Mennonites.

328. Johnston, Paul Keith. "The Confidence of Edmund Wilson." *DAI* 49 (June 1989): 3719A.

Examines Wilson's writing to discover what humanity is and in what manner it creates itself.

329. Jones, DeWitt Grant. "Wade Hampton and the Rhetoric of Race: A Study of the Speaking of Wade Hampton on the Race Issue in South Carolina, 1865–1878." *DAI* 49 (February 1989): 2020A.

Examines the racial rhetoric of Hampton to assess claims that he was a moderate. Analyzes Hampton's rhetorical means for modifying social realities.

330. Joyner, Russell. "Flags, Symbols, and Controversy." *ETC* 46 (Fall 1989): 217–220.

Discusses semantic problems occurring when others use an object symbolically. People must draw inferences carefully from another's behavior and language.

331. Killingsworth, M. Jimmie, and Dean Steffens. "Effectiveness in the Environment Impact Statement: A Study in Public Rhetoric." *WC* 6 (April 1989): 155–180.

Analyzes the rhetorical context of environmental impact statements. Evaluating a statement's effectiveness must take into account its sociocultural context as well as features of the text.

332. Knutson, Roxann L. "Political Partisanship, Ideological Identification, and Rhetorical Community: Attitudes and Preferences in Use of Political Humor." *DAI* 49 (April 1989): 2861A.

Concludes that attitudes and preferences for political humor differ with political partisanship and ideological identification.

333. Leff, Michael C., and Fred J. Kauffeld, eds. *Texts in Context: Critical Dialogues on Significant Episodes in American Political Rhetoric*. Davis, Calif.: Hermagoras Press, 1989. 324 pages

Sixteen studies of modern public address, including six case studies providing paired analyses of key speeches by Burke, Joan of Arc, Nixon, Johnson, and King.

334. Lewis, Claude. "By Any Other Name Poor Is Poor Is Poor." *QRD* 16 (October 1989): 7–8.

Cites euphemisms associated with poverty and blames them on the bureaucratic need to conceal critical problems.

335. Loscalzo, Craig A. "The Rhetoric of Kenneth Burke as a Methodology for Preaching." *DAI* 49 (January 1989): 1851A.

Analyzes Burke's rhetorical theory and concludes that, as a rhetorical methodology, it is viable for Christian preaching.

336. Lutz, William. "No One Died in Tiananmen Square." *QRD* 16 (October 1989): 1.

Reviews Chinese coverage of Tiananmen Square killings to show how propaganda countered eyewitness reports.

337. Madden, Michael Patrick. "A 'Covenant with Death': The President's Epideictic Message of Legitimation and National Sacrifice." *DAI* 50 (October 1989): 828A.

Proposes a new perspective on epideictic messages that focus on power by analyzing President Reagan's eulogies on the Vietnam dead.

338. Madigan, Mary K. "Forever Yours: The Subgenre of the Letter from the Dead to the Living with Thematic Analysis of the Works of Elizabeth Singer Rowe and Meta Klopstock." *DAI* 50 (September 1989): 681A.

Shows that, far from being morbid, the letter from the dead to the living is a new call to life.

339. Magee, Bruce R. "A Rhetorical Analysis of First Corinthians 8:1–11:1 and Romans 14:1–15:13." *DAI* 50 (September 1989): 710A.

Rhetorically analyzes two parallel New Testament passages, concluding that Paul's purpose in both is to gain his readers' adherence to his values.

340. Matchett, Michele, and Mary Louise Ray. "Revising IRS Publications: A Case Study." *TC* 36 (November 1989): 332–340.

Describes the authors' experience in revising the 1040EZ and 1040A instruction booklet. Specifies design choices made to improve readability, legibility, and usefulness.

341. Matthews, Wayne A. "A Multi-Level Dramaturgic Model of Decision Making." *DAI* 49 (January 1989): 1959A.

Develops a model of decision making based upon mutual expectations of roles to be played in a public organization. Contrasts the model with Herbert Simon's "rational choice" model.

342. Mian, Marla Goodman. "A Dramatistic Analysis of the Anti-Tobacco Movement and the Countermovement Response: 1957–1972." *DAI* 49 (February 1989): 2021A.

Uses Burke's dramatism and Griffith's theory of the phases of a social movement's development to analyze the rhetoric of anti-smoking groups.

343. Miller, Keith D. "Voice Merging and Self-Making: The Epistemology of 'I Have a *Dream*.'" *RSQ* 19 (Winter 1989): 23–32.

Discusses King's speech in terms of typology and epistemology of the black folk pulpit.

344. Moore, Mark P. "Reagan's Quest for Freedom in the 1987 State of the Union Address." *WJSC* 53 (Winter 1989): 52–65.

Identifies the quest as a persuasive, archetypal pattern that produces a common vision of the future through mythical appeals to the past.

345. Moss, Beverly J. "The Black Sermon as a Literary Event." *DAI* 50 (August 1989): 434A.

Examines responses of black congregations to features of oral and written sentences.

346. Murray, Paul Edwards. "Paradox and Narrative: The Social Construction of Reality within International Secretariats." *DAI* 50 (October 1989): 990A.

An ethnographic study of the interpretive processes by which the staff in four United Nations secretariats engage, comprehend, and structure organizational life.

347. Nakazawa, Miyori. "A Rhetorical Analysis of the Japanese Student Movement: University of Tokyo Struggle, 1968–1969." *DAI* 50 (October 1989): 828A.

Uses Bormann's fantasy theme analysis to study three stages of the protest and its influence.

348. Nelson, Elizabeth Jean. "To Ethiopia and Beyond: The Primacy of Struggle in Mussolini's Public Discourse." *DAI* 49 (May 1989): 3202A.

Examines the rhetorical situation of Mussolini's war with Ethiopia and the role of struggle in three rhetorical strategies.

349. Nim, Naomi Barbara. "Discourse of an Emerging Culture, Inter-Group Community among Young Adult Friends: Israeli Jews and Palestinian Israeli Arabs." *DAI* 49 (April 1989): 2852A.

Argues that educational change must be coupled with social and political change.

350. Oehlke, Paul William. "Consciousness Creating, Raising, and Sustaining: Communication in the Independent Fundamentalist Rhetoric of the Reverend Jerry Falwell." *DAI* 49 (March 1989): 2452A.

Uses Bormann's symbolic convergence theory to find that Falwell's "Champions for Christ" rhetorical vision is consistent with the independent fundamentalist rhetorical vision.

351. Olson, Gregory Allen. "Mike Mansfield's *Ethos* in the Evolution of U.S. Policy in Indochina." *DAI* 49 (June 1989): 3551A.

Uses a historical and critical approach to focus on *ethos* in assessing the rhetorical effectiveness of Mansfield's public discourse. Also produces a rhetorical biography of Mansfield.

352. Park, Hee Sul. "A Rhetorical Analysis of Archbishop Desmond M. Tutu through the Burkean Pentad." *DAI* 50 (August 1989): 303A.

Analyzes Tutu's rhetorical strategies, finding his use of identification especially successful.

353. Pearce, Stephen Lee. "Roman Education: An Historical Investigation of the Transfer of Advanced Literacy from Greek to Latin." *DAI* 50 (August 1989): 348A.

Details the process by which Romans "transferred" the literacy of Greeks to their youth by starting with Greek language instruction.

354. Petress, Kenneth C. "A Judicial Decision under Pressure: A Dramaturgical Analysis of the Rosenberg Case." *DAI* 49 (February 1989): 2021A.

Uses Burke's dramatistic pentad to analyze the Rosenberg case and the government's rhetorical behavior. Finds relevance for current espionage cases.

355. Pullum, Stephen J. "A Rhetorical Profile of Pentecostal Televangelists: Accounting for the Mass Appeal of Oral Roberts, Jimmy Swaggart, Kenneth Copeland, and Ernest Angley." *DAI* 49 (April 1989): 2863A.

Uses rhetorical criticism to develop a profile of pentecostal televangelists and to account for their appeal.

356. Reed, Fred. "Where Are the Bad Guys in This Ugly Business?" *QRD* 15 (April 1989): 9–10.

Explores why anyone writes a column on the military, concluding that his purpose is to report how we do so much evil with so few evil people. Reprinted from his "Soldiering" column.

357. Reinsdorf, Walter. "The Rhetoric of the Left." *RSQ* 19 (Winter 1989): 33–44.

Discusses the influence of belief on style in leftist newspapers during the Cuban missile crisis.

358. Rieke, Richard D. *Communication in Legal Advocacy*. Studies in Communication Processes. Columbia, S.C.: University of South Carolina Press, 1989. 295 pages

Suggests practical and strategic guides to effective trial advocacy. Provides theoretical insights into trials as socially sanctioned mechanisms for resolving disputes and discusses applied argumentation within the specialized field of law.

359. Robertson, Linda R. "After Such Knowledge: The Rhetoric of the Iran-Contra Fiasco." *RSQ* 19 (Winter 1989): 3–14.

Discusses the role of the critic in analyzing political rhetoric.

360. Rosenberg, Howard. "In the Middle East, a War of Words." *QRD* 15 (April 1989): 10–11.

Analyzes the language used to describe the Arab-Israeli confrontations.

361. Showman, Sharon Ann. "The Rhetoric of a 'Holy Nation': A Fantasy Theme Analysis of the Rhetorical Vision of the Reverend Marion 'Pat' Gordon Robertson." *DAI* 50 (December 1989): 1484A.

Analyzes five speeches and Robertson's books, discussing his use and distortion of biblical and colonial history.

362. Skinner, Anna Moeling. "Writing in a Law Firm: Cognitive Processes and Texts Grounded in Social Knowledge." *DAI* 50 (August 1989): 428A.

Concludes that lawyers' cognitive processes and the texts they compare are grounded in their social knowledge or representation of a problem.

363. Sullivan, Patricia A. "The 1984 Vice-Presidential Debate: A Case Study of Female

and Male Framing in Political Campaigns." *ComQ* 37 (Fall 1989): 329–343.

A rhetorical, metaphoric, and linguistic analysis of the gender differences between Ferraro's and Bush's performances in the 1984 vice-presidential debate.

364. Swanson, David L., and Dan Nimmo, eds. *New Directions in Political Communication: A Resourcebook*. Newbury Park, Calif.: Sage, 1989. 400 pages

A collection of essays that explores the foundations of political communication as a field of study, examines what messages should be viewed as political, provides an institutional perspective on the field, and reviews the field's current approaches and future directions.

365. Swanson, Jon Charles. "The Rhetoric of Evangelization: A Study of Pragmatic Constraints on Organizational Systems of Rhetoric." *DAI* 50 (December 1989): 1484A.

Analyzes the role of rhetoric in maintaining the beliefs, membership, structure, and communicative effectiveness of evangelical organizations.

366. Virgili, Elizabeth S. "Narrative as Expression of Women's Theological Voice." *DAI* 49 (February 1989): 2426A.

Uses a feminist critique of narrative theology to examine the emergence of women's public voice.

367. Watters, Kathleen Brittamart. "Campaign Communication and the Undecided Voter: An Analysis of the Rhetorical Visions of the 1980 Presidential Campaign." *DAI* 50 (August 1989): 304A.

Uses the Q-technique, Q-factor analysis, and Bormann's theory to determine whether campaigners and voters shared rhetorical visions.

368. William, David. "The Concept of Light in the Old Testament: A Semantic Analysis." *DAI* 49 (June 1989): 3707A.

Analyzes the semantic nature of light in the Old Testament.

369. Williams, Daniel Lee. "The Relevance of Classical Rhetorical Canons for Evaluating Twentieth-Century Preaching." *DAI* 49 (January 1989): 1621A.

Uses the canons of truth, ethics, effects, and the artistic to evaluate sermons, finding significant benefits for improving preaching.

370. Young, John Wesley. "Totalitarian Language: Orwell's Newspeak and Its Nazi and Communist Predecessors." *DAI* 49 (May 1989): 3495A.

Analyzes Orwell's newspeak and concludes that it accurately describes the language used by Nazis and Communists.

See also 74, 150, 207, 208, 237, 255, 261, 262, 273, 296, 748, 797, 823, 951, 955, 966

2.4   COMPUTER AND LITERACY STUDIES

371. Adult Literacy and Basic Skills Unit. *Literacy, Numeracy, and Adults: Evidence from the National Child Development Study*. London: Manpower Services Commission, 1987. ERIC ED 303 610. 88 pages

Reports on a survey of 17,000 23-year-old adults in England, finding that 13 percent report some problems with basic skills.

372. Arulampalam, Santha Devi. "A Comparison of Writing Samples of First Graders in Three Different Social Settings with Assigned and Unassigned Topics." *DAI* 50 (November 1989): 1211A.

Data suggest that responses in various social settings differed.

373. Auerbach, Elsa Roberts. "Toward a Social-Contextual Approach to Family Literacy." *HER* 59 (May 1989): 165–181.

Proposes a family literacy program focused on the family's strengths and the cultural practices of the family's community.

374. Baldwin, Elizabeth Frick. "Linguistics and Ideology in the English-Only Movement." *DAI* 49 (January 1989): 1988A.

Analyzes the processes by which dominant classes maintain linguistic hegemony.

375. Batson, Laurie Goodman. "Language without Sound: The Orality or Literacy of the Deaf and American Sign Language." *WI* 8 (Winter 1989): 68–75.

Posits that Ong's and Havelock's theories of orality and literacy perpetuate the myth that deaf signers are "deficient both mentally and culturally."

376. Bloome, David, ed. *Classrooms and Literacy*. Norwood, N.J.: Ablex, 1989. 432 pages

Eleven essays discuss four major themes affecting the relationship between classrooms and literacy: community, cognitive consequences, access, and power.

377. Bode, Barbara A. "The Effect of Using Dialogue Journal Writing with First Graders and Their Parents or Teachers as an Approach to Beginning Literacy Instruction." *DAI* 50 (July 1989): 106A.

Studies ways to enhance the development of beginning literacy by using integrated reading and writing instruction.

378. Borgman, Christine L. "All Users of Information Retrieval Systems Are Not Created Equal: An Exploration into Individual Differences." *IPM* 25 (1989): 237–251.

System design can compensate for differences in information-seeking styles by correlating technical aptitude, personality, and academic discipline.

379. Bowman, Joel P., and Debbie A. Renshaw. "Desktop Publishing: Things Gutenberg Never Taught You." *JBC* 26 (Winter 1989): 57–77.

Discusses the quality and capabilities of desktop publishing, including relative expenses, limitations, problems, and available hardware and software. Includes a glossary.

380. Brandt, Deborah. "The Message Is the Massage: Orality and Literacy Once More." *WC* 6 (January 1989): 31–44.

Criticizes bipolar discussions of literacy, including Tannen's involvement focus and message focus. Contends that message is the embodiment of focus by using an example from cohesion in written texts.

381. Brodkey, Linda. "On the Subjects of Class and Gender in The Literacy Letters." *CE* 51 (February 1989): 125–141.

Examines both the production and reception of self and others by studying correspondence. Concludes that schools tolerate and legitimate classism, racism, and sexism.

382. Cooper, Marilyn, and Michael Holzman. *Writing as Social Action*. Portsmouth, N.H.: Boynton/Cook, 1989. 256 pages

Discusses improvements in teaching strategies, program design, and research opportunities that come from seeing writing as shaped by political, economic, and educational systems.

383. Davies, Patricia A. L. "Children Learning to Write Their Own Names: Exploring a Literacy Event in Playschool." *DAI* 50 (November 1989): 1196A.

Demonstrates that name writing is a process directed by significant others in the environment.

384. Davis, Ken. "Hypertext: A New Medium for Reading and Writing." Paper presented at the CCCC Convention, Seattle, March 1989. ERIC ED 307 625. 11 pages

Describes the nature and functions of hypertext and the ways in which writing specialists can help create hypertexts.

385. Davis, Ken. "Toward a Hypertext on Writing." Paper presented at the Computers and Writing Conference, Minneapolis, May 1989. ERIC ED 307 626. 11 pages

Claims that hypertext, being multidimensional, can combine the product and process approaches to writing, giving students access to various stages in the writing of documents.

386. Dodge, Susan E. "Learning to Write in Kindergarten: Social Processes and Individual Strategies." *DAI* 49 (June 1989): 3701A.

Finds that encouraging children to interact in speech and writing with literate adults and nonliterate peers supports literacy learning.

387. Dorsey, Paul Raymond. "An Investigation of the Effectiveness of Communication between Systems Analysts and End Users in the Design of Large Computer Systems." *DAI* 49 (January 1989): 1875A.

Studies 56 pairs of systems analysts and potential users of a management information system. Finds significant correlations between psychological and communications variables.

388. Ducksworth, Sarah F. Smith. "Social Factors and Classroom Interactional Patterns Affecting Reading Achievement: Case Studies of Four Low-Literate Black Adults." *DAI* 49 (April 1989): 2894A.

Argues that low literacy among black citizens is best comprehended as an outcome of social organizational inequities.

389. Dunn, Bill, and David Reay. "Word Processing and the Keyboard: Comparative Effects of Transcription on Achievement." *JEdR* 82 (March–April 1989): 237–245.

Argues that most studies examining the effects of word processors on writing achievement are seriously flawed.

390. Foss, Carolyn L. "Tools for Reading and Browsing in Hypertext." *IPM* 25 (1989): 407–418.

Describes some tools that help a reader keep track of what information has been searched and what pertinent items have yet to be read.

391. Gallegos, Bernard. "Literacy, Schooling, and Society in Colonial New Mexico: 1692–1821." *DAI* 50 (October 1989): 983A.

Portrays the ways literacy was used by civil and religious authorities to establish and maintain social control.

392. Gambell, Trevor J. "Linguistics and Literacy Teaching." Paper presented at the Eighth World Conference of Applied Linguistics, Sydney, Australia, June 1988. ERIC ED 299 816. 19 pages

Identifies four major contributions applied linguistics has made to literacy teaching in recent years.

393. Garvey, James J., and David H. Lindstrom. "Pros' Prose Meets Writer's Workbench: Analysis of Typical Models for First-Year Writing Courses." *CC* 6 (April 1989): 81–109.

Results of a study suggest that professional models of writing be used to establish statistical norms, thus emphasizing them as models for students to emulate.

394. George, Diana. "The Politics of Social Construction and the Teaching of Writing." *JTW* 8 (Spring-Summer 1989): 1–10.

Discusses the consequences of accepting language as socially constructed.

395. Grimm, Nancy. "Constructing Ideas of the Social Self." *JTW* 8 (Spring-Summer 1989): 11–20.

Explores three constraints on teachers' valuing diversity. Social pressures encourage "veneers of consensus"; social rules create uneven power distribution; and social value differences silence students.

396. Hammond, Jennifer. "Oral and Written Language in the Educational Context." Paper presented at the International Association of Applied Linguistics, Sydney, Australia, August 1987. ERIC ED 301 880. 24 pages

Argues that lessons for childrens' literacy programs should take into account the differences between oral and written language.

397. Harris, William V. *Ancient Literacy.* Cambridge, Mass.: Harvard University Press, 1989. 408 pages

Attempts to establish the extent of Mediterranean literacy across all social levels from the invention of the Greek alphabet to the fifth century A.D. Examines economic, military, medical, personal, and other records and uses of written communication.

398.   Hart, Ellen Louise. "Literacy and the Empowerment of Lesbian and Gay Students." Paper presented at the CCCC Convention, Seattle, March 1989. ERIC ED 304 662. 13 pages

Argues that writing teachers should ensure that their students have access to a fundamental literacy that is truly multicultural.

399.   Hassan, Salah El Mohammed. "Lore of the Traditional *Malam:* Material Culture of Literacy and Ethnography of Writing among the Hausa of Northern Nigeria." *DAI* 50 (July 1989): 227A.

Discusses how the informational, magical, and aesthetic potential of the written word have been adapted in certain local contexts.

400.   Heath, Shirley Brice. "Oral and Literate Traditions among Black Americans Living in Poverty." *AmP* 44 (February 1989): 367–373.

Verbal and literate skills of poor blacks are acquired by a pattern of socialization different from the mainstream. Changes in the workplace assign value to some of these skills.

401.   Hellerstein, Laurel. "Creating Social Reality with Computer-Mediated Communication." *DAI* 50 (November 1989): 1136A.

Concludes that social reality in computer-mediated communication is formed in the same way as in other communication situations.

402.   Hendricks, William A. "Working at Reading and Writing: Academic Literacy for Adults." *DAI* 50 (September 1989): 675A.

An exploratory essay on academic reading and writing addressed to working adults, college students, and their teachers.

403.   Hert, Ronald S. "A Study of One Computer-Driven Text Analysis Package for Collegiate Student Writers." *DAI* 50 (November 1989): 1199A.

Examines the effects of a computer-assisted text-analysis program on students' writing performance, apprehension, processes, and attitudes.

404.   Hull, Glynda, and Mike Rose. "Rethinking Remediation: Toward a Social-Cognitive Understanding of Problematic Reading and Writing." *WC* 6 (April 1989): 139–154.

Analyzes a summary produced by a basic writer, focusing on social and cognitive variables influencing text production. Sets an agenda for future basic writing research.

405.   Joyner, Randy L. "A Comparison of Errors Detected: Video Display Terminals Versus Hardcopy." *DAI* 50 (November 1989): 1187A.

Investigates 72 postsecondary students' abilities to find errors in hardcopy and on terminals.

406.   Kates, Gary. "The Classics of Western Civilization Do Not Belong to Conservatives Alone." *CHE* 35 (5 July 1989): B1-B2.

Argues that an appreciation of "Great Books" does not necessarily define a conservative. These works are also favored by radicals.

407.   Kearns, Richard, and Linda Bannister. "The Rhetoric of Richard Mitchell: Is Literacy a Moral Condition?" Paper presented at the CCCC Convention, Seattle, March 1989. ERIC ED 303 806. 12 pages

Examines the work of Richard Mitchell, the "underground grammarian," suggesting that he links literacy with morality.

408.   Kook, Joong-Kak. "Incorporating Computer Literacy in Korean Colleges of Education: A Study of Faculty Attitudes, Incentives, and Training." *DAI* 50 (September 1989): 665A.

Finds that prior computer experience and workshops affected attitudes.

409. Le, Thao. "Computers as Partners in Writing: A Linguistic Perspective." *JR* 32 (April 1989): 606.

Discusses how the computer facilitates writing and presents a rationale that takes into consideration the linguistic nature of text.

410. Lewis, Junko Yokota. "Home Literacy Environment and Experiences: A Description of Asian American Homes and Recommended Intervention." *DAI* 49 (April 1989): 2982A.

Surveys home environments and rates them high, middle, and low.

411. Li, David Leiwei, and Donald Lazere. "Two Further Comments on E. D. Hirsch [*CE* 50 (March 1988)]." *CE* 51 (February 1989): 210–217.

Li points out inaccuracies in *Cultural Literacy,* and Lazere praises Hirsch's ideas despite some flaws.

412. "Macintosh Becoming Popular Computer for Composition." *CompC* 2 (November 1989): 4–5.

Reports on composition software for the Macintosh, composition research using the Macintosh, and the *Composition Chronicle* editor's experience with the Macintosh.

413. Miller, Richard E. "Teaching Freire and Testing Hirsch: Bringing Literacy into the Classroom." Paper presented at the CCCC Convention, Seattle, March 1989. ERIC ED 304 658. 12 pages

Introduces a pedagogy that promotes a definition of literacy as the production as well as the consumption of texts.

414. Miyoshi, Masao. "Thinking Aloud in Japan." *Raritan* 9 (Fall 1989): 29–44.

Discusses the phenomenon of conversationalism or *zadankai* and its privileging of orality. Links it to the "growing debility of critical discourse in Japan."

415. Moulthrop, Stuart. "In the Zones: Hypertext and the Politics of Interpretation." *WE* 1 (Fall 1989): 18–27.

Calls for a "social theory of hypertext" for considering political ramifications in designing hypertext systems.

416. Pea, Roy D. "Beyond Amplification: Using the Computer to Reorganize Mental Functioning." Paper presented at the AERA, Chicago, April 1985. ERIC ED 297 706. 35 pages

Argues that because technology can cause cultural redefinition the value of educational goals becomes important.

417. Pedersen, Elray L. "The Effectiveness of Writer's Workbench and MacProof." *CAC* 3 (Spring 1989): 92–100.

Concludes that text-analysis software provides meaningful but limited insights into and suggestions for revising student writing.

418. Peek, George S., Tony Eubanks, Claire May, and Patsy Heil. "The Efficacy of Syntax Checkers on the Quality of Accounting Students' Writing." *CC* 6 (August 1989): 47–62.

Finds no significant difference between the writing of intermediate accounting students who had access to a syntax checker and those who did not.

419. Phillips, Steven Raymond. "Electronic Persuasion: The Uses of Electronic Mail for Interpersonal Influence in Organizations." *DAI* 50 (July 1989): 21A.

Discusses strategic or political views of using electronic mail for manipulative, coercive ends.

420. Randsell, Sarah. "Producing Ideas and Text with a Word Processor." *CAC* 3 (Summer 1989): 22–28.

Reports on studies of idea fluency as determined by the type of discourse and by the number of word-processed drafts.

421. Raymond, Chris. "Humanities Researchers Experience a 'Sea Change' in the Use of Computers in Their Disciplines." *CHE* 35 (12 July 1989): A6-A8.

Reports on an informal survey of humanities academics who use computers, especially databases, for research.

422. Robbins, Rosemary A. "Individuality and Literacy: Historical Perspectives." Paper presented at the American Psychological Association, Atlanta, August 1988. ERIC ED 303 768. 8 pages

Suggests that the technology of literacy helps determine the culture of its members. Draws implications for computer literacy.

423. Rogers, Sharon J., and Charlene S. Hurt. "How Scholarly Communication Should Work in the Twenty-First Century." *CHE* 36 (18 October 1989): A56.

A national, computerized, modem-accessed system of scholarly journals could replace our current dependence on the slow, expensive print medium.

424. Rose, Mike. *Lives on the Boundary: The Struggles and Achievements of America's Underprepared*. New York: The Free Press, 1989. 255 pages

A personal exploration of the struggles students belonging to the educational underclass encounter in becoming literate. Rose interweaves his own educational history with stories about his students to examine how we define literacy and success, hindering or enabling students to cross the boundary from one class or culture to another.

425. Severino, Carol Joan. "Helping Non-Traditional Students Achieve College Literacy: A Context-Based Study of the Uses of Text and Teacher-Student Interaction." *DAI* 50 (December 1989): 1585A.

Studies the impact of two contrasting pedagogical approaches to college literacy and their interaction with personality types, attitudes, and features of discourse.

426. Sledd, Andrew E., and James H. Sledd. "Success as Failure and Failure as Success: The Cultural Literacy of E. D. Hirsch, Jr." *WC* 6 (July 1989): 364–389.

Criticizes the logic and rhetoric of Hirsch's *Cultural Literacy*. Suggests that "Hirsch's cultural literacy is in fact cross-cultural literacy." Includes a postscript on *The Dictionary*.

427. Smith, Eric, and Jeanne Smith. "Model Policies on Software Piracy." *CompC* 2 (September 1989): 6–7, 10.

Reprints two policies from the SUNY-Cortland English Department.

428. Stenzel, John, Wes Ingram, and Linda Morris. "Minicomputer Text-Editing in Upper-Division Cross-Disciplinary Courses." *CC* 6 (April 1989): 62–79.

This study showed that writing clearly improved when students used word processing, but the factors leading to these results could not be isolated.

429. Strickland, James. "How the Student Writer Adapts to Computers: A First-Year Student Protocol." *CC* 6 (April 1989): 7–22.

Studies talking-aloud protocols of a first-year college writing student using the computer for the first time. Sees a need to develop programs to assist evaluation and revision.

430. Swilky, Jody D. A. "Competing Approaches to Literacy Instruction: An Examination of Arguments for Writing in the Disciplines." *DAI* 50 (October 1989): 890A.

Advocates a sociological perspective for writing in the disciplines, noting that empowerment and learning come from scrutinizing the self as well as social and academic contexts.

431. Taylor, Charles D. "Transfer of Editing Skills between Two Microcomputer-Based Word Processors." *DAI* 49 (April 1989): 2979A.

Studies the effect of previously learned knowledge on learning new knowledge. Concludes that some computer environments support transfer while some do not.

432. Taylor, Sue S. "Laptop Computers." *CollL* 16 (Fall 1989): 281–286.

A review of five models of laptop computers.

433. Ting-Toomey, Stella, and Felipe Korzenny, eds. *Language, Communication, and Culture: Current Directions*. Annandale, Va.: SCA and Sage, 1989. 271 pages

A collection of 12 essays. Part I examines the relationships among language, context, and cognition; Part II examines language and cross-cultural styles; and Part III examines language and intergroup communication.

434. Trenner, Lesley. "A Comparative Survey of the Friendliness of On-Line Help in Interactive Information Retrieval Systems." *IPM* 25 (1989): 119–136.

Gives six guidelines for designing or evaluating a "help" facility for computerized interactive information retrieval systems. Rates 16 such systems.

435. Troll, Denise A. "Computer Literacy as Ideology: Whose Side Are You On?" *CollM* 7 (February 1989): 52–60.

Examines computer literacy as a literacy issue, giving a history of the concept. Discusses implications for introductory computing courses.

436. Tyler, Barbara Joan. "The Effects of a Whole Language Classroom on the Development and Use of Text Strategies by Retained First Graders." *DAI* 50 (November 1989): 1208A.

Suggests that children's literacy will develop when they are engaged in purposeful and meaningful reading and writing tasks.

437. van Eyken, Harry K. "Fleabite Fundamentals: Promoting More Meaningful Learning." *JCST* 19 (November 1989): 70–72.

Considers some social and educational effects of accessible pocket computers on orality, literacy, and writing instruction.

438. Wakefield, Richard, and Fred Kemp. "Two Comments on 'Readin' Not Riotin': The Politics of Literacy' [*CE* 50 (September 1988)]." *CE* 51 (September 1989): 533–537.

Wakefield and Kemp take issue with Sledd's contention that teachers should attempt to politicize students and criticize his attitude toward computers.

439. Winterowd, W. Ross. *The Culture and Politics of Literacy*. New York: Oxford University Press, 1989. 226 pages

Argues that, since literacy is the key to political access to society, withholding these skills has been used as a means of social control. Explains how people learn to read and write (and why some do not) and critiques current educational methods, suggesting how they can be improved.

440. Woods, Susan M. "The Effects of Teacher Communication and Cooperation on Student Achievement in Written Language and Attitudes towards Computers." *DAI* 49 (April 1989): 2928A.

Finds no statistical differences in scores for computer and noncomputer composers, but does find increased positive attitudes towards computer composing.

441. Wright, Nicholas, and Rosemary Tilley. "The Computer as Style Guide." *EngT* 5 (July 1989): 12–16.

Describes the limitations and advantages of current software packages for checking style.

See also 26, 28, 60, 75, 85, 175, 259, 272, 349, 353, 487, 575, 592, 909, 980, 1554

2.5   ADVERTISING, PUBLIC RELATIONS, AND BUSINESS

442. Adams, Janet Sosebee. "A Role Set Analysis of the Relationship between Communicator Style and Performance for Male and Female Managers in the Banking Industry." *DAI* 50 (August 1989): 481A.

Examines the relationship between communicator styles of men and women managers and their organizational performance.

443. Augustine, Frederick Kelly, Jr. "Assessing the Value of Information and Its Effect on the Performance of the Organization." *DAI* 49 (June 1989): 3784A.

Discovers that changing the timeliness, accuracy, relevance, and reliability of information affects organizational profitability, cost performance, and resource use.

444. Bannister, James W. "Earnings Signals and Inter-Firm Information Transfers." *DAI* 50 (September 1989): 726A.

Examines inter-firm information transfers around earnings signals.

445. Berg, Joyce Ellen. "Informativeness and Value of Public Information: An Experimental Test." *DAI* 49 (February 1989): 2295A.

Examines the use of multiple signals, the controllability of the signal, and framing effects.

446. Blau, Eileen K., Ferne L. Galantai, and Robert T. Sherwin. "Employment Interviewers' Judgments of Business and Technical Writing of Nonnative Speakers of English." *TWT* 16 (Spring 1989): 136–146.

Reports that subjects found syntactic errors more serious than lexical errors. Suggests teaching strategies to eliminate these errors.

447. Bogert, Judith. "Improving the Quality of Writing in the Workplace: A Case Study." *MCQ* 2 (February 1989): 328–356.

Managers can improve the quality of writing in the workplace by creating an open communication environment and by developing a corporate culture that values sound writing practices as a norm.

448. Boller, Gregory William. "Narrative Advertisements: Stories about Consumption Experiences and Their Effects on Meanings about Products." *DAI* 49 (March 1989): 2730A.

Develops a conceptual model of narrative advertisements and contrasts it with a conceptual model of argumentative advertisements.

449. Booher, Elizabeth Kathleen. "From the Desk Of: The Memo as an Index of Power among Corporate Managers." *DAI* 50 (September 1989): 732A.

Examines the adversarial exchange of memos between middle managers in corporations.

450. Buchholz, William J. "The Boston Study: Analysis of a Major Metropolitan Business- and Technical-Communication Market." *JBTC* 3 (January 1989): 5–35.

A year-long study in 1986 identifies a complex market with diverse needs and expected growth in jobs in technical communication, publishing, public relations, marketing, development, and training.

451. Carlson, A. Cheree. "Narrative as the Philosopher's Stone: How Russell H. Conwell Changed Lead into Diamonds." *WJSC* 53 (Fall 1989): 342–355.

A Burkean analysis reveals Conwell's formula for success in winning audiences for over 50 years.

452. Caster, Arthur Bruce. "An Empirical Investigation of the Usefulness of Financial Reporting Information in Predicting Future Cash Flows." *DAI* 50 (August 1989): 479A.

Determines whether or not predictive models based on financial reporting information could predict future cash flows.

453. Cestley, Carolyn L. "Memory and Selective Information Use in Consumer Choice." *DAI* 50 (September 1989): 739A.

Advances knowledge about memory processes and their influence on consumer choice.

454. Corey, Robert John. "A Characterization and Criticism of Promotional Language in a

Business-to-Business Direct Marketing Context." *DAI* 49 (March 1989): 2730A.

Analyzes the use of language in direct marketing catalogs to invite favorable responses from buyers.

455. Cross, Geoffrey A. "Editing in Context: An Ethnographic Exploration of Editor-Writer Revision at a Midwestern Insurance Company." *DAI* 49 (February 1989): 2195A.

Uses Miles and Huberman's qualitative methodology and Bakhtin's language theory to examine how social context influences the collaborative ghost writing of an executive report.

456. Curtis, Dan B., Jerry L. Winsor, and Ronald D. Stephens. "National Preferences in Business and Communication Education." *ComEd* 38 (January 1989): 6–14.

A survey of 1,000 personnel managers indicates that they consider oral and written communication skills priorities when hiring or promoting employees.

457. DeFloria, James Dale. "The Perceptions of Accounting Students as to the Importance of Written Communication Skills for Success in Accounting Careers." *DAI* 50 (September 1989): 727A.

Surveys accounting students' perceptions as to the importance of 11 written communication skills for success in an accounting career.

458. "Doublespeak and the Corporate Annual Report." *QRD* 15 (July 1989): 12.

Provides examples of "really outrageous" doublespeak found in corporate annual reports.

459. Duger, Amitabh. "The Information Content of the Statement of Changes in Financial Position." *DAI* 50 (October 1989): 995A.

Investigates whether cash flow data are marginally informative to equity investors.

460. Earls, Bill. "Corporatespeak." *QRD* 15 (April 1989): 11–12.

A satiric examination of language used in corporations.

461. Eiler, Mary Ann, and David A. Victor. "Genre and Function in the Italian Business Letter." Paper presented at the Eastern Michigan University Conference on Languages for Business and the Professions, Ann Arbor, April 1988. ERIC ED 304 915. 18 pages

A study contrasting the use of openings, summational closings, and closures in Italian and U.S. business letters. Examines the role of culture in communication.

462. Fertig, Doron. "Advertising as a Signal of Product Quality." *DAI* 50 (October 1989): 1027A.

Discusses a model in which advertising or price signals the quality of a monopolist's product and a model in which advertising signals quality in a duopoly. Also presents an empirical study of how movies are distributed.

463. Frank, Jane. "On the Englishes Used in Written Business Communication across Cultures: Can Readers Tell the Difference? And Does It Matter?" Paper presented at the Eastern Michigan University Conference on Languages for Business and the Professions, Ann Arbor, April 1988. ERIC ED 304 907. 21 pages

Describes a survey of native and nonnative speakers that investigates their sensitivity to texts and their intent.

464. Garay, Mary Sue. "Writers Making Points: A Case Study of Executives and College Students Revising Their Own Reports." *DAI* 49 (June 1989): 3645A.

A descriptive study investigating revision and the construction of a writer's points in business writing.

465. Hagge, John, and Charles Kostelnick. "Linguistic Politeness in Professional Prose: A Discourse Analysis of Auditors' Suggestion Letters, with Implications for Business Communication Pedagogy." *WC* 6 (July 1989): 312–339.

Analyzes negative politeness strategies in a suggestion letters manual used by an accounting firm. Contrasts findings with prescriptions found in 10 business communication books.

466. Harcourt, Jules, and A. C. Krizan. "A Comparison of Resume Content Preferences of Fortune 500 Personnel Administrators and Business Communication Instructors." *JBC* 26 (Spring 1989): 177–190.

Surveys 152 personnel directors and 316 business communication teachers on 70 types of resume information. Notes a shift from personal to job-related or academic data.

467. Hargraves, Monica J. "Information Production and Optimal Contracts." *DAI* 50 (July 1989): 225A.

Analyzes the optimal contract structure for agents who produce and transmit information.

468. Helgert, Joseph P. "Determining an Advertising Position in the Japanese Semiconductor Market: A Cultural and Content Analysis." *DAI* 50 (July 1989): 202A.

Japanese purchase factors had the highest correlation with cumulative image, followed by American purchase factors, product orientation, graphs, and abstract illustrations.

469. Hilton, Chadwick B., William H. Motes, and John S. Fielden. "An Experimental Study of the Effects of Style and Organization on Reader Perceptions of Text." *JBC* 26 (Summer 1989): 255–270.

Studies how 26 readers responded to six stylistic or organizational variations of one advertisement. Questionnaires showed that readers' perceptions could be made to match the text's traits.

470. Hussey, Roger. "The Provision of Information to Stakeholders." *DAI* 50 (July 1989): 218A.

Examines the historical perspective of financial reporting to stakeholders. Conducts a review and analysis of existing literature and previous studies.

471. Ice, Richard Joseph, III. "A Rhetorical Analysis of Union Carbide's Justification of the Bhopal Gas Leak." *DAI* 49 (May 1989): 3201A.

Focuses on the rhetoric of organizational justification, used to repair a damaged public image. Identifies its strategies, shifts, and constraints.

472. Insley, Robert Gayle. "A Study of the Effects of Word Processing and Word-Processing Experience on the Quality of Business Writing." *DAI* 50 (October 1989): 857A.

Results reveal few significant differences in quality, regardless of which method of composing was used or how much experience in word processing writers had.

473. Jaffe, Francoise Georgie. "Metaphors and Memory: A Study in Persuasion." *DAI* 49 (February 1989): 2311A.

Examines metaphor as a device in advertising and proposes guidelines for its successful use by advertisers.

474. Lariviere, Elizabeth. "Writing Skills in Business: Implications for Teachers of Technical Writing." *TWT* 16 (Spring 1989): 103–113.

Reports on writing competencies most lacking in secretaries and their bosses. Concludes that the ability to refuse and to criticize need developing in students.

475. "The Leading Advertisers." *QRD* 15 (April 1989): 4.

Describes the 18 September 1988 issue of *Advertising Age* as a valuable resource for researching, teaching, or studying advertising and its impact on society.

476. Livesay, Kathryn Clough-Kelly. "A Study of Foreign Business Card Composition and Usage Patterns." *DAI* 50 (August 1989): 478A.

Finds that etiquette was more important than content.

477. Miles, Thomas H. "The Memo and Disinformation: Beyond Format and Style." *Issues* 2 (Fall-Winter 1989): 42–60.

Uses a series of in-house memos concerning the Three Mile Island incident to illustrate the need for new strategies to ensure that memos are effective.

478. Miller, Laura Ann. "Interethnic Communication in Japan: Interactions between Japanese and American Co-Workers." *DAI* 49 (January 1989): 1864A.

Ethnographic observation indicates that miscommunication between Japanese and Americans results from unshared situational judgments and interpretations.

479. Pindi, Makaya. "Schematic Structures and the Modulation of Proposition in Economics Forecasting Text." *DAI* 49 (March 1989): 2641A.

Uses genre analysis to examine the language of economic forecasting.

480. Place, Frank Melvin. "Information Quality, Country Risk Assessment, and Private Bank Lending to Less-Developed Countries." *DAI* 50 (August 1989): 498A.

Examines how differences in the quality of information pertaining to less-developed countries affect the perception of risk and the supply of money loaned by commercial banks.

481. Ramaglia, Judith Ann. "Structures in the Accounting Lexicon: An Investigation of Similarities, Structures, and Connotative Dimensions in Five Nations." *DAI* 49 (February 1989): 2297A.

Investigates the fidelity of cross-national translations of accounting terms.

482. Redmond, Claire Ellen. "Professional Writers and Word Processing." *DAI* 50 (July 1989): 89A.

An investigation into the influence of word-processing technology on the writing processes of three professional writers at Honeywell Bull.

483. Salmon, Charles Ray. "The Balance Sheet: An American Fable." *ETC* 46 (Spring 1989): 23–29.

Describes how corporations use numerical information to make misstatements. Analyzes the restructuring, understatement, and overstatement of numbers.

484. Sawin, Gregory. "Can They Persuade You?" *ETC* 46 (Summer 1989): 177–179.

Analyzes the ways advertising uses our "time-binding" propensities to persuade us to buy a product. Suggests countering such advertisements with general semantics principles.

485. Smith, Ronald E. "Writing in the Workplace: A Case Study of an Organization." *DAI* 49 (April 1989): 2955A.

Argues for shifting composition research to the workplace. Concludes that workplace research supports a generic writing process modelled on Flower and Hayes.

486. Spilka, Rachel. "Adapting Discourse to Multiple Audiences: Invention Strategies of Seven Corporate Engineers." *DAI* 49 (June 1989): 3648A.

Studies the use of invention in adapting single corporate documents to multiple audiences.

487. Sturges, David L. "Visual Aspects of Internal Correspondence and Their Impact on Communication Effectiveness." *DAI* 50 (August 1989): 485A.

Examines interactions among laser-printer graphic treatment and communication variables as contributors to explaining variance in comprehension.

488. "Technical Writers in the Corporation: A Conversation with Larry Shamus." *Issues* 2 (Fall-Winter 1989): 6–19.

Reports on a conversation with a recruiter of technical writers for IBM. Describes the selection and training of technical writers and the nature of technical writing projects at IBM.

489. Villamil, Anne Patricia. "Essays on Imperfect Information and Monetary Economics." *DAI* 50 (August 1989): 494A.

Two essays on the role of imperfect information in monetary economics.

See also 297, 745, 788, 796, 823

2.6   LITERATURE, FILM, AND THEATER

490. Amore, Adelaide P. "Multiple Perspectives in a Democratic Society: Learning to Understand and Appreciate How American Women Writers' Search for Identity Enriches Our Literary Heritage." *Leaflet* 88 (Winter 1989): 27–36.

Traces the feminine self from the Colonial Period to the twentieth century through the works of women writers.

491. Anderson, Chris, ed. *Literary Nonfiction: Theory, Criticism, Pedagogy.* Carbondale, Ill.: Southern Illinois University Press, 1989. 337 pages

Seventeen essays study the styles and forms of literary nonfiction.

492. Anderson, Mary Janelle. "Toward a Christian Approach to Literature: The Critical Theories of C. S. Lewis as a Model for Christian Literary Criticism." *DAI* 50 (July 1989): 131A.

Explores the literary critical tradition from a Christian perspective and discusses the potential of Lewis's theories to provide a model for Christian literary criticism.

493. Andrews, Rusalyn Herma. "Deaf Theatre Performance: An Aristotelean Approach." *DAI* 50 (December 1989): 1485A.

Analyzes deaf theater performance by translating Aristotle's critical theories into a style that incorporates visually based language.

494. Atwell, Wendy H. "The Application of Reader-Response Theory and Object-Rela-

tions Theory to Three Secondary English Teachers' Reading Experiences and Their Literature Curricula." *DAI* 50 (July 1989): 61A.

A thematic analysis based on texts of teachers' autobiographies and selections from their literature curricula.

495. Austin, Timothy R. "Narrative Discourse and Discoursing in Narratives: Analyzing a Poem from a Sociolinguistic Perspective." *PT* 10 (Winter 1989): 703–728.

Uses techniques of conversation analysis and structural narratology to explain anomalous discourse in a Wordsworth poem and to suggest explanations for nonliterary discourse.

496. Baker, Beverly. "Deconstructionism?—As Thoreau Said, Simplify!" *IlEB* 76 (Winter 1989): 23–29.

A brief introduction to issues in critical theory for those teaching high school and college English.

497. Banks, Carol P. "Playwriting for Different Age Levels." *DAI* 49 (February 1989): 2023A.

Compares the theory and practice of writing plays for adults and plays for young audiences. Identifies problems that lead to the limitations of young people's plays and proposes a solution.

498. Bevan, C. Knatchbull. "The Rhetoric of Syntax in *Pride and Prejudice.*" *Lang&S* 20 (Fall 1987): 396–410.

Examines the characters' and narrator's habitual syntactic patterns to show how syntax provides an index of behavior, thus reinforcing major themes.

499. Biguenet, John, and Rainer Schulte, eds. *The Craft of Translation.* Chicago Guides to Writing, Editing, and Publishing. Chicago: University of Chicago Press, 1989. 176 pages

Collects nine essays discussing the implications of literary translation for critics, scholars, teachers, and students. Translators need both comprehensive scholarly training and broad creativity in recreating the text in a new language.

500. Black, David. "Narrative Film and the Synoptic Tendency." *DAI* 50 (July 1989): 2A.

An inquiry into the cognitive, textual, and cultural significances of the relations between filmic and verbal narrative expression.

501. Booth, Wayne C. *The Company We Keep: An Ethics of Fiction*. Berkeley: University of California Press, 1988. 571 pages

Argues that ethical values must enter into our experience of literature. Readers enter a dialogue with an author that helps them test and understand what they value.

502. Brady, Laura A. "Collaborative Literary Writings: Issues of Authorship and Authority." *DAI* 49 (April 1989): 3016A.

Challenges the notion of the isolated romantic artist and offers composition theory as a model for studying literature in a social and interactive context.

503. Bruss, Neal. "Literary Theory, English Departments, and the Pleasures of Alarm." *CE* 51 (January 1989): 95–98.

Charges that Graff and Gibbons's *Criticism in the University* lacks current reports from English Departments to support its assumption of recent literary theory's harmful effects.

504. Burgard, Peter J. "The Serious Game: Essaying Goethe's Essays." *DAI* 50 (September 1989): 694A.

Studies Goethe's essays in a generic context that accounts for the rhetorical and discursive context.

505. Campbell, Gwyn E. "The Rhetoric of Exemplarity: From Prologue to Censor." *DAI* 49 (January 1989): 1816A.

Examines the *novela corta,* developed in an era of censorship that both created and limited the genre's dynamics.

506. Chamberlain, Lori. "Bombs and Other Exciting Devices; or, The Problem of Teaching Irony." *CE* 51 (January 1989): 29–40.

Associates power and sophisticated literacy with irony. Proposes teaching ironic writing to foster critical thinking, reading, and writing.

507. Clifford, John. "Discerning Theory and Politics." *CE* 51 (September 1989): 517–532.

Reviews three books examining concepts of intellectual Marxism.

508. Colleran, Jeanne Marie. "The Dissenting Writer in South Africa: A Rhetorical Analysis of the Drama of Athol Fugard and the Short Fiction of Nadine Gordimer." *DAI* 49 (March 1989): 2655A.

Uses Burke's principles of rhetorical criticism to determine how Fugard and Gordimer have overcome the legal and social restrictions on their work.

509. Conway, Daniel J. "Erotic Arguments: Rhetoric and Sexuality in Seventeenth-Century English Stage Adaptations of Plutarch." *DAI* 50 (November 1989): 1139A.

Examines the rhetorical functioning of dramatic actions, exploring how stage adaptation can produce arguments different from narrative rhetoric.

510. Cooley, Elizabeth Williams. "One Must Stop to Find a Word: Language and Communication in the Novels of Virginia Woolf." *DAI* 49 (June 1989): 3730A.

Discusses Woolf's fascination and frustration with the power and limitations of the written word.

511. Cotton, Daniel. *Text and Culture: The Politics of Interpretation*. Theory and History of Literature, vol. 62. Minneapolis: University of Minnesota Press, 1989. 200 pages

Examines the political aspects of contemporary disciplines of interpretation, indicating how interpretation may be turned into a more socially responsible practice.

512. Coughlin, Ellen K. "After 'Salinger': Few Feel Sting of Ruling on Use of Papers." *CHE* 36 (15 November 1989): A4, A6-A7.

Following Salinger's court-supported refusal to allow the use of his papers, some scholars confront similar difficulties with other authors' materials.

513. Crawford, Thomas Hugh. "The Rhetoric of Medical Authority: The Early Writings of William Carlos Williams." *DAI* 49 (March 1989): 2657A.

A study of how Williams's work generates poetic authority by invoking the language and values of the medical community. Draws on Burke, Foucault, and Lentricchia.

514. Crowley, Sharon. *A Teacher's Introduction to Deconstruction*. Teacher's Introduction Series. Urbana, Ill.: NCTE, 1989. 63 pages

Provides an overview of Derrida's thought, discusses the major concepts of deconstruction, and examines the implications of deconstructionist theory for teaching, especially for teaching writing.

515. Davidson, Phebe. "Narrative Stance in the Douglass Autobiographies." Paper presented at the CCCC Convention, Seattle, March 1989. ERIC ED 304 686. 26 pages

Posits that the shifting of Frederick Douglass's narrative stance is an index of his intellectual development and of his understanding of himself.

516. Davies, Carole Boyce. "In Their Own Words: Life and Work in South Africa." *CE* 51 (January 1989): 88–94.

Reviews three collections of narratives about life in South Africa. Collectively they reveal that gender and race determine employment satisfaction, possibilities for advancement, salary increases, and control of one's destiny.

517. Davis, Elizabeth H. "The Rhetorical Poetics of Marianne Moore: A Structuralist and Semiotic Analysis of Style." *DAI* 50 (November 1989): 1304A.

Concludes that Moore's rhetorical poetics violates readers' expectations and that intertexts may be used in the composing process as well as in interpretation.

518. de Beaugrande, Robert. *Critical Discourse*. Norwood, N.J.: Ablex, 1988. 496 pages

A survey of 16 contemporary literary theorists.

519. Dingwaney, Anuradha, and Lawrence Needham. "(Un)Creating Taste: Wordsworth's Platonic Defense in the Preface to *Lyrical Ballads*." *RSQ* 19 (Fall 1989): 333–348.

Discusses Wordsworth's Preface as a rhetorically sophisticated defense of the *Ballads* designed to influence the reader's reception of them.

520. Dolan, Marc. " 'True Stories' of 'The Lost Generation': An Exploration of Narrative Truth in Memoirs of Hemingway, Cowley, and Fitzgerald." *DAI* 50 (August 1989): 471A.

Explores the ways in which quasi-factual stories convey historical truth, concentrating on three memoirs of the 1920s.

521. Donovan, Ellen Renee. "Narrative Authority in Nineteenth-Century American Literature: A Study of Dialogic Structures." *DAI* 50 (August 1989): 443A.

Uses a dialogic model and sentence-level analysis to examine the role of narrator and other characters in the reader's construction of narrative.

522. Dyck, Edward Frank. "*Topos* and the Rhetoric of Prairie Poetry." *DAI* 49 (March 1989): 2664A.

A rhetorical analysis of eight, twentieth-century, Canadian prairie poets who treat "place" as *topos* and argument.

523. Ebert, Teresa Lynn. "Patriarchy, Ideology, Subjectivity: Towards a Theory of Femi-

nist Critical Cultural Studies." *DAI* 50 (July 1989): 138A.

Develops postmodern feminist cultural studies through an inquiry into contemporary critical theory.

524. Elbaum, Henry. "Rhetoric and Fiction: Interaction of Verbal Genres in the Soviet Literature of the Twenties and Thirties." *DAI* 50 (July 1989): 158A.

Examines this literature's relationship to other verbal genres, particularly speeches by party leaders, newspaper rhetoric, and political posters.

525. Ernst, Charles Albert Scheuring. "Contextualizing the Character: Generic Studies of Text and Canon, Rhetoric, Style, and Quantitative Analysis in Seventeenth-Century English Prose Character." *DAI* 49 (May 1989): 3367A.

Discusses how character acts as a persuasive instrument. Uses enumerative inventories to model characters.

526. Esonwanne, Uzoma M. "Difference, Interpretation, and Referentiality." *DAI* 49 (February 1989): 2227A.

Examines the influences of culture, history, and authority on readers.

527. Fanto, James A. "The Making of a Literary Critic: Professionalism and the Strategies of Authority." *DAI* 49 (February 1989): 2210A.

Examines systems of power in literary studies, drawing on the theories of Foucault and Bourdieu.

528. Fischlin, Daniel T. "'I Know not what yet that I feele is much': The Rhetoric of Negation in the English Air." *RSQ* 19 (Spring 1989): 153–170.

Discusses types of negation used as structural devices in English poetry.

529. Flachmann, Kim. "From Discord to Harmony: Sound and Punctuation Patterns in Williams's Poetry." *Lang&S* 20 (Fall 1987): 315–341.

A numerical study of Williams's entire corpus shows that he increased assonance, decreased alliteration, and increased parataxis as he matured. Shows the effects of changing patterns on meaning.

530. Foil, Sylvia Lynne. "An Examination of the Conceptual Approach to Film Genre with a Specific Application to the Definition of the Apocalyptic." *DAI* 50 (October 1989): 812A.

Examines the evolution of the cultural model of genre for the purpose of illuminating contemporary precepts of genre while laying the foundation for a conceptual model of genre.

531. Frentz, Thomas S. "Resurrecting the Feminine in *The Name of the Rose*." *Pre/Text* 9 (Fall-Winter 1988): 123–145.

Describes the importance of the repressed feminine semiotic in Eco's repositioning of logocentric, patriarchal rhetoric.

532. Furniss, David West. "Making Sense of the War: Vietnam and American Prose." *DAI* 49 (January 1989): 1861A.

Argues that the Vietnam War changed the way American writers convey the experience of war.

533. Fuss, Diana J. "Essential Theories/Theory's Essentialism: Feminism, Poststructuralism, and Contemporary Literary Criticism." *DAI* 49 (February 1989): 2205A.

Examines the nature and difficulties of contemporary approaches to texts.

534. Gilbert, Sandra M., and Susan Gubar. *The Place of the Woman Writer in the Twentieth Century: Sexchanges*. New Haven: Yale University Press, 1989. 472 pages

Investigates the connections between feminism and modernism, politics and poetics, and gender and genre. Argues that for literary men and women at the turn of the century, sexual battles were associated with radically reconceived gender roles.

535. Gillen, Jay M. "Rhetorical Invention in the Poetry of Robert Browning." *DAI* 49 (January 1989): 1809A.

Labeling Browning's poetry "forensic," this dissertation focuses on the poet's role as artist in creating arguments for social ends.

536. Green, Susan Gale. "The Narrative Construction of Women in Literary Texts." *DAI* 50 (July 1989): 146A.

Examines the proposition that particular narrative practices create particular notions of gender.

537. Greene, Elizabeth. "'Teach the Conflicts' Preaches This Humanist." *CHE* 35 (8 February 1989): A3.

Northwestern University professor Gerald Graff argues that the curriculum would be strengthened if teachers taught the conflicts among critical approaches, rather than merely taking sides.

538. Greer, Michael. "Ideology and Theory in Recent Experimental Writing: or, The Naming of 'Language Poetry.'" *Boundary* 16 (Winter-Spring): 335–355.

Reading avant-garde poets requires reconsidering what it means to read, as attention is callled "to the taken-for-granted nature of reading as process and its reliance on ideology."

539. Hallaq, Ghada Bathish. "Discourse Strategies: The Persuasive Power of Early Khariji Poetry." *DAI* 50 (July 1989): 155A.

Analyzes the arguments, semantic patterns, and language structures of this poetry, which attempts to persuade the audience to act on behalf of the Khariji.

540. Hallett, Nicolette. "New Fashions in Style: Social Ostentation in the Art and Literature of Fifteenth-Century England." *DAI* 49 (January 1989): 1923A.

Studies the influence of cliques of "consumers" in the formulation of literary style.

541. Hantzis, Darlene Marie. "'You Are About to Begin Reading': The Nature and Function of Second-Person Point of View in Narrative." *DAI* 49 (June 1989): 3550A.

Asserts that the second-person point of view challenges traditional concepts of narrative subjectivity and authority. Suggests reasons for the postmodern impulse of this viewpoint.

542. Heidt, Edward R. "Narrative Voice in Autobiographical Writing." *DAI* 50 (July 1989): 147A.

Examines the mimetic and diegetic voices in autobiographies to understand how this writing might stand as a single genre.

543. Heuberger, Dale L. "A Study of the Inner Speech of Seventh Graders Who View a Film." *DAI* 50 (September 1989): 613A.

Analyzes inner speech by examining written responses to film.

544. Hirschkop, Ken, and David Shepherd. *Bakhtin and Cultural Theory*. New York: St. Martin's Press, 1989. 234 pages

Eight essays explore the relevance of Bakhtin's work in areas of cultural studies, including aesthetics, reception theory, the discourse of colonialism, linguistics, women's studies, and theories of the body.

545. Hockley, Luke James. "Detecting the Myth: An Application of C. G. Jung's Analytical Psychology to Film Analysis." *DAI* 50 (November 1989): 1116A.

Uses Jung's theories about conscious and unconscious behavior to develop a model for film analysis.

546. Hogarty, Kenneth W. "Heroes Need Apply: A Critical Study of Appropriating Action in Classrooms Informed by Reader-Response Theory." *DAI* 49 (April 1989): 2955A.

Using Rosenblatt and Ricoeur, concludes that reader-response classroom practices encourage students to become "communicatively competent."

547. Horner, Bruce M. "The Rhetoric of Seventeenth-Century English Songs." *DAI* 49 (January 1989): 1809A.

Using Burke's dramatistic model, this dissertation analyzes seventeenth-century songs as rhetorical "scenes."

548. Jang, Gyung-Ryul. "The Limits of Essentialist Critical Thinking: A Metacritical Study of New Criticism and Its Theoretical Alternatives." *DAI* 50 (July 1989): 140A.

Analyzes critical objectivity in terms of psychological, as opposed to formal, distinctions between the languages of poetry and criticism.

549. Johnson, Cheryl Lynn. "A Womanist Way of Speaking: An Analysis of Language Use in Alice Walker's *The Color Purple,* Toni Morrison's *Tar Baby,* and Gloria Naylor's *The Women of Brewster Place.*" *DAI* 49 (June 1989): 3884A.

Argues that black women speak a "genderlect" that reveals black women's consciousness in the characters of three novels.

550. Johnson, Mary Charlotte. "A Critical Study of the Poetic Voice in the Narratives of Selected Documentary Films of the 1930s." *DAI* 50 (October 1989): 813A.

Examines the inter-animation between words and moving images since many students rely on visual images as the developmental instrument of thought.

551. Jones, Steven Jeffrey. "Criticism, Historicism, and the Rediscovery of Lyricism: Frank Lentricchia's Post-Existential Divagations." *Boundary* 16 (Winter-Spring): 129–160.

Discusses how de Man, Burke, Adorno, Foucault, and Derrida treat linguistic and rhetorical configuration, determinism, and cultural discourse differently from traditional critics.

552. Juhasz, Suzanne. "Reading Dickinson Doubly." *WS* 16 (1989): 217–221.

Suggests that the perspective of a woman writing in a patriarchal structure creates a doubleness of meaning best preserved in the reader's mind by "slow-motion" reading.

553. Katz, Steven Barry. "Teaching the Uncertain: The Application of Reader-Response Criticism to the Teaching of Writing as a New Sophistic." *DAI* 49 (March 1989): 2637A.

Reader-response criticism parallels methods of Cicero, the Sophists, and the new physics by admitting subjectivity and social persuasion in the making of knowledge.

554. Kawaharada, Dennis. "The Rhetoric of Identity in Japanese American Writings, 1948–1988." *DAI* 49 (March 1989): 2659A.

Argues that the rhetoric of ethnicity and protest has promoted sociopolitical participation and created a strong ethnic identity for Japanese Americans.

555. Kelly, Anne Cline. "Conversation: The Tie That Binds." *CEAC* 51 (Winter-Spring 1989): 31–41.

Analyzes Jonathan Swift's "deconstruction" of marriage, emphasizing intellectual discourse as the basis of an ideal union and the importance of reading and verbal interplay in relationships.

556. Kelly, Nancy Webb. "*Homo Ludens, Homo Aestheticus:* The Transformation of 'Free Play' in the Rise of Literary Criticism." *DAI* 49 (March 1989): 2644A.

Addresses the rhetorical significance of free play in the literary criticism of Schiller, Coleridge, Arnold, Richards, Huizinga, Gadamer, and Derrida.

557. Klein, Roxanne Veronica. "Reading and Writing the Place of Difference: Mary Wollstonecraft, Mary Shelley, and Women's Discourse in Late Eighteenth- and Early Nineteenth-Century Britain." *DAI* 49 (June 1989): 3719A.

Considers Wollstonecraft's and Shelley's strategies for constructing a place for females or any figures of difference.

558. Kraemer, Donald James. "Creating and Controlling Plurality: A Critique of Some Attempts to Unify the Profession of Literary Studies." *DAI* 49 (June 1989): 3712A.

Using the theories of Booth, Jameson, and Fish, this study considers the role of literary studies and its potential for changing society.

559. Lanier, Douglas Mercer. "'Better Markes': Towards a Rhetoric of Jonsonian Authority." *DAI* 49 (March 1989): 2669A.

Argues that Jonson struggled "to create an anti-rhetorical rhetoric of poetic selfhood."

560. Larabee, Ann E. "First-Wave Feminist Theatre, 1890–1930." *DAI* 49 (February 1989): 2426A.

Explores women's use of theater in the first-wave feminist struggle for personal and political freedom.

561. Levine, George. "Graff Revisited." *Raritan* 8 (Spring 1989): 121–133.

A review of *Professing Literature* that argues for "contextualization" as the chief principle determining the English curriculum.

562. Levy, Anita Beth. "The Reevaluation at Home: Domestic Fictions in the Human Sciences." *DAI* 49 (May 1989): 3370A.

Suggests that writing established the notion of gender as the primary means whereby modern individuals came to know and evaluate themselves in England.

563. Lewis, Jayne Elizabeth. "The Voluble Body: Re-Inventing the Neoclassical Fable." *DAI* 50 (July 1989): 148A.

Views fable as a signifying strategy that both demonstrates the identification between the body and linguistic order and inculcates particular epistemological dispositions in readers.

564. Marshall, Brenda K. DeVore. "A Semiotic Phenomenology of Directing." *DAI* 50 (August 1989): 306A.

Argues that theater is a collaborative art. The successful director must consider the nature of human communication within the theatrical rite of passage from pre-performing to performing.

565. Marshall, Gary T. "An Exploration of William Stafford's Writing Process." Paper presented at the Midwest Regional Conference of English in the Two-Year College, Urbana, Ill., February 1988. ERIC ED 299 562. 22 pages

Argues that the poet's experimentation with open form shows that writing is discovery and process rather than plan and product.

566. Martin, Jerry Jon. "Hawthorne, Melville, and Poe." *DAI* 49 (June 1989): 3725A.

Examines how self-delusion works in the rhetorical strategies of Hawthorne, Poe, and Melville.

567. McGuiness, Ilona Maria Kuehnhackle. "Only Connections: Rhetoric as Collaborative Impulse in E. M. Forster's Nonfiction." *DAI* 49 (February 1989): 2232A.

Examines Forster's rhetorical and stylistic strategies, used to make readers collaborators in the construction of his texts.

568. McKerrow, Raymie E. "Critical Rhetoric: Theory and *Praxis*." *ComM* 56 (June 1989): 91–111.

Sets out a theoretical rationale for a critical rhetoric. Presents eight principles that orient the critic toward the act of criticism.

569. McNarie, Alan D. "The Gospel of St. Thomas: An Exploration of Roleplaying and the Creative Process." *DAI* 49 (March 1989): 2644A.

Draws on speech-act theory, reader-response theory, and modern dramaturgy to examine the heuristics of roleplaying in fiction writing.

570. Miller, Cristanne. "Approaches to Reading Dickinson." *WS* 16 (1989): 223–228.

Illustrates the power of language to close and open meaning by discussing the syntactic gaps in Dickinson's poems, which the reader has to fill.

571. Miyake, Lynne K. "Woman's Voice in Japanese Literature: Expanding the Feminine." *WS* 17 (1989): 87–100.

Describes the development of a distinct female discourse in personal and lyrical forms of Japanese literature.

572. Morris, Mary Josephine. "Evelyn Waugh: The Novel and Its Relation to Other Media." *DAI* 50 (July 1989): 149A.

Waugh's novels parody futuristic art, Hollywood filmmaking, journalism, lyric poetry, Victorian narrative painting, and radio broadcasting.

573. Murphy, Patrick D. "The Verse Novel: A Modern American Poetic Genre." *CE* 51 (January 1989): 57–72.

Describes the verse novel as a self-conscious genre tending toward the polyphonic and dialogical and resembling the novel in plot, theme, characterization, and length.

574. Murray, Frank J., Jr. "Speaking the Unspeakable: Theatrical Language in the Plays of Samuel Beckett and Sam Shepard." *DAI* 49 (March 1989): 2454A.

Uses semiology, phenomenology, hermeneutics, reader-response theory, and performance theory to examine the problematic relationship between words and other types of expression in Beckett's and Shepard's works.

575. Olson, Jon. "Frederick Douglass and a Process of Cultural Literacy Empowerment." *DAI* 50 (July 1989): 141A.

Examines Douglass's persona in three autobiographies. Traces his movement, through literacy, from a subordinate to a dominant culture without alienation from his original culture.

576. Radcliffe, David Hill. "Meditations and Literary History, 1600–1750." *DAI* 50 (July 1989): 149A.

Discusses the importance of meditational genres in articulating philosophical, religious, and social positions.

577. Radner, Hilary Ann. "Shopping Around: Locating Feminine Enunciation through Textual Practice." *DAI* 49 (May 1989): 3530A.

Examines narratives associated with feminine activities, investigating the production and deployment of gender in the romance, the novel, the women's magazine, and the self-help book.

578. Ratcliffe, Krista L. "Words of One's Own: Toward a Rhetoric of Feminism in Selected Essays of Virginia Woolf and Adrienne Rich." *DAI* 49 (March 1989): 2653A.

Studies how Woolf and Rich transcend the traditional rhetorical strategies of a "phallogocentric language" to develop their own rhetoric of feminism.

579. Reed, Melissa Ann. "Recurring Images of Symbolic Action in Shakespeare's *Tragedy of Romeo and Juliet:* Initiating the Bard." *DAI* 49 (February 1989): 2028A.

Argues that theater is symbolic action. Uses four interpreting processes—clustering, storying, ceiling, and conjuring—to examine Shakespeare's composition process.

580. Richter, David H., ed. *The Critical Tradition: Classic Texts and Contemporary Trends.* New York: St. Martin's Press, 1989. 1488 pages

Documents the evolution of critical theory from Plato to the 1980s through selections by 35 major figures. Includes 108 selections representing seven schools of criticism and treats two significant critical issues, the literary canon and authorial intention. Authors of the selections are not indexed separately in this volume.

581. Robe, Margaret Ann. "Conceiving a Self in Autobiography by Women." *DAI* 49 (June 1989): 3720A.

Considers theories of gender, genre, and representation in autobiography and their implications for the theory and practice of women's autobiography.

582. Rosenberg, Brian C. "Character and the Demands of Structure: The Example of Dickens." *CEAC* 51 (Winter-Spring 1989): 42–54.

A study of the power of language to create extra-textual reality. Characters like Scrooge transcend the text to assume an independent existence in the popular imagination.

583. Ryan, Frank L. "Democracy and Books." *Leaflet* 88 (Winter 1989): 14–16.

Contrasts Emerson's comments on books with those of Ellison to illustrate the changed role of books in a democracy.

584. Salvatori, Mariolina. "Recuperative Readings." *CE* 51 (February 1989): 201–209.

Reviews Weinsheimer's and Wertsch's critical readings of Gadamer and Vygotsky, respectively. Finds that they extend the conversation about knowledge.

585. Schultz, Jane Ellen. "Women at the Front: Gender and Genre in the Literature of the American Civil War." *DAI* 49 (February 1989): 2282A.

Explores the impact of assumptions about femininity on historical genres and examines the development of gender consciousness in diaries, memoirs, and letters.

586. Seamon, Roger. "Poetics against Itself: On the Self-Destruction of Modern Scientific Criticism." *PMLA* 104 (May 1989): 294–305.

Argues that criticism is primarily neither science nor interpretation but an act of assertion in an exchange of texts.

587. Smith, Kathy Overhulse. "Making Much of Time: Rhetorical Strategies of Renaissance *Carpe Diem* Poetry." *DAI* 49 (May 1989): 3372A.

Describes rhetorical strategies in the poems and relates them to Renaissance rhetoric in general. Ties the fate of *carpe diem* poetry to the fate of formal rhetoric.

588. Stam, Robert. *Subversive Pleasures: Bakhtin, Cultural Criticism, and Film*. Baltimore: The Johns Hopkins University Press, 1989. 282 pages

Offers an extended application of Bakhtin's critical methods. Analyzes eroticism in the cinema and applies textual dialogism to mass media.

589. Steig, Michael. *Stories of Reading: Subjectivity and Literary Understanding*. Baltimore: The Johns Hopkins University Press, 1989. 272 pages

Argues for a method of reading that explores the intersection of the reader's subjective response, the text's intrinsic qualities, and such extrinsic factors as author and source.

590. Stewart, Matthew C. "Making Sense of Chaos: Prose Writing, Fictional Kind, and the Reality of Vietnam." *DAI* 50 (July 1989): 141A.

Regards realism as a viable aesthetic in conveying the chaotic realities of American involvement in Southeast Asia into a variety of styles.

591. Straayer, Amy Christine. "Sexual Subjects: Signification, Viewership, and Pleasure in Film and Video." *DAI* 50 (October 1989): 813A.

Studies sexuality, representation, and narrative in film, emphasizing that the conflation of sex and gender is a social construct.

592. Sullivan, Dale Lee. "A Rhetoric of Children's Literature as Epideictic Discourse." *DAI* 49 (May 1989): 3204A.

Develops a multi-faceted theory of epideictic rhetoric to analyze C. S. Lewis's *The Chronicles of Narnia*. Argues for the importance of epideictic rhetoric in establishing cultural values.

593. Todd, Loreto. *The Classroom of Irish Literature*. Edited by N. F. Blake. Language of Literature. New York: St. Martin's Press, 1989. 209 pages

Discusses Irish literature in terms of historical linguistic contacts in Ireland. Describes the development of English varieties in Ireland, the nature of Irish and Irish varieties of English, and the oral tradition of songs, stories, prose, poetry, and drama.

594. Tuchman, Gaye, and Nina E. Fortin. *Edging Women Out: Victorian Novelists, Publishers, and Social Change*. New Haven: Yale University Press, 1989. 288 pages

Both a sociological study of occupational gender transformation and a historical study of writing. Documents how men supplanted women as novelists once novel-writing was perceived as profitable.

595. Vickers, Brian. *Classical Rhetoric in English Poetry*. Carbondale, Ill.: Southern Illinois University Press, 1989. 186 pages

A history of rhetoric as it relates to structure, genre, and style, with special reference to English literature and literary criticism from ancient Greece to the end of the eighteenth century. Argues that rhetoric was a stylized representation of language and human feelings. Originally published in 1970.

596. Vosevich, Kathi A. "The Rhetoric of Shakespeare's Women: Figures, Sense, and Structure." *DAI* 49 (January 1989): 1812A.

Examines how the rhetorical figures of *interrogatio, provocatio,* and *negatio* fit heroines and genres in Shakespeare's works.

597. Wald, Patricia B. "Writing America: The Rhetoric of Self-Authorization in Early Modern American Literature." *DAI* 50 (November 1989): 1307A.

Uses psychoanalytic theories of narrative to argue for the force of the social critique in formal properties of self-reflective texts such as *In Our Time*.

598. Weightman, John. "On Not Understanding Michel Foucault." *ASch* (Summer 1989): 383–406.

Offers a critique of *Les Mots et Les Choses,* exploring Foucault's treatment of issues regarding language and perception.

599. Wilson, Elizabeth Anne. "Criticism, Inc.: A Reconsideration of New Criticism and the Profession, 1935–1955." *DAI* 50 (July 1989): 142A.

Examines the external forces that rendered traditional literary studies vulnerable to change.

600. Wilson, Susan R. "Adrienne Rich: The Conscious Rhetorician." *DAI* 49 (February 1989): 2223A.

Argues that Rich's critics largely ignore her shift from a new critical mode, her influence on the larger rhetorical situation, and her own rhetorical changes.

601. Winterowd, W. Ross. "Reading (and Rehabilitating) the Literature of Fact." *RR* 8 (Fall 1989): 44–59.

Argues that "nonfiction literature is as rich and valuable as fiction." Gives theoretical support, illustrating with a critique of *The Snow Leopard*.

602. Wood, Michael. "Montaigne and the Mirror of Example." *P&L* 13 (April 1989): 1–15.

Explores the purposes of examples by contrasting argument and example. Examples are a source of life in literature.

603. Zinman, Jane Ann. "Readers, Writers, and the Grounds for a Textual Divorce." *DAI* 49 (February 1989): 2206A.

Examines the consequences of a reader's inability to accept the rhetorical invitations extended by an author.

See also 72, 89, 142, 156, 178, 199, 202, 208, 209, 248, 253, 256, 285, 289, 292, 299, 635, 943, 950, 975, 1191, 1222, 1225, 1545

2.7   READING

604. Allison, Vicie. "A Comparison of the Effects of Four Methods of Repeated Readings on Reading Comprehension, Vocabulary, and Attitude." *DAI* 50 (July 1989): 106A.

Compares the effects of oral interpretive readings, repeated listenings, partner readings, and repeated silent readings.

605. Andrews, Sally. "Frequency and Neighborhood Effects on Lexical Access: Activation or Search?" *JEPL* 15 (September 1989): 802–814.

Lexical access is "sensitive to word frequency" and influenced by the number of words that can be constructed by changing one letter.

606. Bahr, Damon L. "The Relationship between Reading Using Full Graphemic Cues and Spelling Ability." *DAI* 49 (April 1989): 2924A.

Suggests that spelling achievement results from a knowledge of letter-sound correspondences determined by verbal IQ.

607. Bentin, Shlomo. "Orthography and Phonology in Lexical Decision: Evidence from Repetition Effects at Different Lags." *JEPL* 15 (January 1989): 61–72.

Finds that lexical access for voweled and unvoweled Hebrew words is mediated by phonemic and orthographic codes.

608. Blum, Abraham, and Moshe Azencot. "Small Farmers Habits of Reading Agricultural Extension Publications: The Case of Moshav Farmers in Israel." *JTWC* 19 (1989): 381–393.

Interviews with 171 farmers explore how they read agricultural and extension publications, how they use such materials, and what problems they encounter with them.

609. Brady, Susan, Erika Poggie, and Michele Merlo Rapala. "Speech Repetition Abilities in Children Who Differ in Reading Skill." *L&S* 32 (April–June 1989): 109–122.

Results show that phonological encoding difficulties contribute to memory deficits characteristic of poor readers.

610. Burgess, Curt, Michael K. Tanenhaus, and Mark S. Seidenberg. "Context and Lexical Access: Implications of Nonword Interference for Lexical Ambiguity Resolution." *JEPL* 15 (July 1989): 620–632.

Reports on the "effects of contextual information on lexical decisions to misspelled nonword targets."

611. Carr, Thomas H., Joseph S. Brown, and Alkistis Charalambous. "Repetition and Reading: Perceptual Encoding Mechanisms Are Very Abstract but Not Very Interactive." *JEPL* 15 (September 1989): 763–778.

Reports on four experiments testing the effects of variations in surface form and context.

612. Clayton, Keith, and David Chattin. "Spatial and Semantic Priming Effects in Tests of Spatial Knowledge." *JEPL* 15 (May 1989): 495–506.

Compares spatial knowledge with semantic memory to show that semantic priming is not automatic with word processing.

613. Corder, Jim W. "Hunting for *Ethos* Where They Say It Can't Be Found." *RR* 7 (Spring 1989): 299–316.

Explores the implications of whether we find meaning in the text or in the reading strategies of an interpretive community.

614. Davis, Sara N. "A Dialectical Approach to Reader Response." Paper presented at the American Psychological Association, Atlanta, August 1988. ERIC ED 304 676. 14 pages

Introduces the "interruption method" for investigating reader-text relationships.

615. de Groot, Annette M. B. "Representational Aspects of Word Imageability and Word Frequency as Assessed through Word Association." *JEPL* 15 (September 1989): 824–845.

Imageability is a strong influence on word association whereas word frequency is a weak influence. "Concept nodes of concrete words contain more information than those of abstract nodes."

616. Dosher, Barbara Anne, Brian McElree, R. Mark Hood, and Glenda Rosedale. "Retrieval Dynamics of Priming in Recognition Memory: Bias and Discrimination Analysis." *JEPL* 15 (September 1989): 868–886.

"Analyzes the nature of semantic priming in item recognition." Discusses implications for lexical and recognition domains.

617. Dosher, Barbara Anne, and Glenda Rosedale. "Integrated Retrieval Cues as a Mechanism for Priming in Retrieval from Memory." *JEPG* 118 (June 1989): 191–211.

Examines associative memory judgments using words as the cue.

618. Duffy, Susan A., John M. Henderson, and Robin K. Morris. "Semantic Facilitation of Lexical Access during Sentence Processing." *JEPL* 15 (September 1989): 791–801.

Neither words alone nor syntactic relations can account for the improvement words together have on lexical access.

619. Duffy, Thomas M., Lorraine Higgins, Brad Mehlenbacher, Cynthia Cochran, David Wallace, Charles Hill, Diane Haugen, Margaret McCaffrey, Rebecca Burnett, Sarah Sloane, and Suzanne Smith. "Models for the Design of Instructional Text." *RRQ* 24 (Fall 1989): 434–457.

Eleventh graders found a high school history textbook that had been revised by composition teachers more effective than textbooks revised by text linguists and Time-Life writers.

620. Entes, Judith. "College Students in Remedial Reading Classes Interacting with Stories Written in Chronological Time Order and Time-Shift." *DAI* 50 (November 1989): 1263A.

Hypothesizes and discusses two stances taken in the reading process: engagement and disengagement.

621. Fang, Sheng-Ping, and Pichun Wu. "Illusory Conjunctions in the Perception of Chinese Characters." *JEPH* 15 (August 1989): 434–447.

The probability of seeing illusory characters is not governed by lexicality, pro-

nounceability, or character frequency but by familiarity and context.

622. Garner, Ruth, Mark G. Gillingham, and C. Stephen White. "Effects of 'Seductive Details' on Macroprocessing and Microprocessing in Adults and Children." *CI* 6 (January 1989): 41–57.

The presentation of interesting but unimportant information in expository texts inhibited the recall of main ideas generally but affected microprocessing in children alone.

623. Gerard, Linda D., and Don L. Scarborough. "Language-Specific Lexical Access of Homographs by Bilinguals." *JEPL* 15 (March 1989): 305–315.

Using results from Spanish-English bilinguals, reports support for the hypothesis that word recognition requires searching the language-appropriate lexicon.

624. Gerrig, Richard J. "Suspense in the Absence of Uncertainty." *JML* 28 (December 1989): 633–648.

Readers can become immersed in stories to the point that they express uncertainty with respect to outcomes they have certain knowledge about.

625. Gibbs, Raymond W., Jr., Nandini P. Nayak, and Cooper Cutting. "How to Kick the Bucket and Not Decompose: Analyzability and Idiom Processing." *JML* 28 (October 1989): 576–593.

Suggests that idioms and literal language are processed similarly, though it is unnecessary to analyze literal meanings to understand figurative phrases.

626. Glaser, Wilhelm R., and Margrit O. Glaser. "Context Effects in Stroop-Like Word and Picture Processing." *JEPG* 118 (March 1989): 13–42.

Studies the effects of context. Finds that distracting words disturb naming but not reading and that word processing is disturbed by picture distractors.

627. Gregory, Monica E. "Metaphor Comprehension: In Search of Literal Truth, Sense, and Meaning." *DAI* 50 (December 1989): 2650B.

Studies how subjects process metaphor. Concludes that a variety of strategies are used to make sense of metaphoric expressions.

628. Guri-Rozenblit, Sarah. "Effects of a Tree Diagram on Students' Comprehension of Main Ideas in an Expository Text with Multiple Themes." *RRQ* 24 (Spring 1989): 236–247.

Finds that a tree diagram illustrating points in a social science textbook helped 167 Israeli undergraduates better perceive relationships.

629. Haberlandt, Karl F., and Arthur C. Graesser. "Buffering New Information during Reading." *DPr* 12 (October–December 1989): 479–494.

Reading times increased for content words, especially for nouns used for the first time in a text.

630. Haberlandt, Karl F., Arthur C. Graesser, and Nancy J. Schneider. "Reading Strategies of Fast and Slow Readers." *JEPL* 15 (September 1989): 815–823.

Studies reading rates relative to grouping words, to single versus many argument strategies, and to physical versus linguistic strategies.

631. Hague, Sally Ann. "The Effects of Top-Level Rhetorical Structure on the Recall and Retention of Expository Prose on Readers of a Foreign Language." *DAI* 49 (May 1989): 3317A.

Findings indicate that an awareness of rhetorical structures aided in retaining information.

632. Hall, William S. "Reading Comprehension." *AmP* 44 (February 1989): 157–161.

Asserts that prior knowledge and cognitive and metacognitive processes are critical for developing reading comprehension. Suggests that instruction in underlying processes can improve comprehension skills.

633. Harste, Jerome C. *New Policy Guidelines for Reading: Connecting Research and Practice.* Urbana, Ill.: NCTE and ERIC/RCS, 1989. 81 pages

Makes recommendations for improving policy, research, and instruction in reading. Includes 20 guidelines focused specifically on instruction. Extensive bibliography.

634. Hartman, Marilyn, David S. Knopman, and Mary Jo Nissen. "Implicit Learning of New Verbal Associations." *JEPL* 15 (November 1989): 1070–1082.

Demonstrates that implicit learning occurs in the verbal domain if minimal attention is present.

635. Hauptmeier, Helmut, Dietrich Meutsch, and Reinhold Viehoff. "Empirical Research on Understanding Literature." *PT* 10 (Fall 1989): 563–604.

Surveys empirical research to determine if textual factors can explain literary reading guided by aesthetic conventions. Proposes a theory and model of "communicate construction."

636. Herdman, Chris M., and Allen R. Dobbs. "Attentional Demands of Visual Word Recognition." *JEPH* 15 (February 1989): 124–132.

Shows that visual word recognition requires attentional resources and that the demands of recognition vary with word frequency.

637. Huba, M. E., S. S. Robinson, and S. Kontos. "Prereaders' Understanding of the Purposes of Print and Subsequent Reading Achievement." *JEdR* 82 (March–April 1989): 210–215.

Findings indicate a positive correlation between early understanding and subsequent achievement.

638. Hynds, Susan. "Bringing Life to Literature and Literature to Life: Social Constructs and Contexts of Four Adolescent Readers." *RTE* 23 (February 1989): 30–61.

Studies the interplay of readers' social experience and social constructs in the reading process. Argues for more attention to social factors in the assessment of reading competence.

639. Hyona, Jukka, Pekka Niemi, and Geoffrey Underwood. "Reading Long Words Embedded in Sentences: Informativeness of Word Halves Affects Eye Movements." *JEPH* 15 (February 1989): 142–152.

Shows that readers of Finnish initially fixate the first part of the word regardless of its informativeness and sometimes skip the second half of the word.

640. Inhoff, Albrecht Werner. "Parafoveal Processing of Words and Saccade Computation during Eye Fixations in Reading." *JEPH* 15 (August 1989): 544–555.

Seeks to compare preview benefits from word beginnings with word endings and to determine whether functionally related or autonomous processes control reading.

641. Inhoff, Albrecht Werner, and Kevin Fleming. "Probe-Detection Times during the Reading of Easy and Difficult Text." *JEPL* 15 (March 1989): 339–351.

Experimentally demonstrates that reading difficult texts requires more capacity than reading easy texts.

642. Jacoby, Larry L., and Kevin Whitehouse. "An Illusion of Memory: False Recognition Influenced by Unconscious Perception." *JEPG* 118 (June 1989): 126–135.

Considers the effects of context and attribution.

643. Jacoby, Larry L., Vera Woloshyn, and Colleen Kelley. "Becoming Famous without Being Recognized: Unconscious Influences of Memory Produced by Dividing Attention." *JEPG* 118 (June 1989): 115–125.

Reading tasks show that conscious recollection helps to avoid the misleading effects of the past and is an attention-demanding act distinct from other memory.

644. Jahnke, John C., Susan T. Davis, and Ray E. Bower. "Position and Order Information in Recognition Memory." *JEPL* 15 (September 1989): 859–867.

The closer transposed letters are to one another, the more difficult they are to identify. Uncertainty about position "appears to determine other information."

645. Keysar, Boaz. "On the Function Equivalence of Literal and Metaphorical Interpretations in Discourse." *JML* 28 (August 1989): 375–385.

Suggests that nonliteral meanings are automatically generated and integrated with context whenever a coherent interpretation can be formed.

646. Koda, Keiko. "Effects of L1 Orthographic Representation on L2 Phonological Coding Strategies." *JPsyR* 18 (1989): 201–222.

Studies L1 orthographic impact on cognitive processing involved in L2 reading. Findings suggest a strong relationship between orthography and cognition.

647. Koriat, Asher, and Joel Norman. "Why Is Word Recognition Impaired by Disorientation While the Identification of Single Letters Is Not?" *JEPH* 15 (February 1989): 153–163.

Reports that differences in the two tasks are related to the number of visual elements that have to be processed, not to inherent differences in tasks.

648. Levy, Betty Ann, and Kim Kirsner. "Reprocessing Text: Indirect Measures of Word and Message Level Processes." *JEPL* 15 (May 1989): 407–417.

Raises two issues: the use of indirect measures to analyze skilled reading and the relations between surface and message clues for judging transfer of skill.

649. Long, Shirley A., Peter N. Winograd, and Connie A. Bridge. "The Effects of Reader and Text Characteristics on Imagery Reported

during and after Reading." *RRQ* 24 (Summer 1989): 353–372.

Finds that imagery may increase the capacity of working memory, may help match schematic and textual information, and may help organize information.

650. Lupker, Stephen J., and Bonnie A. Williams. "Rhyme Priming of Pictures and Words: A Lexical Activation Account." *JEPL* 15 (November 1989): 1033–1046.

Reports on various ways pictures and words affect the processing of new information.

651. Lysynchuk, Linda M., Michael Pressley, Hsiao d'Ailly, Michael Smith, and Heather Cake. "A Methodological Analysis of Experimental Studies of Comprehension Instruction." *RRQ* 24 (Fall 1989): 458–470.

Identifies six weaknesses in studies of reading comprehension.

652. MacDonald, Maryellen C., and Marcel Adam Just. "Changes in Activation Levels with Negation." *JEPL* 15 (July 1989): 633–642.

Negation has differing effects depending on the complexity of comprehension. The reading time for initial encoding was not affected, but analyzing the truth value was greatly influenced.

653. MacLeod, Colin M. "Word Context during Initial Exposure Influences Degree of Priming in Word Fragment Completion." *JEPL* 15 (May 1989): 398–406.

"Context plays a critical role in priming." Words contextually bound in meaningful discourse are more likely to show priming than words in lists.

654. Macruso, Paul, Eva Bar-Shalom, Stephen Crain, and Donald Shankweiler. "Comprehension of Temporal Cues by Good and Poor Readers." *L&S* 32 (January-March 1989): 45–67.

Tests of second-graders show that poor readers misinterpretations may result from poor verbal memory and not from a delay in acquiring syntactic knowledge.

655. Martin-Wambu, Judith. "Case Studies of Nine Community College Good Writers/Poor Readers." *DAI* 50 (July 1989): 108A.

Examines four areas that have an impact on students' reading and writing: verbal ability, processing of text, and the artifacts and affective considerations of the testing situation.

656. McConkie, G. W., P. W. Kerr, M. D. Reddix, and D. Zola. *Eye Movement Control during Reading: Frequency of Refixating a Word.* University of Illinois Center for the Study of Reading Technical Report, no. 469. Urbana, Ill.: University of Illinois Center for the Study of Reading, 1989. ERIC ED 307 592. 28 pages

Investigates 66 college students who fixated over 40,000 times. Concludes that a word refixation curve existed.

657. McKoon, Gail, and Roger Ratcliff. "Inferences about Contextually Defined Categories." *JEPL* 15 (November 1989): 1134–1146.

Investigates encoded meanings. Studies inference processes occurring during reading. Examines how the structure of semantic memory affects discourse processing.

658. McKoon, Gail, and Roger Ratcliff. "Semantic Associations and Elaborative Inference." *JEPL* 15 (March 1989): 326–338.

Inferences vary in degree of specificity, in the strength with which they are encoded, and in how quickly they are available.

659. McKoon, Gail, Roger Ratcliff, and Colleen Seifert. "Making the Connection: Generalized Knowledge Structures in Story Understanding." *JML* 28 (December 1989): 711–734.

Memory organization packets (MOPs) or shared knowledge structures allowed a phrase from one story to recall a phrase from another.

660. Monsell, S., M. C. Doyle, and P. N. Haggard. "Effects of Frequency on Visual Word Recognition Tasks: Where Are They?" *JEPG* 118 (March 1989): 43–71.

Supports the idea that lexical identification is strongly sensitive to word frequency. Argues that parallel-distributed processing accounts for this phenomenon.

661. Morrow, Daniel G., Gordon H. Bower, and Steven L. Greenspan. "Updating Situation Models during Narrative Comprehension." *JML* 28 (June 1989): 292–312.

Readers focused more on a protagonist's "mental location" than on the physical location.

662. Mozer, Michael. "Types and Tokens in Visual Letter Perception." *JEPH* 15 (May 1989): 287–303.

Explains the difficulty of distinguishing NTEST[1]+1 from NTEST1[1]+1. Concludes that some visual processing requires serial, not parallel, processing.

663. Mullin, Paul A., and Howard E. Egeth. "Capacity Limitations in Visual Word Processing." *JEPH* 15 (February 1989): 111–123.

Argues against the unlimited capacity, parallel processing hypothesis.

664. Nagy, William, Richard C. Anderson, Marlene Schommer, Judith Ann Scott, and Anne C. Stallman. "Morphological Families in the Internal Lexicon." *RRQ* 24 (Summer 1989): 262–282.

Studies whether college students recognize words faster if they are related by inflections (*stair/stairs*) or by nonmorphological relatives (*fee/feet*).

665. Neely, James H., Dennis E. Keefe, and Kent L. Ross. "Semantic Priming in the Lexical Decision Task: Roles of Prospective Prime-Generated Expectancies and Retrospective Semantic Matching." *JEPL* 15 (November 1989): 1003–1019.

Studies whether "the relatedness proportion effect in the lexical decision task is mediated by a prelexical expectancy mechanism, a postlexical semantic matching mechanism, or both."

666. Nelson, Douglas L., Patricia D. Keelean, and Maura Negrao. "Word-Fragment Cuing: The Lexical Search Hypothesis." *JEPL* 15 (May 1989): 388–397.

Argues that meaning is not recovered by word-fragment cues. Discusses the effects of rhyme and of instructions about the methods of recall.

667. Niles, Jerome A., and Larry A. Harris, eds. *Changing Perspectives on Research in Reading/Language Processing and Instruction*. Thirty-Third Yearbook of the National Reading Conference. Chicago: National Reading Conference, 1983. ERIC ED 298 466. 332 pages

Presents 51 papers from the National Reading Conference, Austin, Texas, December 1983.

668. Niles, Jerome A., and Rosary V. Lalik, eds. *Solving Problems in Literacy: Learners, Teachers, and Researchers*. Thirty-Fifth Yearbook of the National Reading Conference. Chicago: National Reading Conference, 1986. ERIC ED 298 459. 422 pages

Presents 59 papers from the National Reading Conference, San Diego, December 1985.

669. O'Seaghdha, Padraig G. "The Dependence of Lexical Relatedness Effects on Syntactic Connectedness." *JEPL* 15 (January 1989): 73–87.

Studies text comprehension, considering the impact of both words and topics.

670. Perkins, Kyle, Sheila R. Brutten, and John T. Pohlman. "First and Second Language Reading Comprehension." Paper presented at the TESOL Conference, Chicago, March 1988. ERIC ED 304 875. 25 pages

Finds evidence for a "threshold competence ceiling" at which first language reading abilities transferred to second language reading abilities.

671. Peterson, Robert R., and Greg B. Simpson. "Effect of Backward Priming on Word Recognition in Single-Word and Sentence Contexts." *JEPL* 15 (November 1989): 1020–1032.

   Presents experimental results showing backward priming with words but not with sentences. Discusses implications for sentence comprehension research.

672. Peynircioglu, Zehra F. "Part-Set Cuing Effect with Word-Fragment Cuing: Evidence against the Strategy Disruption and Increased-List-Length Explanations." *JEPL* 15 (January 1989): 147–152.

   Cues that compel people to use strategies different from their usual ways of recalling words reduce people's ability to remember.

673. Ratcliff, Roger, Gail McKoon, and Marjolein Verwoerd. "A Bias Interpretation of Facilitation in Perceptual Identification." *JEPL* 15 (May 1989): 378–387.

   Improvements in word recognition after priming are shown to be the result of bias, not of changed perception. Discusses implications for word recognition models and amnesia.

674. Rayner, Keith, and Lyn Frazier. "Selection Mechanisms in Reading Lexically Ambiguous Words." *JEPL* 15 (September 1989): 779–790.

   Uses gaze durations. Presents results that are counter to selective access and multiple access models of reading but that are consistent with integration.

675. Read, Charles. *Adults Who Read like Children: The Psycholinguistic Bases*. Madison: Wisconsin Center for Education Research, 1988. ERIC ED 303 781. 47 pages

   After testing the reading abilities of 88 male prison inmates, finds that poor readers had a "hidden deficit," the need to sound out words.

676. Read, Charles. *Phonological Awareness and Adult Readers*. Madison: Wisconsin Center for Education Research, 1988. ERIC ED 303 782. 18 pages

   Tests the phonemic awareness of adult readers. Notes among other findings that the belief that English orthography reflects sound, although illusory, seems essential for skilled reading.

677. Readence, John E., and R. Scott Baldwin, eds. *Research in Literacy: Merging Perspectives*. Thirty-Sixth Yearbook of the National Reading Conference. Chicago: National Reading Conference, 1987. ERIC ED 298 454. 336 pages

   Presents 30 papers from the National Reading Conference, Austin, Texas, December 1986.

678. Reed, Keflyn X. "A Statewide Readability Study." *TETYC* 16 (May 1989): 116–120.

   Finds that readability levels of textbooks in Alabama two-year college content courses were above students' average reading abilities.

679. Reese, Diane Jones. "Effect of Training in Expository Text Structure on Reading Comprehension." *DAI* 50 (July 1989): 69A.

   Schema theory, text structure analysis, and comprehension strategies were the basis for this study involving instruction in the awareness and use of five expository structures.

680. Roberts, David D. "Readers' Comprehension Responses in Informative Discourse: Toward Connecting Reading and Writing in Technical Communication." *JTWC* 19 (1989): 135–148.

   Using reading protocols, this study attempts to describe and analyze "what readers do when they seek information."

681. Schwanenflugel, Paula J., and Randall W. Stowe. "Context Availability and the Processing of Abstract and Concrete Words in Sentences." *RRQ* 24 (Winter 1989): 114–126.

Concludes that college students comprehend slowly abstract words in nonsupportive contexts.

682. Schwartz, Barbara Lyn. "Effects of Generation on Indirect Measures of Memory." *JEPL* 15 (November 1989): 1119–1128.

Finds that word identification performance was lower for words generated than read. Word completion performance was indistinguishable.

683. Shimamura, Arthur P., and Larry R. Squire. "Impaired Priming of New Associations in Amnesia." *JEPL* 15 (July 1989): 721–728.

Finds that newly associated word cues did not improve word completion. Context priming inversely correlated with the severity of amnesia.

684. Simonsen, Stephen W. "The Generalizability of Metacognition from the Writing to the Reading Mode." *DAI* 49 (February 1989): 2135A.

Examines metacognitive structures and their relation to skills learned in writing that generalize to reading.

685. Simpson, Greg B., Robert R. Peterson, Mark A. Casteel, and Curt Burgess. "Lexical and Sentence Context Effects in Word Recognition." *JEPL* 15 (January 1989): 88–97.

Shows that the ideas in a sentence aid recognition of subsequent words.

686. Sinclair, Grant P., Alice F. Healy, and Lyle E. Bourne, Jr. "Facilitating Text Memory with Additional Processing Opportunities in Rapid Sequential Reading." *JEPL* 15 (May 1989): 418–431.

Pauses at linguistic boundaries are not necessary for efficient text comprehension and memory. Total reading time available is more important than distribution.

687. Smith, Dean R., A. Jackson Stenner, Ivan Horabin, and Malbert Smith. *The Lexile Scale in Theory and Practice: Final Report*. Wash-

ington, D.C.: MetaMetrics, 1989. ERIC ED 307 577. 46 pages

Reports on a correlational study of the explanatory power of the Lexile theory of reading comprehension.

688. Smith, Marilyn C., Colin M. MacLeod, John D. Bain, and Richard B. Hoppe. "Lexical Decision as an Indirect Test of Memory: Repetition Priming and List-Wide Priming as a Function of Type of Encoding." *JEPL* 15 (November 1989): 1109–1118.

Tests the dissociation between type of encoding and later memory performance. Finds that lexical decisions, unlike recognition, were either unaffected by or aided by nonsemantic processing.

689. Spivey, Nancy Nelson, and James R. King. "Readers as Writers Composing from Sources." *RRQ* 24 (Winter 1989): 7–26.

In writing informational reports based on three sources, 60 students in sixth, eighth, and tenth grades revealed that general reading ability and success at synthesizing overlap.

690. Spyridakis, Jan H. "Signaling Effects: Increased Content Retention and New Answers, Part II." *JTWC* 19 (1989): 395–415.

"This study supports the hypothesis that signals"—headings, previews, and logical connectives—"can influence retention of text-based information, particularly with long, unfamiliar, or difficult passages."

691. Spyridakis, Jan H. "Signaling Effects: A Review of the Research, Part I." *JTWC* 19 (1989): 227–240.

Critiques previous methods employed to study the effects of structural cues on a reader's comprehension of expository prose. Suggests a refined research design.

692. Stahl, Steven A., Michael G. Jacobson, Charlotte E. Davis, and Robin L. Davis. "Prior Knowledge and Difficult Vocabulary in the Comprehension of Unfamiliar Text." *RRQ* 24 (Winter 1989): 27–43.

Vocabulary difficulty and preteaching may function independently, not interactively.

693. Stanovich, Keith E., and Richard F. West. "Exposure to Print and Orthographic Processing." *RRQ* 24 (Fall 1989): 402–433.

Finds that variation in children's and adults' abilities to form, store, or access orthographic representations causes individual differences in reading and spelling.

694. Tardif, Twila, and Fergus I. M. Clark. "Reading a Week Later: Perceptual and Conceptual Factors." *JML* 28 (February 1989): 107–125.

Researchers found no evidence that specific perceptual information had been retained after one week.

695. Tierney, Robert J., Anna Soter, John F. O'Flahavan, and William McGinley. "The Effects of Reading and Writing upon Thinking Critically." *RRQ* 24 (Spring 1989): 134–173.

A study of 137 undergraduates finds that reading and writing together are more likely to promote critical thinking than either activity alone.

696. van der Velde, Frank, A. H. C. van der Heijden, and Robert Schreuder. "Context-Dependent Migrations in Visual Word Perception." *JEPH* 15 (February 1989): 133–141.

Argues that higher-order word knowledge, in the form of semantic relations between words, influences the migration.

697. Walter-Burnham, Molly L. "A Comparison of the Oral and Written Compositions of Remedial and Conventional Freshman Writers: Using the Herber Reading Comprehension Model to Expand the Description of Freshman Writers and Their Comprehension Levels for Two Short Stories." *DAI* 49 (February 1989): 2136A.

Examines differences between remedial and conventional freshmen as readers and writers.

698. Whitlow, J. W., Jr., and Alberto Cebollero. "The Nature of Word Frequency Effects on Perceptual Identification." *JEPL* 15 (July 1989): 643–656.

Finds "that word frequency is not a major determinant of perceptual identification accuracy." Words and pseudowords differ significantly in their effect on perception.

699. Wolf, Yuval, Joel Walters, and Susan Holzman. "Integration of Semantic and Structural Constraints in Narrative Comprehension." *DPr* 12 (April–June 1989): 149–167.

Subjects' evaluations of texts had both semantic and syntactic bases and thus support theories of comprehension in which both types of constraints play a role.

See also 25, 78, 107, 159, 168, 200, 743, 765, 815, 828, 839, 866, 916

2.8 LINGUISTICS, GRAMMATICAL THEORY, AND SEMANTICS

700. Aarts, Bas. "Clauses of Concession in Written Present-Day British English." *JEngL* 21 (April 1988): 39–57.

Discusses the semantic notion of concession and analyzes the distribution of concessive clauses over 12 text categories.

701. Ahmed, Mohammed K. "Speaking as a Cognitive Regulation: A Study of L1 and L2 Dyadic Problem-Solving Activity." *DAI* 49 (June 1989): 3699A.

Uses Vygotskyan psycholinguistic theory to analyze task-based conversations of native and nonnative speakers of English.

702. Arnold, Doug, Martin Atkinson, Jacques Durand, Claire Grover, and Louisa Sadler. *Essays on Grammatical Theory and Universal Grammar*. New York: Oxford University Press, 1989. 300 pages

Collects nine essays on grammatical theory. Discusses the semantic basis for syntactic categories and relations, the search for linguistic universals and the study of language typology, and detailed descriptions of particular phenomena.

703. Barnlund, Dean C. *Communicative Styles of Japanese and Americans: Images and Realities.* Belmont. Calif.: Wadsworth, 1989. 218 pages

> Discusses issues of intercultural communication to provide a context for comparing Japanese and American cultures. Treats the personal, social, and cultural functions of communication in each society.

704. Baron, Dennis. *Declining Grammar and Other Essays on the English Vocabulary.* Urbana, Ill.: NCTE, 1989. 240 pages

> Twenty-five essays examine some of the myths that affect our attitudes toward language, controversial trends in English vocabulary, questions of meaning and usage, and linguistic politics.

705. Baron, Dennis. "Going out of Style?" *EngT* 5 (January 1989): 6–11.

> Argues that passive voice is a natural part of English sentence structure despite current resistance to it.

706. Benson, James D., and William S. Greaves, eds. *Systemic Functional Approaches to Discourse: Selected Papers from the Twelfth International Systemic Workshop.* Advances in Discourse Processes, vol. 26. Norwood, N.J.: Ablex, 1988. 384 pages

> Eighteen papers propose criteria for evaluating system networks, illustrate the range of discourse topics of interest to systemicists, and show how the study of discourse stimulates the development of systemic linguistics as an analytic tool.

707. Bourland, D. David, Jr. "To Be or Not to Be: E-Prime as a Tool for Critical Thinking." *ETC* 46 (Fall 1989): 202–211.

> Discusses the philosophical, linguistic, and semantic advantages of eliminating "to be" forms from English usage.

708. Bowers, Bege K., Danna Bozick, Jean Engle, George Letchworth, Joan Philipp, and Victor Wan-Tatah. *Guidelines for Nonsexist Communication.* Youngstown, Ohio: Youngstown State University Special Task Force on Sexism in Communication, 1988. ERIC ED 303 841. 21 pages

> Offers guidelines for nonsexist communication. Designed for teachers, students, and administrators.

709. Breidenstein, Patricia Ann. "On the Creation of Organizational Fold Theories: An Analysis of Storytelling and Language Behavior." *DAI* 50 (September 1989): 571A.

> Studies how organizational language structures meaning.

710. Brody, Miriam B. "Advice to Writers: The Poetics of Gender in Rhetoric and Composition." *DAI* 49 (June 1989): 3598A.

> Studies the rhetorical use of gender in composition and how composition textbooks treat the issue of gender.

711. Brunot, William. "What Is General Semantics? Another Answer." *ETC* 46 (Spring 1989): 41–42.

> Defines the field as concerning itself with the tests for and the substance of successful communication. Projects new directions for inquiry.

712. Butt, David. *Talking and Thinking: The Patterns of Behavior.* Language Education. Edited by Frances Christie. New York: Oxford University Press, 1989. 104 pages

> Discusses the Saussurean theory of signs, its implications for what thinking means in specific communities, and how point of view alters meaning within a community.

713. "Canadian Council of Teachers of English Doublespeak Award." *QRD* 15 (January 1989): 12.

> Announces the Doublespeak and Plain English awards for 1988.

714. "Canadian Council of Teachers of English Doublespeak Award." *QRD* 16 (October 1989): 11–12.

> Announces Doublespeak and Plain English awards and invites nominations.

715. Chapman, Robert L., ed. *Thesaurus of American Slang*. New York: Harper & Row, 1989. 448 pages

Cites synonyms for more than 17,000 slang words.

716. Chen, Guo-Ming. "Relationships of the Dimensions of Intercultural Communication Competence." *ComQ* 37 (Spring 1989): 118–133.

Although the study of communication competence can be traced to Aristotle, few scholars consider cultural factors affecting it. Factors considered include the sojourner's characteristics and behaviors.

717. Christie, Frances. *Language Education*. Language Education. Edited by Frances Christie. New York: Oxford University Press, 1989. 50 pages

Explores the significance of language in personal development and learning. Demonstrates that interpreting and communicating ideas through language is essential to successful participation in any society.

718. Clancy, Patricia. "A Case Study in Language Socialization: Korean Wh-Questions." *DPr* 12 (April–June 1989): 169–191.

Among the most frequent questions asked of two preschoolers were those eliciting information, testing knowledge, prompting reading, or facilitating activities.

719. Collinge, N. E., ed. *An Encyclopaedia of Language*. New York: Routledge, 1989. 1000 pages

A reference source comprised of 26 articles grouped into three sections: Inner Nature of Language, the Larger Province of Language, and Special Aspects of Language.

720. Crowley, Anthony E. "*Standard English:* The History of the Term and Concept in the Nineteenth and Early Twentieth Centuries." *DAI* 49 (February 1989): 2198A.

Examines the often ambiguous definition and use of British Standard English and its sociopolitical implications.

721. Crowley, Sharon. "Linguistics and Composition Instruction: 1950–1980." *WC* 6 (October 1989): 480–505.

Traces the influence of then-current linguistic theory on instruction in grammar and usage, in improving sentence structure and style, and in teaching invention.

722. Daniels, Harvey, Courtney Cazden, Victor Villanueva, and Geneva Smitherman. *Taking the English Language to Heart: Critical Issues in English*. Urbana, Ill.: NCTE, 1988.

Four speakers discuss language diversity and how it relates to education. A cassette recorded during the 1988 NCTE Convention in St. Louis.

723. Dijkstra, Ton, Robert Schreuder, and Uli H. Frauenfelder. "Grapheme Context Effects on Phonemic Processing." *L&S* 32 (April–June 1989): 89–108.

Supports the hypothesis of automatic grapheme-to-phoneme activation before word recognition.

724. Dobrich, Wanda. "Phonological Development in Preschoolers: Learning to Speak English by Speaking English." *DAI* 49 (April 1989): 4572B.

Analyzes consonant usage in a sample of children's and adults' speech. Finds no differences in the phonemic content and complexity of words attempted.

725. Domowitz, Susan. "An Ethnography of Storytelling in Two Anyi Communities." *DAI* 50 (October 1989): 1047A.

A description and analysis of a changing oral narrative tradition in two Anyi communities in the Ivory Coast.

726. "Doublespeak and Iran Air Flight 655." *QRD* 15 (January 1989): 10–11.

Analyzes a report and press conference for examples of omission, distortion, contradiction, and misdirection, all characteristics of doublespeak.

727. "Doublespeak Here and There." *QRD* 15 (January 1989): 4–10.

Notes examples of doublespeak in business, education, foreign countries, government, medicine, military, and other professions.

728. "Doublespeak Here and There." *QRD* 15 (July 1989): 1–10.

Notes examples of doublespeak in business, education, foreign countries, government, law, medicine, military, and other professions.

729. "Doublespeak Here and There." *QRD* 16 (October 1989): 2–7.

Notes examples of doublespeak in business, education, foreign countries, government, medicine, military, and other professions.

730. Dryer, Matthew S. "Large Linguistic Areas and Language Sampling." *SLang* 13 (1989): 257–292.

Finds that continental linguistic areas may exist and that many languages from each continent may reflect areal phenomena rather than linguistic preferences.

731. Dumesnil, James, and Bruce Dorval. "The Development of Talk-Activity Frames That Foster Perspective-Focused Talk among Peers." *DPr* 12 (April–June 1989): 193–225.

Comparing conversations of ninth graders, twelfth graders, and college students suggests a developmental sequence in the way conversations are structured.

732. Duques, Susan L. "Grammatical Deficiencies in Writing: An Investigation of Learning-Disabled College Students." *DAI* 49 (February 1989): 2153A.

Examines the linguistic and orthographic demands made on learning-disabled writers. Reviews teaching approaches designed to accommodate these students.

733. Eble, Connie. *College Slang 101*. Georgetown, Conn.: Spectacle Lane Press, 1989. 97 pages

Collects more than 1,000 slang words, terms, and definitions, relating their origins

to the social, academic, and psychological aspects of college life during the past 20 years.

734. Edmiston, Cynthia D. "English Grammar as a Stratified System of Signs." *DAI* 49 (April 1989): 3013A.

Adopts a four-strata linguistic structure: graphic, morphemic, lexemic, and sememic.

735. Elshershabi, Muhammad A. "Substitution and Lexical Cohesion in the Editorial Argumentative Discourse of Arabic and American English." *DAI* 49 (January 1989): 1786A.

Expands Halliday and Hasan's cohesion model and offers a potentially universal description of cohesion and rhetorical cohesive choices.

736. Faltz, Leonard M. "A Role for Inference in Meaning Change." *SLang* 13 (1989): 317–331.

Examines the notion that inference provides a channel for semantic change by focusing on how the English morpheme *self* changes from emphatic to reflexive meaning.

737. Fareh, Shehdeh I. "Paragraph Structure in Arabic and English Expository Discourse." *DAI* 50 (November 1989): 1292A.

Tagmemic analysis shows that paragraphs in Arabic and English differ in topic placement and cohesion methods.

738. Farris, Catherine S. "Language and Sex Role Acquisition in a Taiwanese Kindergarten: A Semiotic Analysis." *DAI* 49 (February 1989): 2288A.

Examines how gender as a meaning system is encoded in Standard Chinese and how these meanings are learned in the sex role socialization process.

739. Ferreira, Elrod S. "A Systematic Critique of Three Language Acquisition Epistemologies: Toward a Unifying Epistemology of Language Acquisition." *DAI* 49 (February 1989): 2199A.

Compares the theories of Piaget, Fodor, and the Soviets, proposing a method of critique and offering unifying suggestions.

740. Fersh, Seymour. "General Semantics and the Study of Cultures." *ETC* 46 (Fall 1989): 231–235.

Shows how a knowledge of general semantics can improve our study of and interactions with those of other cultures.

741. Fine, Jonathan, ed. *Second Language Discourse: A Textbook of Current Research*. Advances in Discourse Processes, vol. 25. Norwood, N.J.: Ablex, 1988. 208 pages

Eight studies examine the interaction of factors in second language acquisition and use.

742. Flege, James Emil. "Differences in Inventory Size Affect the Location but Not the Precision of Tongue Positioning in Vowel Production." *L&S* 32 (April–June 1989): 123–147.

Discusses whether or not native speakers whose language has a high vowel inventory maximize phonetic distances by using a wide range of tongue positions.

743. Foy, Judith G. "Event-Related Brain Potential Correlates of Psycholinguistic Manipulations during Discourse Processing." *DAI* 49 (January 1989): 2897B.

Investigates how changing linguistic information affects reading times and discovers that factual information is processed separately from semantic and syntactic data.

744. Frank, Francine Wattman, and Paula A. Treichler. *Language, Gender, and Professional Writing*. New York: MLA, 1989. 341 pages

Analyzes research on sexism in language and offers guidelines for nondiscriminatory usage.

745. "Further Adventures in Nukespeak." *QRD* 15 (April 1989): 7.

Reports on doublespeak relating to nuclear power plants.

746. Galbraith, John Kenneth. "Interest Groups, By Any Other Name." *QRD* 15 (April 1989): 8.

Analyzes how doublespeak is at work in defining the term "interest group."

747. Gee, James. "Two Styles of Narrative Construction and Their Linguistic and Educational Implications." *DPr* 12 (July–September 1989): 287–307.

Compares the styles of two females, one black and one white, the former using more expressive and fewer informative lines than the latter.

748. Gonzalez-Pineiro, Manuel. "The Structure of Ideology in Written Texts: A Linguistic Analysis." *DAI* 49 (January 1989): 1786A.

Uses a linguistic-based ideological structural analysis to detect the presence of structure-distorting devices in advocacy literature.

749. Gozzi, Raymond, Jr. "Metaphors That Undermine Human Identity." *ETC* 46 (Spring 1989): 49–53.

Shows how the careless use of machinery metaphors can undermine and undervalue our sense of humanity. Suggests maintaining control of language, especially metaphorical choices.

750. Graves, William, III. "The Sociocultural Construction of Grammar: A Metalinguistic Case Study." *DAI* 50 (August 1989): 430A.

Studies an Arizona Indian community and finds that factors such as social and personal concerns, generally considered peripheral to the description of language, are actually central.

751. Grosjean, Francois. "Neurolinguists, Beware! The Bilingual Is Not Two Monolinguals in One Person." *BL* 36 (January 1989): 3–15.

Presents two views of bilingualism, but supports the holistic view that bilingual speakers are more than the sum of the parts.

752. Gu, Yuegue. "Towards a Model of Conversational Rhetoric: An Investigation of the

Perlocutionary Movement in Conversation."
DAI 50 (December 1989): 1482A.

Uses the rhetorical concept of persuasion and negotiation to revise the current understanding of the speech act.

753. Gunawardena, C. N. "The Present Perfect in the Rhetorical Divisions of Biology and Biochemistry Journal Articles." *ESP* 8 (1989): 265–273.

Studies the use of the present perfect in biology and biochemistry journals, determining that it serves varied purposes and rhetorical functions in science articles.

754. Halliday, M. A. K. *Spoken and Written Language*. Language Education. Edited by Frances Christie. New York: Oxford University Press, 1989. 110 pages

Identifies important differences between speaking and writing, contrasting the prosodic features and grammatical intricacy of speech with the high lexical density and grammatical metaphor of writing.

755. Halliday, M. A. K., and Ruquiya Hasan. *Language, Context, and Text: Aspects of Language in a Social-Semiotic Perspective*. Language Education. Edited by Frances Christie. New York: Oxford University Press, 1989. 126 pages

Deals with the linguistic study of texts as a way of understanding how language functions in its varied range of social contexts.

756. Harris, R. Allen. "Argumentation in Chomsky's *Syntactic Structures:* An Exercise in Rhetoric of Science." *RSQ* 19 (Spring 1989): 105–130.

Analyzes the system of argumentation Chomsky uses.

757. Hasan, Ruquiya. *Linguistics, Language, and Verbal Art*. Language Education. Edited by Frances Christie. New York: Oxford University Press, 1989. 124 pages

Analyzes how verbal art is constructed out of language.

758. Hasan, Ruquiya, and James R. Martin, eds. *Language Development: Learning Language, Learning Culture*. Advances in Discourse Processes, vol. 27. Norwood, N.J.: Ablex, 1989. 400 pages

Eight articles explore Halliday's functional theories of language development, approaching language as a resource for meaning. The volume argues that educational theory and practice must consider the social perspective in language development.

759. Heller, Monica. "Speech Economy and Social Selection in Educational Contexts: A Franco-Ontarian Case Study." *DPr* 12 (July–September 1989): 377–390.

Social background affects children's performance in interviews that determine the ability of Francophone children to participate in French language programs.

760. Hemphill, Lowry. "Topic Development, Syntax, and Social Class." *DPr* 12 (July-September 1989): 267–286.

Middle-class and working-class conversational styles differ in turn-taking, anaphoric reference, ellipses, and syntactic subordination.

761. Hendrikse, A. P. "Syntactic Structures as Pragmatic Options." *SLang* 13 (1989): 333–379.

Sees conceptual schemas rather than linguistic structures as the basis for syntactic analysis. Claims that language acquisition and cognitive development are intimately related.

762. Hilles, Sharon Lee. "Access to Universal Grammar in Second Language Acquisition." *DAI* 50 (August 1989): 430A.

Examines the interlanguage of two children, two adolescents, and two adults learning English as a second language to determine the extent of their access to universal grammar.

763. Horn, Lawrence R. *A Natural History of Negation*. Chicago: University of Chicago Press, 1989. 664 pages

Treats the structure, use, and meaning of negation in natural language. Although standard logic shows symmetry between affirmative and negative propositions, no apparent comparable symmetry exists in ordinary language, which instead reflects complexity in the form and function of negative statements.

764. Hubbard, Maki Hirano. "Repetition and Ellipsis in Japanese Conversational Discourse: A Study of the Cognitive Domain of Conversational Interaction." *DAI* 49 (June 1989): 3704A.

A study of when and why repetition and ellipsis are used in Japanese conversation.

765. Hubbell, James Alvin. "The Effects of Metaphorical and Literal Processing on Subsequent Lexical Decision Latencies of Sentence Components." *DAI* 50 (July 1989): 362B.

Replicates Camac and Gluckberg's study, concluding that components drawn from apt metaphors show different lexical priming effects than those in semantically associated pairs.

766. Hwang, Shin Ja Joo. "Recursion in the Paragraph as a Unit of Discourse." *DPr* 12 (October–December 1989): 461–477.

Paragraphs have their own structural characteristics, which recur in texts such as narratives in English and in Korean.

767. Jacobs, Suzanne E. "From Syntax to Genre: Writers Use of Definite Constructions in 15 Editorials." *WC* 6 (October 1989): 528–544.

Using taxonomy from Brown and Yule, analyzes definite constructions in 15 editorials. Discusses pragmatic concerns influencing the writer's choice of definite constructions.

768. Johnston, Paul Dennithorne. "Escape from a Frozen Universe: Discovering General Semantics." *ETC* 46 (Summer 1989): 136–140.

A writer's personal account of coming to understand linguistic sources of conflicting realities and truths, allowing him to experience life as process.

769. Kehl, Del. "A New Grandfather Clause: The Doublespeak of Ageism." *QRD* 15 (April 1989): 2–3.

Argues that euphemisms for aging are manipulative doublespeak.

770. Kellerman, Kathy, Scott Broetzmann, Tae-Seop Lim, and Kenji Kitao. "The Conversation MOP: Scenes in the Stream of Discourse." *DPr* 12 (January–March 1989): 27–61.

American undergraduates appear to structure conversations through memory organization packets (MOPs) consisting of imagined topics and scenes organized into a limited number of scripts.

771. Khosroshahi, Fatemeh. "Penguins Don't Care, but Women Do: A Social Identity Analysis of a Whorfian Problem." *LSoc* 18 (December 1989): 505–525.

Suggests that encountering gender-neutral language tends to change concepts of gender only in readers who make conscious use of such language themselves.

772. Koskensalo, Annikki. "The Development of Interlanguage." Paper presented at the International Association of Applied Linguistics, Sydney, Australia, August 1987. ERIC ED 304 008. 14 pages

Examines the role of interlanguage in the error patterns of 432 essays in German, written by 38 speakers of Finnish.

773. Kress, Gunther. *Linguistic Processes in Sociocultural Practice*. Language Education. Edited by Frances Christie. New York: Oxford University Press, 1989. 102 pages

Explores the interconnectedness of linguistic and social matters in texts ranging from casual conversations to extracts from coursebooks.

774. Kristeva, Julia. *Language: The Unknown*. Translated by Anne M. Menke. New York: Columbia University Press, 1989. 328 pages

Investigates the evolution of linguistics as a science and traces postmodernist contemporary linguistic theory back to its roots.

775. Lawler, John M. "Lexical Semantics in the Commercial Transaction Frame: Value, Worth, Cost, and Price." *SLang* 13 (1989): 381–404.

Claims that the frame can be used both as the basis of metaphor and the definitional context for a large set of common lexical items.

776. Lehrer, Adrienne. "Remembering and Representing Prose: Quoted Speech as a Data Source." *DPr* 12 (January–March 1989): 105–125.

Verbatim recall is especially weak for hedges, intensifiers, conjunctions, and other words not tightly integrated into a clause.

777. Lin, Hwei-Bing, and Bruno H. Repp. "Cues to the Perception of Taiwanese Tones." *L&S* 32 (January–March 1989): 25–44.

Describes to what extent two dimensions of frequency—height/movement and syllable duration—provide cues to tonal distinctions.

778. Longacre, Robert. "Two Hypotheses regarding Text Generation and Analysis." *DPr* 12 (October–December 1989): 413–460.

Languages use a limited set of constructions to code the main line of discourse development. This set of constructions provides a basis for text analysis.

779. Lutz, William. *Doublespeak*. New York: Harper & Row, 1989. 256 pages

Discusses how government, business, advertisers, and others use deceptive language.

780. Lutz, William, ed. *Beyond Nineteen Eighty-Four: Doublespeak in a Post-Orwellian Age*. Urbana, Ill.: NCTE, 1989. 220 pages

Eighteen essays that discuss how doublespeak has invaded every sector of society and how it functions to manipulate and mislead people. Appendixes list annual recipients of the Orwell and Doublespeak awards.

781. Macaruso, Paul A. "Lexical Organization of Inflected Words." *DAI* 50 (November 1989): 2186B.

Examines how inflected words are lexically organized. Proposes a processing model to account for the cross-model facilitation effects shown in the study.

782. Maggio, Rosalie. *The Nonsexist Word Finder: A Dictionary of Gender Usage*. Boston: Beacon Press, 1989. 224 pages

Offers alternatives to words often used in sexist contexts.

783. Mair, Christian. "In Defense of 'the Fact That': A Corpus-Based Study of Current British Usage." *JEngL* 21 (April 1988): 59–71.

Defends the suppletive role of "the fact that" following some prepositional verbs and expressions.

784. Manning, Alan D. "The Relevance of Visual Models in Linguistic Theory and Discourse." *DAI* 49 (June 1989): 3705A.

Reviews five articles that use visual analogies to explain textual organization, perception, and analysis.

785. Manning, Alan D. "The Semantics of Technical Graphics." *JTWC* 19 (1989): 31–51.

Discusses the meanings of the terms *table, graph, chart,* and *diagram* and clarifies the relationship of these types of graphics to one another.

786. Mathews, Robert C., Ray R. Buss, William B. Stanley, Fredda Blanchard-Fields, Jeung Ryeul Cho, and Barry Druhan. "Role of Implicit and Explicit Processes in Learning from Examples: A Synergistic Effect." *JEPL* 15 (November 1989): 1083–1100.

Shows that experience with examples of a grammar is sufficient for people to learn it. Explains the situation through implicit, memory-based processing.

787. McArthur, Tom. "The Long-Neglected Phrasal Verb." *EngT* 5 (April 1989): 38–43.

Reviews the grammar and history of the verbal phrase and notes its current increased use.

788. "Mechanically Separated Meat." *QRD* 15 (April 1989): 5.

Points to examples of doublespeak in the food processing industry.

789. Melara, Robert D. "Dimensional Interaction between Color and Pitch." *JEPH* 15 (February 1989): 69–79.

Considers whether semantic considerations account for faster classification when color and pitch are presented jointly.

790. Michelini, Edward Lewis. "Adaptive Computer-Assisted Instruction for Rule Acquisition of English Sentence Punctuation Based upon the Right-Wrong Pattern of Learner Response." *DAI* 49 (March 1989): 2525A.

Studies the effects of different instructional management decision algorithms on teaching English punctuation rules to 228 college freshmen.

791. Morrow, Phillip R. "Conjunct Use in Business News Stories and Academic Journal Articles: A Comparative Study." *ESP* 8 (1989): 239–254.

Compares the use of conjunct connectives in business news stories and economics journal articles. Recommends that ESP business courses consider these findings.

792. Neale, Stephen R. "Descriptions." *DAI* 50 (July 1989): 165A.

Articulates, defends, and extends Russell's theory of descriptions, demonstrating that the theory accounts for pronominal anaphora in natural language.

793. "New Speakers' Bureau List Available." *QRD* 15 (April 1989): 6.

Announces the Speakers' Bureau as a resource for talks relating to doublespeak and explains how to get a free copy of the list of speakers.

794. "Nominations for Orwell and Doublespeak Awards." *QRD* 15 (July 1989): 11.

Invites nominations and provides guidelines for both the Orwell and Doublespeak awards.

795. Norrick, Neal R. "How Paradox Means." *PT* 10 (Fall 1989): 551–562.

Paradoxes yoke two contradictory frames of reference at the text-semantic level and are interpreted using three basic strategies that impose a higher-level schema.

796. "On Recalling Defective Language." *QRD* 15 (April 1989): 4.

Cites a recall letter as an example of how "corporate bureaucrats, government bureaucrats, and lawyers" create doublespeak.

797. "Out of the Loop." *QRD* 15 (April 1989): 5–6.

Cites "out of the loop" as an example of governmental doublespeak.

798. Perkins, Revere D. "Statistical Techniques for Determining Language Sample Size." *SLang* 13 (1989): 293–315.

Offers a set of heuristics to conduct cross-linguistic research.

799. Pitthan, Ingeborg Maria. "A History of Russian/Soviet Ideas about Language: Background to Soviet Foreign Language Pedagogy." *DAI* 50 (July 1989): 86A.

Acquaints Western students with ideas concerning linguistics, psychology, and pedagogy in a country with different political orientations and socioeconomic conditions.

800. "The Plain English Campaign in England." *QRD* 16 (October 1989): 11.

Reports on a group that awards prizes to organizations producing clear documents and gives the Golden Bull Award for gobbledygook.

801. Presby-Kodish, Susan. "Resolving Tensions with General Semantics." *ETC* 46 (Summer 1989): 142–146.

Shows how learning to distinguish between facts and inferences can be used to overcome such difficulties as writer's block, phobias, and problems in communication.

802. *QRD* 15 (January 1989): 1–4.

Announces the 1988 Orwell and Doublespeak awards, discussing nominations for each category and providing the text of William Lutz's speech announcing the awards.

803. Regan, Vincent D. "A Conception of Language Embodied in the Dictionary." *DAI* 49 (March 1989): 2642A.

Establishes the dictionary's indebtedness to written language and its maintenance, historically, of a formalist literary standard of language.

804. Renfrew, Colin. "The Origins of Indo-European Languages." *SAm* 261 (October 1989): 106–114.

Argues that linguistic similarities among Indo-European languages result from written records reflecting agricultural interdependence, not from the spoken interaction of military conquest.

805. Room, Adrian. "Axing the Apostrophe." *EngT* 5 (July 1989): 21–23.

Considers the origin of the apostrophe, reviews its current use and abuse, and speculates about the advantages of eliminating the apostrophe from English.

806. Said, Hanan Asa'd. "The Cohesive Role of Reference, Substitution, and Ellipsis in Two Genres of Modern Literary Arabic." *DAI* 49 (May 1989): 3352A.

Examines the type and frequency of cohesion devices in Arabic short stories and essays and compares findings to English usage.

807. Saito-Fukunaga, Mitsuko. "General Semantics and Intercultural Communication." *ETC* 46 (Winter 1989): 295–297.

Uses principles of general semantics to analyze sources of intercultural miscommunication. Suggests strategies for avoiding such problems.

808. Sakakini, Adel Omar. "The Effect of Context Clues and Grammatical Classes on the Ability of Undergraduate International Students to Identify Meanings of Unfamiliar Words in English Texts." *DAI* 49 (March 1989): 2603A.

Uses an instrument devised by Dulin (1968) to examine how undergraduate international students identify unfamiliar words from context.

809. Schiappa, Edward. "The Rhetoric of Nukespeak." *ComM* 56 (September 1989): 253–272.

Nukespeak uses metaphor, euphemism, technical jargon, and acronyms to portray nuclear concepts in a neutral or positive way.

810. Seliger, Herbert, and Elena Shohamy. *Second Language Research Methods.* Language Education. Edited by Frances Christie. New York: Oxford University Press, 1989. 280 pages

A comprehensive guide to research methods in second language learning and bilingualism.

811. Shalinksy, Allison. "A Cognitive Semantics for First-Person Statements." *DAI* 49 (March 1989): 2688A.

Investigates linguistic data associated with first-person statements. Concludes that semantic theory can successfully account for such statements.

812. Skinner, B. F. "The Origins of Cognitive Thought." *AmP* 44 (January 1989): 13–18.

Provides etymologies of words relating to feelings, then shows how those words have come to be used in cognitive psychology.

813.   Slator, Brian M. "Lexical Semantics and Preference Semantics Analysis." *DAI* 50 (July 1989): 252B.

Describes a computational system used to analyze English prose under the Preference Semantics Theory of language understanding.

814.   Steiner, Erich H., and Robert Veltman, eds. *Pragmatics, Discourse, and Text: Some Systemic Approaches*. Advances in Discourse Processes, vol. 37. Norwood, N.J.: Ablex, 1988. 256 pages

Twelve essays report on recent progress in applying systemic linguistics to discourse analysis and text structure.

815.   Streim, Nancy W. "The Effects of Syntactic Priming on the Production of Active and Passive Sentences." *DAI* 49 (February 1989): 3474B.

Examines how syntactic priming affects the selection of grammatical voice, concluding that an abstract syntactic production rule exists, at least in adult readers.

816.   Stuart, David, and Stephen D. Houston. "Maya Writing." *SAm* 261 (August 1989): 82–89.

Examines how translations of Mayan writing suggest that linguistic patterns are related to Mayan social patterns.

817.   Svorou, Soteria. "The Experiential Basis of the Grammar of Space: Evidence from the Language of the World." *DAI* 49 (June 1989): 3707A.

Investigates the way in which different languages express spatial relations of location and direction.

818.   Tannen, Deborah, ed. *Linguistics in Context: Connecting Observation and Understanding*. Advances in Discourse Processes, vol. 29. Norwood, N.J.: Ablex, 1988. 352 pages

Prints 13 lectures from the 1985 LSA-TESOL Institute. Treats humanistic approaches to linguistic analysis, the nature and use of language, language learning and teaching, and poetry.

819.   Taylor, Hanni U. *Standard English, Black English, and Bidialectalism: A Controversy*. American University Studies. New York: Peter Lang, 1989. 235 pages

A five-chapter discussion of the need for multicultural language instruction. Treats relevant research, subliminal barriers to interracial communication, and techniques and attitudes that can lead black students to academic success.

820.   Taylor, John R. *Linguistic Categorization: Prototypes in Linguistic Theory*. New York: Oxford University Press, 1989. 304 pages

Provides an introduction to the cognitive paradigm in linguistics, exploring its potential for studying word meaning, syntax, and phonology.

821.   Tiancharoen, Supanee. "A Comparative Study of Spoken and Written Thai: Linguistic and Sociolinguistic Perspectives." *DAI* 49 (January 1989): 1790A.

Finds spoken and written texts too broad to compare. Also judges sociolinguistic context more important than modality in determining linguistic features.

822.   Trabasso, Tom, Paul van den Broek, and Young Suh So. "Logical Necessity and Transitivity of Causal Relations in Stories." *DPr* 12 (January–March 1989): 1–25.

The strength of relations between clauses is a function of the causal distance between them.

823.   Trowbridge, T. R. "On Euphemisms; or, Through the Dark, Glassily." *QRD* 15 (April 1989): 8–9.

Argues that the 1980s are the decade of euphemisms. Provides examples from air travel, museums, law, and government.

824. Turner, Elise, and Richard E. Cullingford. "Using Conversation MOPs in Natural Language Interfaces." *DPr* 12 (January–March 1989): 63–90.

Artificial intelligence systems can model the intentionality in conversations through memory organization packets (MOPs) consisting of scripts with imagined topics and scenes.

825. Vihman, Marilyn M., and Shelley L. Velleman. "Phonological Reorganization: A Case Study." *L&S* 32 (April–June 1989): 149–170.

Between 10 months and 16 months of age, the child in this study showed no transition from whole-word to segmental phonology.

826. Warner, John D. "A Theory of Grammatical Intuition." *DAI* 50 (October 1989): 1674B.

Investigates the origins of grammatical intuition, finding that several kinds of information besides syntactic are incorporated into intuition.

827. Weinberger, Steven Howard. "Theoretical Foundations of Second Language Phonology." *DAI* 50 (July 1989): 129A.

Argues that acquiring phonology involves more than the transfer of surface items. Invokes recoverability to account for the differential use of two functionally related syllable simplification processes in L2 phonology.

828. White, William Howard. "Vocabulary Acquisition from Reading and the ESL Learner." *DAI* 50 (July 1989): 129A.

Examines the hypothesis that first language vocabulary is acquired incidentally through reading. Applies the hypothesis to second language vocabulary acquisition.

829. Wierzbicka, Anna. "Prototypes in Semantics and Pragmatics: Explicating Attitudinal Meanings in Terms of Prototypes." *Ling* 27 (1989): 731–769.

Shows how "pragmatic meanings" encoded in different forms of address can be portrayed in a rigorous and illuminating way in a natural semantic metalanguage.

830. Wilson, Robert Anton. "Toward Understanding E-Prime." *ETC* 46 (Winter 1989): 316–319.

Discusses various meanings of "to be" verbs and ways of misusing them. Advocates using E-Prime, English without "to be" verbs.

831. Wisniewski, Edward, and Gregory Murphy. "Superordinate and Basic Category Names in Discourse: A Textual Analysis." *DPr* 12 (April–June 1989): 245–261.

Analysis of a computerized corpus shows that basic category names (*hammer*) frequently designate single objects, whereas superordinate terms (*tool*) designate classes of objects.

832. Wolf, Dennie, and Deborah Hicks. "The Voices within Narratives: The Development of Intertextuality in Young Children's Stories." *DPr* 12 (July–September 1989): 329–351.

By age three, children's stories show the simultaneous use of stage-managing, dialogue among characters, and narrative commentary. Such devices support the notion of linguistic polyphony.

See also 44, 90, 105, 133, 171, 180, 187, 201, 208, 240, 392, 433, 478, 493, 495, 517, 593, 664, 696, 843, 869, 877, 896, 897, 904, 906, 921, 973, 990, 1298, 1715

2.9 PSYCHOLOGY

833. Alexander, Michael P., D. Frank Benson, and Donald T. Stuss. "Frontal Lobes and Language." *BL* 37 (November 1989): 656–691.

Discusses the specific modal and supramodal functions of the frontal lobes with respect to language and communication.

834. Allen, Mike, and James B. Stiff. "Testing Three Models for the Sleeper Effect." *WJSC* 53 (Fall 1989): 411–426.

A meta-analysis of the long-term effects of a low-credible source on attitude change suggests that a sleeper effect does exist. Offers suggestions for practitioners and theorists.

835. Aune, Robert Kelly. "Effects of the Need for Cognition, Attribution of Intent, and Quality of Argument on Persuasion." *DAI* 49 (June 1989): 3548A.

Investigates the interaction among cognition, the level of mindfulness, an arguments quality, and changes in attitude.

836. Banaji, Mahzarin R., and Robert G. Crowder. "The Bankruptcy of Everyday Memory." *AmP* 44 (September 1989): 1185–1193.

Values laboratory experimentation over naturalistic observation because the former is high in generalizibility.

837. Barnes, Michael L., and Robert J. Sternberg. "Social Intelligence and Decoding of Nonverbal Cues." *Intell* 13 (July–September 1989): 263–287.

Concludes that these constructs are related. They require one to extract, weigh, and combine relevant features as well as to formulate and execute appropriate strategies.

838. Becker, Barbara Jean. "The Effect of Mands and Tacts on Conversational Units and Other Verbal Operants." *DAI* 50 (September 1989): 571A.

Examines verbal behavior as a product of mands and tacts.

839. Benderly, Beryl Lieff. "Everyday Intuition." *PsyT* 23 (September 1989): 35–40.

Defines intuition as the expert's ability to chunk information into meaningful patterns that allow quick insight. Uses the process of reading to illustrate.

840. Braiker, Harriet B. "The Power of Self-Talk." *PsyT* 23 (December 1989): 23–27.

Analyzes the effects of inner dialogue on emotion and motivation, emphasizes the cognitive traps in negative "self-talk," and

provides techniques for capturing and responding to this inner voice.

841. Braswell, Robert Don. "An Exploration of the Warp Factor in Galileo Theory as a Measure of Cognitive Dissonance." *DAI* 49 (February 1989): 2008A.

Uses student-written attitudinal essays to examine the usefulness of warp factor as a measure of dissonance.

842. Brems, Christiane, and Mark E. Johnson. "Problem-Solving Appraisal and Coping Style: The Influence of Sex-Role Orientation and Gender." *JPsy* 123 (March 1989): 187–194.

Suggests that men have greater confidence than women in solving problems. Men cope via denial while women turn against the self.

843. Brody, Nathan. "Unconscious Learning of Rules: Comment on Reber's Analysis of Implicit Learning [*JEPG* 118 (September 1989)]." *JEPG* 118 (September 1989): 236–238.

Suggests that the ability to acquire knowledge without being aware of the process of acquisition constitutes a rebuttal to Reber's thesis.

844. Brueggemann, Brenda Jo. "Whole Brains, Half Brains, and Writing." *RR* 8 (Fall 1989): 127–136.

Reviews research and suggests that writing is complex, requiring both types of hemisphere use.

845. Buss, Arnold H. "Personality as Traits." *AmP* 44 (November 1989): 1378–1388.

Discusses the importance of personality traits in determining behavior.

846. Catanzaro, Salvatore J. "Effects of Enhancement Expectancies on Expectancy and Minimal Goal Statements." *JPsy* 123 (January 1989): 91–100.

Examines students' enjoyment of achievement tasks in relation to a level of self-set goals and to a knowledge of other students' enjoyment of the task.

847. Clark, Herbert H., and Edward F. Schaefer. "Contributing to Discourse." *CSc* 13 (1989): 259–294.

For people to contribute to discourse, they must add to their common ground in an orderly way by establishing for each utterance the mutual belief that the addressees have understood the speaker.

848. Collins, Allan, and Ryszard Michalski. "The Logic of Plausible Reasoning: A Core Theory." *CSc* 13 (1989): 1–49.

Presents a core theory of human reasoning that addresses both the semantic and parametric aspects of the kind of everyday reasoning that pervades all human discourse.

849. Cotman, Carl W., and Gary S. Lynch. "The Neurobiology of Learning and Memory." *Cognition* 33 (1989): 201–241.

Discusses progress in using models to describe molecular and anatomical details of the brain that transfer to studies of memory and learning.

850. Daly, John, David Weber, Anita Vangelisti, Madeline Maxwell, and Heather Neel. "Concurrent Cognitions during Conversations: Protocol Analysis as a Means of Exploring Conversations." *DPr* 12 (April–June 1989): 227–244.

New insights about speech-act theory come from think-aloud protocols combined with records of communications betweeen individuals on a computer network.

851. Demoss, David Jay. "Compatibilism, Practical Wisdom, and the Narrative Self; or, If I Had Had My Act Together, I Could Have Done Otherwise." *DAI* 49 (May 1989): 3383A.

Examines the relations between intentional actions and reasons for actions, between intentional actions and action plans, and between intentional actions and free actions. Focuses on a web of attitudes in defining free action and the self.

852. Derr, Richard L. "Insights on the Nature of Intelligence from Ordinary Discourse." *Intell* 13 (April June 1989): 113–118.

Identifies four properties of intelligence. Draws implications for research in psychology and for educational practices.

853. Detterman, Douglas K. "The Future of Intelligence Research." *Intell* 13 (July-September 1989): 199–203.

Stresses a necessary future emphasis on large N research, corrections of correlations, reliability, formal theories, and the biological grounding of models.

854. Dixon, Kathleen G. "Intellectual Development and the Place of Narrative in Basic and Freshman Composition." *JBW* 8 (Spring 1989): 3–20.

Questions the applicability of "the Piagetian-Perry stage model" of development. Calls for reconsidering what "development" itself means and supports the value of narrative writing.

855. Dormen, Lesley, and Peter Edidin. "Original Spin." *PsyT* 23 (July–August 1989): 46–52.

Defines creativity as a basic human endowment seen in the ability to adapt to change, to break mindsets and play with perspectives, and to focus on process rather than outcome.

856. Dyck, Joachim. "Rhetoric and Psychoanalysis." *RSQ* 19 (Spring 1989): 95–105.

A conversation about argumentation between a rhetorician and a psychiatrist.

857. Farah, Martha J. "Semantic and Perceptual Priming: How Similar Are the Underlying Mechanisms?" *JEPH* 15 (February 1989): 188–194.

Argues that perceptual priming reflects a sensitivity change while semantic priming reflects a bias change.

858. Flisser, Grace Anne. "A Phenomenological Inquiry into Insight in Writing." *DAI* 49 (March 1989): 2519A.

Focuses on "insight as lived in writing experiences." Describes the relationship of insight to larger contexts of meaning in writing, including cognitive acts.

859. Garner, Ruth, and Patricia A. Alexander. "Metacognition: Answered and Unanswered Questions." *EdPsy* 24 (Spring 1989): 143–158.

Summarizes and explains recent research on metacognition, focusing on four central questions about measuring and evaluating knowledge and about relationships among kinds of knowledge.

860. Gibbs, Raymond W. "Understanding and Literal Meaning." *CSc* 13 (1989): 259–294.

Argues that the widely accepted distinctions between literal and metaphoric meanings and between semantics and pragmatics have little utility for psycholinguistic theories.

861. Gintner, Gary G., John D. West, and John J. Zarski. "Learned Resourcefulness and Situation-Specific Coping with Stress." *JPsy* 123 (May 1989): 295–304.

Finds that "problem-focused coping" results in lower stress levels among students.

862. Goodson, Linda K. "The Relationship between Data Gathering Preferences of Young Adult Students as Reported by the Myers-Briggs Type Indicator and the Content of Their Creative Compositions." *DAI* 49 (April 1989): 2895A.

Finds a relationship between personality type and data gathering preferences.

863. Greeno, James G. "A Perspective on Thinking." *AmP* 44 (February 1989): 134–141.

Regards an individual's intuitive conceptual understanding and beliefs about knowledge, learning, and intelligence as important factors in thinking activity.

864. Halford, Graeme S. "Reflections on 25 Years of Piagetian Cognitive Developmental Psychology, 1963–1988." *HD* 32 (November 1989): 325–357.

Discusses Piagetian theory, concluding that "Piaget's empirical work has held up better than is often thought but that his conceptualization of cognitive development is inadequate."

865. Hatcher, Donald. "Is Critical Thinking Guilty of Unwarranted Reductionism?" *JT* 24 (Spring-Summer 1989): 94–111.

Denies the contextualist argument. Asserts that teachers of critical thinking "should show students that such claims are very problematic, probably incoherent, and ultimately unintelligible."

866. Horn, Christy A., Duane Shell, and M. T. H. Benkofske. "Effects of Cognitive Development Level on the Relationship between Self-Efficacy, Causal Attribution, and Outcome Expectancy and Performance in Reading and Writing." Paper presented at the National Reading Conference, Tucson, December 1988. ERIC ED 304 659. 10 pages

Studies 150 undergraduates between the ages of 18 and 23.

867. Iran-Nejad, Asghar. "A Nonconnectionist Schema Theory of Understanding Surprise-Ending Stories." *DPr* 12 (April–June 1989): 127–148.

Subjects' interpretations of ambiguous stories support a theory positing that the same neural microsystems are involved in interpretations that contradict each other.

868. Jacklin, Carol Nagy. "Female and Male: Issues of Gender." *AmP* 44 (February 1989): 127–133.

Discusses gender in terms of biology and behavior, social processes, and measuring intellectual abilities.

869. Javier, Rafael A., and Luis R. Marcos. "The Role of Stress on the Language-Independence and Code-Switching Phenomena." *JPsyR* 18 (1989): 449–472.

Studies the extent to which stress affects the assumed functional separation of coordinate bilinguals' linguistic organization.

870. Jensen, George H., and John K. DiTiberio. *Personality and the Teaching of Composition*. Advances in Writing Research. Edited by Marcia Farr. Norwood, N.J.: Ablex, 1989. 224 pages

Applies Jungian personality theory to explain individual differences in writing processes and texts. Includes handouts for students and an appendix on learning styles.

871. Johnson, Janice, Veronica Fabian, and Juan Pascual-Leone. "Quantitative Hardware Stages That Constrain Language Development." *HD* 32 (September 1989): 245–271.

Two studies using Pascual-Leone's theory of constructive operators support the idea of general cognitive-processing constraints on, and cognitive-developmental stages in, linguistic performance.

872. Johnson, Neal F., Kenneth R. Pough, and Anthony J. Blum. "More on the Way We 'See' Letters from Words within Memory." *JML* 28 (April 1989): 155–163.

Concludes that words are processed holistically, that the perceiver is not in direct control, and that letter information must be derived from memory of word-level representation.

873. Judge, Lisa Clare. "The Therapeutic Writing Process: A Case Study." *DAI* 50 (August 1989): 363A.

Compares stages of the writing process with stages of the psychotherapeutic process. Concludes from a six-year study that personal writing can be therapeutic.

874. Krainer, Elizabeth. "Challenges in a Psychotherapy Group: Reflections of Direct and Indirect Discourse Strategies." *DAI* 49 (May 1989): 3350A.

Examines the pragmatic functions of challenges in expressing and negotiating interactional conflict.

875. Larson, Gerald E., and Dennis P. Saccuzzo. "Cognitive Correlates of General Intelligence: Towards a Process Theory of *g*." *Intell* 13 (January–March 1989): 5–31.

Concludes that "more intelligent individuals . . . more flexibly and consistently reconfigure the 'contents of consciousness.'" They are more agile in manipulating symbols during cognitive processing.

876. Levander, Maria, Sten E. Levander, and Daisey Schalling. "Hand Preference and Sex as Determinants of Neuropsychological Skill, Solving Strategy, and Side Preference." *Intell* 13 (January–March 1989): 93–111.

Discovered "small, scattered" differences for handedness. Males were faster with most tasks, but less accurate; females excelled with most verbal skills, showing same side preferences.

877. Lewicki, Pawel, and Thomas Hill. "On the Status of Nonconscious Processes in Human Cognition: Comment on Reber [*JEPG* 118 (September 1989)]." *JEPG* 118 (September 1989): 239–241.

Discusses the generality of nonconscious acquisition of knowledge and its status in contemporary cognitive psychology.

878. Lundell, James Walfred. "Knowledge Extraction and the Modelling of Expertise in a Diagnostic Task." *DAI* 50 (July 1989): 364B.

Investigates three strategies—extraction of rules, extraction of prototypical knowledge, and induction through exemplars—and considers the implications of this research for developing computerized expert systems.

879. MacNeal, Edward. "MacNeal's Master Atlas of Decision Making: Appendices." *ETC* 46 (Fall 1989): 250–262.

Summarizes decision-making patterns presented in previous articles. Defines patterns, gives applications, and includes a glossary of terms.

880. MacNeal, Edward. "MacNeal's Master Atlas of Decision Making: Appendices." *ETC* 46 (Winter 1989): 334–351.

Includes a sample demalogical analysis of a speech to show how decision-making clues are inherent in language. Also contains sample dictionary entries, a thesaurus, and a bibliography.

881. MacNeal, Edward. "MacNeal's Master Atlas of Decision Making: Applying Demalogics." *ETC* 46 (Spring 1989): 7–20.

Discusses general considerations in selecting decision-making strategies: sources of error, habitual limitations of strategies, an awareness of using demalogics, and practice in forecasting.

882. MacNeal, Edward. "MacNeal's Master Atlas of Decision Making: Applying Demalogics." *ETC* 46 (Summer 1989): 101–113.

Analyzes advantages of practicing the repertoire of decision-making strategies, enabling practitioners to recognize another's patterns and their own errors.

883. Massaro, Dominic W. *Experimental Psychology: An Information-Processing Approach*. San Diego: Harcourt Brace Jovanovich, 1989. 512 pages

Examines methods for investigating mental phenomena and cognitive processes involved in language, memory, and thought. Stressing experimental procedures, applies these methods to specific cases and researchers.

884. Massaro, Dominic W. "Testing between the TRACE Model and the Fuzzy Logical Model of Speech Perception." *CPsy* 21 (July 1989): 398–421.

Contrasts the TRACE Model with the Fuzzy Logical Model in an attempt to "account for the influence of multiple sources of information on perceptual judgement."

885. Mayer, John D., David R. Caruso, Edward Zigler, and Julia I. Dreyden. "Intelligence and Intelligence-Related Personality Traits." *Intell* 13 (April–June 1989): 119–133.

Identifies "three intellect-related personality traits: Absorption, Pleasure, and Apathy." Demonstrates differences across groups that differ by age and by giftedness.

886. McCombs, Barbara L., and Jo Sue Whisler. "The Role of Affective Variables in Autonomous Learning." *EdPsy* 24 (Summer 1989): 277–306.

Proposes a causal model for facilitating autonomous learning. The model is based on the supposition that autonomous learning is preceded by positive affect, motivation, and the expectation of success.

887. McMahan, Charles R. "Differences in Levels of Evaluation and Verbal Reinforcement Chosen by Communication Apprehensives." *DAI* 49 (April 1989): 2862A.

Studies 31 males and 31 females and finds high apprehensives giving more positive reinforcement to video-taped speakers than did low apprehensives.

888. Mikulincer, Mario. "Self-Serving Biases in the Perception of Freedom: The Impact of Previously Experienced Failure." *JPsy* 123 (January 1989): 25–41.

Five experiments indicate that students protected self-esteem by attributing failure to a lack of freedom during assigned tasks.

889. Modarressi, Ali Asghar. "Learned Helplessness, Attributions, and Depression: A Correlational Study." *DAI* 50 (July 1989): 349B.

Examines the relationship between attributional style, depression, and gender as a means of testing the reformulated learned helplessness theory.

890. Naglieri, Jack A. "A Cognitive Processing Theory for the Measurement of Intelligence." *EdPsy* 24 (Spring 1989): 185–206.

Prompted by the limitations of current intelligence tests, this essay proposes an alternative means of measuring intelligence based on the work of Luria and Das.

891. Newton, Deborah Anne. "Influence Strategies Used by Relational Partners during Disagreements." *DAI* 49 (May 1989): 3202A.

Discusses interpersonal strategies and tactics during arguments. In close relationships, influence is used to attain instrumental goals and to manage and maintain identity.

892. Potts, George R., Mark F. St. John, and Donald Kirson. "Incorporating New Information into Existing World Knowledge." *CPsy* 21 (July 1989): 303–333.

Suggests that new information is incorporated when it is easy to retrieve and use in a variety of contexts.

893. Preiss, Raymond W. "A Narrative and Meta-Analytic Review of Receiver Apprehension Outcomes: The Consolidation and Extension of the Literature." *DAI* 49 (April 1989): 2863A.

Finds that receiver apprehension correlated positively with alienation, communication and test anxiety, intolerance for ambiguity, and rigidity of personal habits.

894. Ramsey, William M. "Parallelism and Functionalism." *CSc* 13 (1989): 139–144.

Argues that parallel distributed processing models do not inherently undermine functionalism.

895. Ransdell, Sarah Ellen, and Ira Fischler. "Effects of Concreteness and Task Context on Recall of Prose among Bilingual and Monolingual Speakers." *JML* 28 (June 1989): 278–291.

The language of prose can act as a context specifier for bilinguals.

896. Reber, Arthur S. "Implicit Learning and Tacit Knowledge." *JEPG* 118 (September 1989): 219–235.

Considers the acquisition of a complex knowledge. Using a synthetic grammar, finds that implicit learning is independent of consciousness.

897. Reber, Arthur S. "More Thoughts on the Unconscious: Reply to Brody and to Lewicki and Hill [*JEPG* 118 (September 1989)]." *JEPG* 118 (September 1989): 242–244.

Defends his methodology in studies on implicit unconscious learning. Reviews arguments related to evolutionary forces that influence learning.

898. Reinitz, Mark Tippens, Eve Wright, and Geoffrey Loftus. "Effects of Semantic Priming on Visual Encoding of Pictures." *JEPG* 118 (September 1989): 280–297.

Argues that primes affect information acquisition, not just late cognitive processes.

899. Robertson, Carolyn Seils. "The Role of Metaphor in Comprehension Processes." *DAI* 49 (March 1989): 2603A.

Investigates among 80 freshman students and four professors whether and how a metaphor connects an already held concept to a new one.

900. Rosnow, Ralph L., and Robert Rosenthal. "Statistical Procedures and the Justification of Knowledge in Psychological Science." *AmP* 44 (October 1989): 1276–1284.

Examines the rhetoric of justification.

901. Rushton, J. Philippe. "Japanese Inbreeding Depression Scores: Predictors of Cognitive Differences between Blacks and Whites." *Intell* 13 (January–March 1989): 43–51.

Concludes that the "genetic contribution to racial differences in cognitive performance may be more robust . . . than has been considered to date."

902. Salomon, Gayriel, and David N. Perkins. "Rocky Roads to Transfer: Rethinking Mechanisms of a Neglected Phenomenon." *EdPsy* 24 (Spring 1989): 113–142.

Proposes a model of transfer based on two mechanisms: the nearly automatic transfer of a practiced behavior and a deliberate, "mindful abstraction" of a principle.

903. Samuel, Valerie J., and Stephen J. Dollinger. "Self-Focused Attention and the Recognition of Psychological Implications." *JPsy* 123 (November 1989): 623–625.

Examines the effects on research subjects of using cameras or one-way mirrors.

904. Sanders, Geoff, Helen V. Wright, and Carol Ellis. "Cerebral Lateralization of Language in Deaf and Hearing People." *BL* 36 (May 1989): 555–579.

Explores differences in deaf and hearing adolescents with regard to language acquisition and a left or right visual field advantage.

905. Siegal, Marjorie, and Robert F. Carey. *Critical Thinking: A Semiotic Perspective.* Monographs on Teaching Critical Thinking. Bloomington, Ind.: NCTE and ERIC/RCS, 1989. ERIC ED 303 802. 64 pages

Encourages teachers at all levels to foster critical thinking. Examines relationships between language and thinking, discussing how semiotics functions in language making.

906. Sies, Luther F., and Martin R. Gitterman. "Neurolinguistic Processing and Brain Function: A General Semantics Perspective." *ETC* 46 (Winter 1989): 328–333.

Reviews in light of current mind-brain research Korzybski's claim that language affects neurological functions. Concludes that current research supports Korzybski's claim.

907. Stacks, Don W., and Peter A. Andersen. "The Modular Mind: Implications for Intrapersonal Communication." *SCJ* 54 (Spring 1989): 273–293.

Extends the right brain-left brain argument by examining specific interhemispheric and intermodular processes and their effects on language and communication.

908. Sternberg, Robert J., and Joyce Gastel. "Coping with Novelty in Human Intelligence: An Empirical Investigation." *Intell* 13 (April–June 1989): 187–197.

"The ability to cope with novelty" correlated significantly with two fluid ability tests, supporting the notion that it is an important aspect of intelligence.

909. Stewart, Abigail J., and Joseph M. Healy, Jr. "Linking Individual Developmental and Social Changes." *AmP* 44 (January 1989): 30–42.

Argues that social history and personality development are linked. Presents a model that compares the impact of social events to life style.

910. Strauss, Claudia Rae. "Culture, Discourse, and Cognition: Forms of Belief in Some Rhode Island Working Men's Talk about Success." *DAI* 49 (April 1989): 3073A.

Challenges assumptions about consistency of beliefs in individual cognitive schema theories.

911. Strickland, Bonnie R. "Internal-External Control Expectancies: From Contingencies to Creativity." *AmP* 44 (January 1989): 1–12.

Reviews theory and research behind internal-external expectancies. Concludes that self-theory will be enhanced if contingencies are better understood and new patterns created.

912. Tappan, Mark B. "Stories Lived and Stories Told: The Narrative Structure of Late Adolescent Moral Development." *HD* 32 (September 1989): 300–315.

Compares the narrative structures of Kohlberg's and Perry's theoretical accounts with two late adolescents' narrative structures of personal accounts. Finds Perry's account more accurate.

913. Teasdale, T. W., and David R. Owen. "Continuing Secular Increases in Intelligence and a Stable Prevalence of High Intelligence Levels." *Intell* 13 (July–September 1989): 255–262.

Found that gains continuing among lower intelligence levels were due not to ceiling levels on tests but to the egalitarian nature of Danish schools.

914. Tobias, Sigmund. "Another Look at Research on the Adaptation of Instruction to Student Characteristics." *EdPsy* 24 (Summer 1989): 213–227.

Reviews and evaluates the value of aptitude treatment interaction studies to cognition and students' learning styles. Recommends alterations in current methods.

915. Torney-Purta, Judith. "Political Cognition and Its Restructuring in Young People." *HD* 32 (January 1989): 14–23.

Uses the Piagetian concept of accommodation to study political learning in children and adolescents. Offers suggestions for cognitive analysis of political socialization.

916. Turner, Marilyn L., and Randall W. Engle. "Is Working Memory Capacity Task Dependent?" *JML* 28 (April 1989): 127–154.

Experiments showed that working memory storage capacity was task independent. Reading comprehension was unaffected by processing concurrent tasks unrelated to reading skills.

917. Walczyk, Jeffrey J., and Vernon C. Hall. "Is the Failure of Monitor Comprehension an Instance of Cognitive Impulsivity?" *JEdP* 81 (September 1989): 294–298.

Reports on the measurement of third and fifth graders' abilities to monitor comprehension. Cognitively impulsive and reflective children were identified via the Matching Familiar Figures Test.

918. White, Aaronette Michelle. "A Social-Cognitive Approach toward the Measurement of Racio-Ethnic Identification among Afro-Americans." *DAI* 50 (July 1989): 374B.

Conducts a meta-analytic review of literature investigating ethnic identification among Afro-Americans. Discusses the development and testing of an instrument for measuring ethnic identity.

919. Woods, Donald R. "Teaching Thinking and Ideas about Assessment." *JCST* 18 (March–April 1989): 338–340.

Summarizes Lauren Resnick's *Education and Learning to Think* (1987) and suggests applications for teaching higher-order thinking skills.

920. Wyche-Smith, Susan L. "The Magic Circle: Writers and Ritual." *DAI* 49 (March 1989): 2645A.

Connects ritual with the psychophysiological concept of emotion as an active agent in cognition. Explores its implications for composition research and teaching.

921. Zatorre, Robert J. "On the Representation of Multiple Languages in the Brain: Old Problems and New Directions." *BL* 36 (January 1989): 127–147.

Argues that the right hemisphere is more involved in language production in multilingual speakers than in unilingual speakers.

See also 10, 40, 207, 217, 617, 646, 662, 684, 699, 761, 770, 812, 824, 933, 1011, 1351, 1352, 1790

2.10　EDUCATION

922. Banks, James A., and Cherry A. McGee Banks, eds. *Multicultural Education: Issues and Perspectives*. Needham Heights, Mass.: Allyn & Bacon, 1989. 337 pages

Sixteen essays identify major issues and define concepts relevant to multicultural education. Explores issues such as social class, religion, ethnicity and language, and exceptionality. Presents suggestions for school reform.

923. Braun, Joseph A., Jr., ed. *Reforming Teacher Education: Issues and New Directions*. Source Books on Education, vol. 20. New York: Garland, 1989. 362 pages

A collection of 16 essays that examine issues raised by reform proposals and propose new directions for teacher education.

924. Cohen, Arthur M., and Florence B. Brawer. *The American Community College*. 2d ed. Higher Education Series. San Francisco: Jossey-Bass, 1989. 440 pages

Reviews the background, purpose, and social role of the community college; analyzes enrollment trends, hiring practices, instructional methods, and academic programs; and discusses the future of community colleges.

925. Cremin, Lawrence. *Popular Education and Its Discontents*. New York: Harper & Row, 1989. 144 pages

Based on a series of lectures, reflects on the achievements and problems of American education.

926. Kimball, Roger. *Tenured Radicals: How Politics Has Corrupted Our High Education*. New York: Harper & Row, 1989. 224 pages

Argues that individuals, universities, and politically motivated groups such as deconstructionists and feminists are responsible for the present disarray of the liberal arts.

927. Marton, Ference. "Towards a Pedagogy of Content." *EdPsy* 24 (Winter 1989): 1–23.

Investigates the relationship between educational research and practice by examining its past and current relevance and by predicting the future relevance of research to pedagogy.

928. National Center for Education Statistics. *Digest of Education Statistics, 1989*. Washington, D.C.: U.S. Government Printing Office, 1989. 462 pages

Provides abstracts of statistical information concerning American education from prekindergarten through graduate school. Covers such subjects as the numbers of schools and colleges, teachers, enrollments, funding, educational attainment, libraries, and employment of graduates.

929. Puckett, John L. *Foxfire Reconsidered: A 20-Year Experiment in Progressive Education*. Champaign, Ill.: University of Illinois Press, 1989. 376 pages

Discusses the contribution the Foxfire program has made to schooling.

930. *Recruiting Minority Teachers: A Practical Guide*. Washington, D.C.: American Association of Colleges for Teacher Education, 1989. 31 pages

Suggests strategies for recruiting minority-group members as students in teacher education programs.

931. Russell, David R. "The Cooperation Movement: Language across the Curriculum and Mass Education, 1900–1930." *RTE* 23 (December 1989): 399–423.

Describes an early twentieth-century attempt to broaden responsibility for language instruction. It had little effect on writing instruction but offered a base for later reform.

932. Schubert, William. "On the Practical Value of Practical Inquiry for Teachers and Students." *JT* 24 (Spring-Summer 1989): 41–74.

Discusses the curriculum theory of Joseph Schwab, particularly his ideas relating to practical inquiry, curricular collaboration, *arete* (versus *techne*) reflection, and situational context.

933. Sewall, Timothy John. "A Factor Analysis of Three Learning Styles Instruments: A Test of the Curry Model of Learning Style Characteristics." *DAI* 50 (July 1989): 54A.

Examines the Myers-Briggs Type Indicator, the Kolb Learning Style Indicator, and the Canfield Learning Styles Indicator in the context of the Curry model.

934. Shea, Stephanie B. "The Scientific Study of Education: Its Status, Development, and Alternatives." *DAI* 50 (July 1989): 95A.

Considers which model of inquiry—natural science or naturalistic—is most appropriate and productive for the educational research community.

935. Tillis, Linda Lancaster. "Expanding Rhetorical Boundaries: A Paradigm for Categories of Expressive Discourse in a Student Development Context." *DAI* 49 (April 1989): 2956A.

Analyzes the journals of 39 resident assistants.

936. Wigginton, Eliot. "Foxfire Grows Up." *HER* 59 (February 1989): 24–49.

Redefines the Foxfire approach of publishing oral histories, identifying the philosophy behind such works and suggesting pedagogical techniques for teachers.

937. Winne, Philip H. "Theories of Instruction and of Intelligence for Designing Artificially Intelligent Tutoring Systems." *EdPsy* 24 (Summer 1989): 229–259.

Suggests that designers of artificially intelligent systems adapt programs to a previously articulated theory of instruction. Proposes one such model.

938. Zanardi, William. "Higher Education and the Crisis of Historicism." *JT* 24 (Spring-Summer 1989): 75–93.

Recommends an approach, given the influence of relativism and historicism, that would alert students to issues, offer them directions, and make responsible judgments possible.

See also 235, 408, 424, 852, 913, 949, 1005, 1051, 1065, 1076, 1102, 1188, 1806

2.11 JOURNALISM, PUBLISHING, TELEVISION, AND RADIO

939. Allen, Julia M. "The Women Writers of *The Masses:* The Rhetorical Use of Multiple Social Languages." *DAI* 50 (August 1989): 441A.

Studies the discourse patterns of women writing for *The Masses,* a socialist periodical published between 1911 and 1917.

940. Allen, Martha Leslie. "The Development of Communication Networks among Women, 1963–1983." *DAI* 49 (March 1989): 2743A.

Studies the development of mass media and communication networks that emerged in the 1960s essentially independent of male control.

941. Bryski, Bruce G. "The Rhetoric of Television News: '60 Minutes' as Media Presentation." *DAI* 49 (April 1989): 2861A.

Uses Burke's dramatism and on-site observation to analyze the verbal and visual strategies "60 Minutes" employs to construct a visually persuasive and symbolic reality.

942. Carey, John. "From Eyewitness to History." *ETC* 46 (Spring 1989): 35–40.

Contrasts bad reportage, which uses language to retreat, with good reportage, which uses the power of language to confront. Reports must be individual, powerful, and literal.

943. Coughlin, Ellen K. "On 'Dynasty,' the Audience and the TV Show Overlap." *CHE* 35 (7 June 1989): A5.

Using reader-response theory, Jane Feuer of the University of Pittsburgh argues that "Dynasty" produces a stronger viewer response than literature such as *Ulysses.*

944. Crouthamel, James L. *Bennett's New York Herald and the Rise of the Popular Press.* Syracuse: Syracuse University Press, 1989. 224 pages

Studies James Gordon Bennett's role in developing the mass-circulation metropolitan newspaper. Treats his use of sensationalism and his applying new technology to make the *Herald* one of the most important newspapers of its time.

945. De Vito, Joseph A. "The Author and the Reviewer." *ETC* 46 (Winter 1989): 308–311.

Discusses assumptions that make dealing with reviewers' comments, including teachers' comments, easy and difficult.

946. Duffy, Bernard K., and Mark Royden Winchell. " 'Speak the Speech, I Pray You': The Practice and Perils of Literary and Oratorical Ghostwriting." *SCJ* 55 (Fall 1989): 102–115.

Four ghostwriters discuss ghostwriting books and speeches. Treats the process, relationships, ethics, authenticity, historical data, and career prospects.

947. Ellis, Donald G., and G. Blake Armstrong. "Class, Gender, and Code on Prime-Time Television." *ComQ* 37 (Summer 1989): 157–169.

Research identifies the nature of linguistic codes relating to gender and social class used on prime-time television.

948. Fair, Jo E. "A Meta-Research of Mass Media Effects on Audiences in Developing Countries from 1958 through 1986." *DAI* 49 (April 1989): 2854A.

Surveys more than 200 research articles, papers, chapters, and dissertations.

949. Fisher, John R. "Print Media Coverage of Educational Policy Making." *DAI* 49 (April 1989): 2854A.

Surveys education officials and analyzes newspaper and magazine articles.

950. Gelderman, Carol. "The Lure and the Lore of Trying to Write a Serious Book That Makes a Fortune." *CHE* 35 (12 April 1989): B2.

The author recounts her experiences researching and publishing biographies of Henry Ford and Mary McCarthy.

951. Gibson, Walker. "A Note on Willie Horton." *QRD* 15 (April 1989): 1.

Identifies four separate voices—quadruplespeak—in the Willie Horton commercial that Bush campaigners ran against Dukakis.

952. Graffy, Julian, and Geoffrey A. Hosking, eds. *Culture and Media in the USSR Today.* New York: St. Martin's Press, 1989. 208 pages

Seven essays describe and analyze the effect in all areas of the arts and media of new intellectual and institutional upheavals introduced by *glasnost.*

953. Haines, Duane E., and Charles W. Mitchell. "Strengthening Textbook Proposals." *AM* 64 (September 1989): 516–517.

Provides practical advice on preparing and submitting textbook proposals.

954. Haynes, W. Lance. "Shifting Media, Shifting Paradigms, and the Growing Utility of Narrative as Metaphor." *ComS* 40 (Summer 1989): 109–126.

Reviews the influence of writing-based cognition on rhetorical practice and theory in media. An increase in competing media requires reexamining the utility of current rhetorical theories.

955. "It All Depends on Who's Running." *QRD* 15 (April 1989): 1–2.

Quotes without comment a media critic's contradictory statements about the press's responsibility for reporting on the private lives of political candidates. Reprinted from *Extra!* (September–October 1988).

956. Mbaatyo, Akpe A. "The New Telecommunications Technology and the Human Factor: The Impact of Video Conferencing on Perceived Group Cohesiveness." *DAI* 49 (April 1989): 2862A.

Applies the Integrated Cohesiveness Measure to five organizations that engage in teleconferencing.

957. McCleary, Bill. "So You're Thinking of Writing a Textbook." *CompC* 2 (November 1989): 6–7, 12.

Describes how to get a publisher, write the book, and edit the manuscript. Includes information on noncommercial publishing.

958. Murphy, Keith B. "A Rhetorical and Cultural Analysis of the Protest Rock Movement, 1964–1971." *DAI* 49 (April 1989): 2862A.

Applies Foucault's "epistemological rupture" and Marxist analysis to media coverage of rock music.

959. Parsons, Paul. *Getting Published: The Acquisitions Process at University Presses.* Knoxville: The University of Tennessee Press, 1989. 243 pages

Explains the practices and philosophies controlling the selection of manuscripts by university presses.

960. Pickering, Miles. "So You're Thinking of Publishing a Lab Manual." *JCST* 18 (February 1989): 223–224.

Offers practical advice for manual publication as an antidote to "pen lust."

961. "Project Censored." *QRD* 15 (July 1989): 11–12.

Reports on the top 10 stories selected by Project Censored, stories that the national news media ignored but should not have.

962. Roffey-Mitchell, Napier James. "Towards a Semiotic Rhetoric: The Communication of Visual Analogs of the Figure of Speech in Magazine and Television Advertisements." *DAI* 50 (October 1989): 829A.

Uses Dondis's elements of the visual and Burke's theory to develop a "detailed visual taxonomy of the figures."

963. Schroeder, Eric James. "Interview with Michael Herr: We've All Been There." *WE* 1 (Fall 1989): 39–54.

Herr discusses the writing of *Dispatches* and its connection to new journalism.

964. Shanken Skwersky, Serena. "The Dialogical Imaginings of Adolescent and Youth: Discourses on Gender, Language, and Power in Student Literary Magazines from 1900 to 1929." *DAI* 50 (July 1989): 276A.

Examines the images and discourses of gender and power in student-authored stories and compares them to adult literary constructions.

965. Sides, Margaret N. "Harry Golden's Rhetoric: The Persona, the Message, the Audience." *DAI* 49 (February 1989): 2222A.

Examines Golden's rhetorical emphasis on audience by focusing on proofs of *ethos, logos,* and *pathos* in his civil rights speeches, correspondence, and essays.

966. Simons, Herbert W., Don J. Stewart, and David Harvey. "Effects of Network Treatments of Perceptions of a Political Campaign Film: Can Rhetorical Criticism Make a Difference?" *ComQ* 37 (Summer 1989): 184–198.

Assesses the uses and limitations of rhetorical criticism in the television coverage of political campaigns.

967. Streitmatten, Rodger Allan. "Front Page from the White House: A Quantitative Study of Personal News Coverage from Teddy Roosevelt to Ronald Reagan." *DAI* 49 (June 1989): 3852A.

Shows that, contrary to the general impression, early twentieth-century presidents received more personal news coverage than did recent presidents.

968. Turner, Judith Axler. "With the Aid of Computers, New Publishing Ventures Allow Professors to Create Customized Textbooks." *CHE* 36 (15 November 1989): A19, A25.

Textbooks can now be generated quickly from the professor's notes and from the publisher's database of articles and book chapters.

969. Weber, Robert L. "Wanted: An Author-Publisher Fair Practice Code." *JCST* 18 (February 1989): 220–222.

Relates anecdotes about the unfair treatment of authors. Suggests nine steps for authors seeking publication.

970. Winterowd, W. Ross. "Composition Textbooks: Publisher-Author Relationships." *CCC* 40 (May 1989): 139–151.

Discusses legalities in publishing composition textbooks.

See also 17, 205, 208, 355, 1146, 1158, 1609, 1616

2.12 PHILOSOPHY

971. Alcoff, Linda S. "New Versions of the Coherence Theory: Gadamer, Davidson, Foucault, and Putnam." *DAI* 49 (February 1989): 2249A.

Examines four contemporary accounts of knowledge and epistemology.

972. Barwise, Jon. *The Situation in Logic*. Chicago: University of Chicago Press, 1989. 200 pages

Treats the relations among logic, situation theory, and situation semantics.

973. Cranmer, Robin. "Fundamental Aspects of Wittgenstein's Later Conception of Language." *DAI* 49 (February 1989): 2198A.

Examines and evaluates four basic language concepts found in Wittgenstein's works.

974. Cudd, Ann Elizabeth. "Common Knowledge and the Theory of Interaction." *DAI* 50 (September 1989): 701A.

Uses game theory to analyze and evaluate common knowledge.

975. Dasenbrock, Reed Way. *Redrawing the Lines: Analytic Philosophy, Deconstruction, and Literary Theory*. Minneapolis: University of Minnesota Press, 1989. 300 pages

Ten essays chart the debate between Anglo-American analytic and Continental philosophers.

976. Dubsky, Richard. "A Comparison of Heidegger and Wittgenstein's Departure from Traditional Formulations of World, Language, and Truth." *DAI* 49 (May 1989): 3384A.

Deals with rhetoric in terms of applied language. Both writers inspected ordinary behavior closely before concluding that language is not a picture of facts.

977. Eiland, Howard. "The Pedagogy of Shadow: Heidegger and Plato." *Boundary* 16 (Winter-Spring 1989): 13–39.

Discusses Plato's *Republic,* the cave, the metaphor of kingship, the perception of experience, the discovery of reality, and the idea of mind as linguistic grammar.

978. Horne, Janet. "Rhetoric after Rorty." *WJSC* 53 (Summer 1989): 247–259.

Outlines the general features of Rorty's postfoundational philosophy, citing some consequences for rhetoric of his pragmatist position.

979. Hughes, John. "Philosophy and Style: Wittgenstein and Russell." *P&L* 13 (October 1989): 332–339.

Explores connections between the language philosophers use in writing and their philosophical styles. Contrasts Russell's subjection of the reader with Wittgenstein's respect for the reader.

980. Kingsley, Patricia Eiline. "The Dialectics of Decision Making: Rules, Acts, and Propositions in Practical Logic." *DAI* 49 (February 1989): 2021A.

Constructs an epistemological paradigm for dialectics, practical logic, and modern semiotics that is compared with fourth-generation computer language.

981. Krajewski, Bruce J. "Traveling with Hermes: Hermeneutics and Rhetoric." *DAI* 49 (February 1989): 2205A.

A series of essays that examine the nexus between rhetoric and hermeneutics as discussed by Gadamer.

982. Lofgren, Christine Ruth Plapp. "A Deductive Reasoning Task: Performance, Including Logical Anomalies." *DAI* 50 (July 1989): 363B.

Suggests a new paradigm for studying deductive reasoning and problem solving. Formalizes a hypothesis elimination scheme representing internal task states and an information processing model.

983. McGowan, Thomas G. "The Sociological Significance of Gadamer's Hermeneutics." *DAI* 50 (September 1989): 806A.

Analyzes Gadamer's work on interpretation, examining applications to many fields.

984. Newstead, Stephen E. "Interpretational Errors in Syllogistic Reasoning." *JML* 28 (February 1989): 78–91.

> Researchers concluded that most syllogistic reasoning errors were caused by misinterpreting premises.

985. Novitz, David. "Art, Narrative, and Human Nature." *P&L* 13 (April 1989): 57–74.

> Explores connections between narrative and imaging, shows how a self-image and life story emerge from picturing, and concludes that literary arts are fundamentally connected to visual arts.

986. Sebberson, David. "Investigations for a Critical Theory of Rhetoric: Issues in Practical Reasoning and Rhetorical Proof." *DAI* 49 (March 1989): 2637A.

> Challenges Hobbes's and Habermas's critiques of practical reasoning. Argues that rhetorical proofs are legitimate means of argument with theoretical and philosophical underpinnings.

987. Silverberg, Arnold Steven. "Anti-Realism in Semantics and Logic." *DAI* 50 (July 1989): 166A.

> Studies Dummett's notion that our epistemological limitations impose constraints on theories of meaning, thereby undermining the semantic justification of classical logic.

988. Stewart, Robert Scott. "The Epistemological Function of Platonic Myth." *P&R* 22 (1989): 259–280.

> Defines Platonic myth, arguing that only through myth could Plato write of that about which he was most serious. Explores myth within an epistemic hierarchy.

989. Willett, Cynthia J. "Tropes of Orientation: Between Dialectic and Deconstruction." *DAI* 49 (March 1989): 2689A.

> Locates a post-Hegelian response to the question of orientation by isolating nondialectical tropes in Hegel and finding those same orienting tropes in Derrida.

See also 47, 48, 80, 83, 113, 125, 131, 132, 134, 152, 161, 163, 175, 177, 203, 213, 216, 253, 266, 270, 280, 287, 288, 763

2.13   SCIENCE AND MEDICINE

990. Ali, Mohammed Z. "The Translation of English Scientific Texts into Habasa Malaysia: A Study in Contrastive Textualization." *DAI* 49 (February 1989): 2195A.

> Compares the translation equivalencies of rhetorical functions and techniques in scientific discourse to determine differences in textualization across two languages.

991. Almeida, Lucia Q. "Clinical Interpretation and the Reframing of Experience: Evidence from Therapeutic Discourse." *DAI* 49 (February 1989): 2196A.

> Uses frame analysis of videotaped psychotherapy interviews to isolate and analyze interpretive structures. Finds frequent violation of Grice's quantity maxims.

992. Anderson, Charles M. *Richard Selzer and the Rhetoric of Surgery*. Carbondale, Ill.: Southern Illinois University Press, 1989. 160 pages

> Examines Selzer's writing, particularly "Jonah and the Whale" and *Mortal Lessons,* to determine why a surgeon would write. Focuses on the context from which Selzer writes and his concepts of language.

993. Ashmore, Malcolm. *The Reflexive Thesis: Wrighting Sociology of Scientific Knowledge*. Chicago: University of Chicago Press, 1989. 318 pages

> Discusses the problem of reflexivity in the sociology of scientific knowledge, focusing on the play between thesis-as-argument and thesis-as-an-occasioned-academic-product. Uses case studies to deconstruct

deconstruction in the sociology of scientific knowledge.

994. Campbell, John Angus. "The Invisible Rhetorician: Charles Darwin's 'Third Party' Strategy." *Rhetorica* 7 (Winter 1989): 55–85.

By examining letters, argues that Darwin indirectly engineered the public defense of *The Origin*. He evolved from a scientist to a rhetorician torn by ethical tension.

995. Ceccio, Joseph F. "The Organizational Language of AIDS: A Case Analysis." *BABC* 52 (March 1989): 17–23.

Analyzes organizational communications about a hospital employee who had contracted AIDS.

996. Comprone, Joseph J. "Narrative Topic and the Contemporary Science Essay: A Lesson from Loren Eiseley's Notebooks." *JAC* 9 (1989): 112–123.

The "science essay" practiced by Eiseley and others presents scientific insights for lay readers by using narrative not as mode but as topic.

997. Crismore, Avon, and Rodney Farnsworth. "Mr. Darwin and His Readers: Exploring Interpersonal Metadiscourse as a Dimension of *Ethos*." *RR* 8 (Fall 1989): 91–112.

Analyzes how interpersonal language establishes Darwin as the "cautious, tentative scientist."

998. Fraser, David W., and Leah J. Smith. "Unmet Needs and Unused Skills: Physicians' Reflections on Their Liberal Arts Education." *AM* 64 (September 1989): 532–537.

Physicians surveyed wished they had taken more liberal arts courses and had developed better critical and communicative skills while in college.

999. Friedman, Miriam, M. Prywes, and J. Benbassat. "Variability in Doctors' Problem-Solving as Measured by Open-Ended Written Patient Simulations." *MEd* 23 (May 1989): 270–275.

Experts' written answers to medical problems varied widely because their interpretations differed. Discusses the legal and pedagogical ramifications of such variation.

1000. Griffith, Belver C. "Understanding Science: Studies of Communication and Information." *ComR* 16 (October 1989): 600–614.

Examines communication's role in the social and cognitive processes of science.

1001. Gross, Alan G. "Discourse on Method: The Rhetorical Analysis of Scientific Texts." *Pre/Text* 9 (Fall-Winter 1988): 169–185.

Proposes a classically based rhetoric of science, emphasizing the centrality of persuasion in its texts.

1002. Hallberg, Lillian Mae. "Rhetorical Dimensions of Institutional Language: A Case Study of Women Alcoholics." *DAI* 50 (October 1989): 1113A.

Examines the language of alcoholism in organizations like Alcoholics Anonymous.

1003. Haynes, R. Brian, Michael Ramsden, K. Ann McKibbon, Cynthia J. Walker, and Nancy C. Ryan. "A Review of Medical Information and Medical Informatics." *AM* 64 (April 1989): 207–212.

Describes those aspects of informatics most helpful to students and academics faced with collecting and interpreting a variety of data.

1004. Hunter, Kathryn Montgomery. "Making a Case." *L&M* 7 (1988): 66–79.

Examines tradition and innovation in the rhetoric of medical case histories as a genre.

1005. Jackson, Robert Neil. "Coping with the Reality of AIDS: A Rhetorical Analysis of Kokomo, Indiana's Response to the Ryan White-Western Schools Corporation Controversy." *DAI* 49 (June 1989): 3550A.

Uses fantasy theme analysis and focus group interviewing techniques to analyze five groups' differing reactions to the controversy.

1006. Kaufmann, James Michael. "The Rhetoric of Medical Writing: Case Studies of Physicians Writing for Journal Publication." *DAI* 50 (August 1989): 427A.

Investigates how physicians who write for publication conceive of the rhetorical situation as well as how they see themselves, their audience, and their subject matter.

1007. Lightman, Alan P. "Magic on the Mind: Physicists' Use of Metaphor." *ASch* (Winter 1989): 97–101.

Explores metaphors in modern science, using Newton, Bohr, and others to discuss the reasons for metaphors' being essential to science and scientific writing.

1008. Masys, Daniel R. "Medical Informatics: Glimpses of the Promised Land." *AM* 64 (January 1989): 13–14.

Outlines the four basic fields of informatics and defines this new field.

1009. Mosley, Philip. "The Healthy Text." *L&M* 6 (1987): 35–42.

Uses Foucault, Laing, Sontag, and Lacan to delineate language appropriate to the healthy text.

1010. Neal, Mary Kathryn. "Balancing Passion and Reason: A Symbolic Analysis of the Communications Strategies of the Physicians' Movement against Nuclear Weapons." *DAI* 49 (March 1989): 2708A.

Uses rhetorical theory as well as medical and social anthropology to show how the Physicians' Movement against Nuclear Weapons mobilized "the technical reason and human passion of medicine."

1011. O'Reilly, Edmund Bernard. "Toward Rhetorical Immunity: Narratives of Alcoholism and Recovery." *DAI* 49 (March 1989): 2771A.

Examines narratives and interviews of Alcoholics Anonymous members to clarify

the ways in which rhetorical and behavioral modalities are interlaced.

1012. Percy, Walker. "Walker Percy, a Physician Turned Novelist, Chastises the Scientists for Failing to Explicate the Human Mind." *CHE* 35 (10 May 1989): A5, A7.

Novelist Percy argues that, although skillful at studying body parts, the sciences fail at explicating the humanness of human beings.

1013. Pettinari, Catherine Johnson. *Task, Talk, and Text in the Operating Room: A Study in Medical Discourse*. Advances in Discourse Processes, vol. 33. Norwood, N.J.: Ablex, 1988. 192 pages

Examines the roles of surgical residents in producing operative reports, the relationship between operations and reports, the text's internal structure, and changes in reporting styles over time.

1014. Prelli, Lawrence J. *A Rhetoric of Science: Inventing Scientific Discourse*. Studies in Rhetoric/Communication. Columbia, S.C.: University of South Carolina Press, 1989. 325 pages

Addresses the process by which scientific claims are legitimated. Moves beyond the general idea that science has rhetorical dimensions to outline in detail an informal rhetorical logic that constrains scientific discourse.

1015. Psaty, Bruce M. "Literature and Medicine as a Critical Discourse." *L&M* 6 (1987): 13–14.

Uses the dichotomy between subject and object as a vehicle to argue for a dialogue-based rhetoric of scientific exposition.

1016. Reynolds, John Frederick, and David Mair. "Patient Records in the Mental Health Disciplines." *JTWC* 19 (1989): 245–254.

Describes the types of "reports regularly written in mental hospitals and community mental centers." Studies the major rhetorical problems associated with these types of reports.

1017. Segal, Judith Zelda. "Reading Medical Prose as Rhetoric: A Study in the Rhetoric of Science." *DAI* 49 (June 1989): 3551A.

Examines the rhetoric of science, or the persuasive means of scientific communication, in 35 medical articles. Holds that medical journals should be read critically, as rhetoric.

1018. Sturgell, Charles Wesley. "Evolution of the Concept of an Antarctic Region Based on Narrative and Cartographic Documents from 1772 to 1872." *DAI* 50 (July 1989): 228A.

An account of the evolution of the concept of the Antarctic as a geographic region.

1019. Yanoff, Karin L. "The Rhetoric of Medical Discourse: An Analysis of Major Genres." *DAI* 49 (April 1989): 3011A.

Describes the rhetorical features of six major genres of medical discourse.

1020. Zappen, James P. "Francis Bacon and the Historiography of Scientific Rhetoric." *RR* 8 (Fall 1989): 74–88.

Reviews twentieth-century interpretations of Bacon's science and rhetoric. Claims that each reflects a different ideology and view of what science is and ought to be.

See also 144, 145, 151, 160, 207, 208, 225, 277, 293, 319, 342, 513, 683, 753, 906, 1562

2.14   CROSS-DISCIPLINARY STUDIES

1021. Burke, Carol. "Vision Narratives of Women in Prison: A Study in Women's Folklore." *DAI* 49 (January 1989): 1994A.

Examines the place of narratives of visions and dreams in the community of a women's prison.

1022. Doyle, Mary Agnes. "Games of Lamentation: The Irish Wake Performance Tradition." *DAI* 49 (February 1989): 2346A.

Reevaluates the performance tradition of the games of lamentation in Ireland after 1,500 years of ecclesiastical censorship.

1023. Kirshenblatt-Gimblett, Barbara. "Authoring Lives." *JFR* 26 (May–August 1989): 123–149.

Analyzes various approaches to self-authoring life histories: literary, ethnographic, folkloristic, and rhetorical.

1024. Lim, Tae-Seop. "A New Model of Politeness in Discourse." *DAI* 49 (April 1989): 2862A.

Analyzes Brown and Levinson's model to explore its effectiveness in observing politeness in face-threatening situations.

1025. Ngole, Jean-Pierre. "Bargaining Strategies as Performance: An Ethnographic and Sociolinguistic Study of Women Fishsellers in Congo." *DAI* 50 (October 1989): 1048A.

Examines salient folkloric, linguistic, and literary features embedded in the bargaining performance of women fishsellers in the People's Republic of Congo.

1026. Reichwein, Jeffrey Charles. "Native American Response to Euro-American Contact in the Columbia Plateau of Northwestern North America, 1840 to 1914: An Anthropological Interpretation Based on Written and Pictorial Ethnohistorical Data." *DAI* 50 (August 1989): 473A.

An anthropological interpretation of events associated with the contact between Euro-American and Native American groups in the Columbia Plateau from 1840 to 1914.

1027. Smith, Paul. "Variations in the Manner of Adoption of Cultural Traditions: A Conceptual Framework and Application." *DAI* 50 (September 1989): 768A.

Identifies the factors affecting the adoption, nonadoption, and manner of adoption of cultural traditions.

See also 66, 138

2.15   OTHER

1028. Allen, Laura Warantz. "The Art of Persuasion: Narrative Structure, Imagery, and Meaning in the 'Saigyo Monogatari Emaki.' " *DAI* 50 (October 1989): 814A.

Uses rhetorical concepts such as persuasion, narrative structure, and meaning to analyze the work of twelfth-century scroll artist Saigyo.

1029. Baxter, Paola Tinagli. "Vasari's 'Ragionamenti': The Text as a Key to the Decorations of Palazzo Vecchio." *DAI* 49 (April 1989): 2846A.

Argues that Vasari's "Ragionamenti" should be viewed in light of sixteenth-century Italian politics. Supports the view that meaning is best found hidden within another contextual image.

1030. Cheney, Lynne V. "Current Fashions in Scholarship Diminish the Value of the Humanities." *CHE* 35 (8 February 1989): A40.

The NEH chair identifies some strengths of humanistic studies.

1031. Etzel, Crystal Lorinda. "The Evolution of Rhetorical Strategies: A Critical Essay on Contemporary Christian Music." *DAI* 50 (August 1989): 301A.

Uses five rhetorical strategies—relationship, antithetical construction, redundancy, metaphor, and image—to analyze changes in the music of 10 writers during the past 20 years.

1032. Haddad, Ziyad Salem. "The Jordanian Contemporary Art Criticism: A Methodological Analysis of Critical Practices." *DAI* 49 (February 1989): 2002A.

Critically assesses the writings of contemporary Jordanian art critics. Introduces a metacritical methodology for scrutinizing art criticism.

1033. Kalisperis, Loukas Nickolas. "A Conceptual Framework for Computing in Architectural Design." *DAI* 50 (August 1989): 277A.

Emerging social problem-solving paradigms seek to construct a cognitive psychology of problem solving and have a direct reference to architectural design.

1034. Kauffman, Kathy Coventon. "The Belief System of the Avant-Garde." *DAI* 50 (November 1989): 1119A.

Argues that avant-garde art is controlled by a definite belief system with roots in Western society, which makes apparently unstructured art highly structured.

1035. Parker, Rodney Douglas. "Rhetoric as a Conceptual Framework for Architectural Design and Criticism." *DAI* 49 (January 1989): 1602A.

Rhetoric adds coherence and clarity to architectural theory by providing constructs for analyzing clientele-audience relationships as well as a frame of reference for assimilating other disciplines.

1036. Perkins, Janet Blair. "Images of Movement and Dance in Ancient Greek Art: A Qualitative Approach." *DAI* 49 (June 1989): 3535A.

Discusses attempts to capture in language the visual images created by dance. Concludes that the works of Plato and Aristotle support a broad definition of dance.

1037. Tamuz, Michal. "Monitoring Dangers in the Air: Studies in Ambiguity and Information." *DAI* 49 (June 1989): 3876A.

Examines the ways in which organizations gather and record information, under differing conditions of ambiguity, about near accidents in the air.

1038. Trimbur, John. "Censorship and Self-Policing in the Art World." *QRD* 16 (October 1989): 9–10.

> Uses the controversy over the Mapplethorpe exhibit to argue that censorship was not imposed on the art world but was enacted from within.

1039. Wallace, W. A. "The Influence of Design Team Communication Content upon the Architectural Decision-Making Process in the Pre-Contract Design Stages." *DAI* 50 (July 1989): 2A.

> Considers patterns of communication in the decision-making process of design team architects, showing that interaction in pre-contract stages affects the entire design process.

1040. Willumson, Glenn Gardner. "W. Eugene Smith: A Critical Analysis of Four Photographic Essays." *DAI* 50 (August 1989): 281A.

> Using Smith's work, this study demonstrates the variability of interpretation possible with sequenced photographs.

3
Teacher Education, Administration, and Social Roles

3.1   TEACHER EDUCATION

1041. Allen, R. R., and Theodore Rueter. *Teaching Assistant Strategies: An Introduction to College Teaching.* Dubuque, Iowa: Kendall/Hunt, 1989. 160 pages

A guide to college teaching for graduate students holding teaching assistantships. Discusses teaching styles, instructional planning, effective lectures and class presentations, assessing students' progress, and the instructor's relationship to students, course directors, and support staff.

1042. Amore, Adelaide P. "How Faculty Learn to Become Better Coaches of Writing and Thinking: A Case Study of Workshops in Writing across the Disciplines at Smith College, Northhampton, Massachusetts." *DAI* 49 (March 1989): 2549A.

Investigates how four workshops in writing across the disciplines held at Smith College between 1981 and 1987 affected faculty members as writing coaches.

1043. Aschauer, Mary Ann. "Reinforcing Successive Gains: Collaborative Projects for Writing Faculty." *WPA* 12 (Spring 1989): 57–61.

Explores the lack of ongoing collaboration and dialogue among college writing faculty members and offers suggestions for fostering such exchange.

1044. Aschauer, Mary Ann. "Reinforcing Successive Gains: Collaborative Writing Faculty Projects." Paper presented at the CCCC Convention, St. Louis, March 1988. ERIC ED 297 328. 11 pages

Argues that collaborative projects allow writing teachers the opportunity to exchange ideas and to participate in the ongoing concerns of the field.

1045. Batson, Laurie Goodman. "Defining Ourselves as Woman (in the Profession)." *Pre/Text* 9 (Fall-Winter 1988): 207–209.

Explains the difficulty of resisting the process of homogenizing "woman" as composition professionals.

1046. Bishop, Wendy. "A Microethnography with Case Studies of Teacher Development through a Graduate Training Course in Writing." *DAI* 49 (May 1989): 3347A.

Describes the affective, cognitive, and pedagogical changes in teachers introduced to a process-oriented, whole language, writing workshop model.

1047. Bishop, Wendy. "Teachers as Learners: Negotiated Roles in College Writing Teachers' Learning Logs." Paper presented at the CCCC Convention, Seattle, March 1989. ERIC ED 304 690. 22 pages

Reports on a study that analyzed teachers' dialogue learning logs. Discusses the teachers' response patterns.

1048. Bishop, Wendy. "Writing Teacher as Researcher: More Than Jargon." *ArEB* 31 (Winter 1989): 17–19.

Offers procedures for teachers to use in beginning research.

1049. Blake, Veronica M., and Sarah M. Dinham. *Teaching Guidebook: An Introduction to Some Basics*. Bloomington, Ind.: ERIC/RCS, 1988. ERIC ED 301 106. 24 pages

Provides a general guide to help teaching assistants carry out instructional responsibilities.

1050. Bomer, Randy. "Thinking Small to Think Big: The Teachers College Writing Project." *CompC* 2 (December 1989): 4–6.

Strengths of the program are mentor relationships between staff members and teachers and the transformation of classrooms into writing studios.

1051. Booth, Wayne C. *The Vocation of a Teacher: Rhetorical Occasions, 1967–1988*. Chicago: University of Chicago Press, 1988. 354 pages

A collection of articles, speeches, and journal entries that celebrates teaching as a vocation, argues for rhetoric as the center of a liberal education, and exposes the political and economic scandals that frustrate dedicated educators.

1052. Burrows, Thais J. "Teachers' Perceptions of Their Motivation While Writing: A Phenomenological Study." *DAI* 49 (February 1989): 2180A.

Views the teaching of writing from the perspective of learning theory, especially in relation to the training of teachers, their composing processes, and their motivations for writing.

1053. Byrd, Patricia, Janet C. Constantinides, and Martha C. Pennington. *The Foreign Teaching Assistant's Manual*. New York: Collier Macmillan, 1989. 195 pages

A guide to help foreign teaching assistants conduct classes and interact effectively with American students. Five sections treat the purposes of American education, planning classes and assignments, improving pronunciation and listening skills, managing classroom communication, and observing how American students and teachers interact.

1054. Cazden, Courtney, Judy Diamondstone, and Paul Naso. "Teachers and Researchers: Roles and Relationships." *CSWQ* 11 (Fall 1989): 1–3, 25–27.

Examines four edited volumes of teacher research, discussing their two purposes, to solve problems or test new ideas and to describe learners or classroom events.

1055. Crowley, Sharon. "Three Heroines: An Oral History." *Pre/Text* 9 (Fall-Winter 1988): 202–206.

Describes the professional career paths of Lynn Bloom, Maxine Hairston, and Winifred Horner.

1056. Daiker, Donald A., and Max Morenberg, eds. *The Writing Teacher as Researcher: Essays in the Theory and Practice of Class-Based Research*. Portsmouth, N.H.: Boynton/Cook, 1989. 384 pages

Twenty-five essays discuss how the teaching of writing improves when the teacher becomes engaged in studies of actual classroom practices.

1057. Dunstan, Angus, Judy Kirscht, John Reiff, Majorie Roemer, and Nick Tingle. "Working in the Classroom: Teachers Talk about What They Do." *EEd* 24 (February 1989): 39–52.

Five, nontenure track, English faculty members report on a collaborative project in which they watched each other teach, hoping to answer the questions, "What is composition and how is it taught?"

1058. Faille, Rachida Carolyn. "Interactive Research and Development on Teaching: A Collaborative Model for Teachers of Students from Diverse Cultures." *DAI* 50 (July 1989): 63A.

Urges the development of sensitivity to and instructional strategies for multicultural classroom settings.

1059. Fishman, Andrea R., and Elizabeth J. Raver. "Maybe I'm Just Not Teacher Material: Dialogue Journals in the Student Teaching Experience." *EEd* 21 (May 1989): 92–109.

Dialogue journals helped a student teacher and cooperating teacher to create knowledge, assisting them to become more effective professionals.

1060. Franke, Johannah S. "Coaching, Dancing, and Writing: Parallel Skills." *TETYC* 16 (December 1989): 274–279.

Two physical education instructors, training to teach composition by taking an English 102 course, discover similarities between training athletes and writers.

1061. Fulwiler, Toby. "Writing Workshops and the Mechanics of Change." *WPA* 12 (Spring 1989): 7–20.

Gives detailed lists of materials and procedures for conducting writing workshops that train teachers to provide student-centered writing instruction.

1062. Hales, John. "Learning to Teach in the Ivory Tower." *CalE* 25 (January–February 1989): 16–17, 29.

College teaching helps prepare apprentice teachers to teach in secondary schools.

1063. Harrington, David V. "Sustaining an English Faculty Seminar." *BADE* 94 (Winter 1989): 45–48.

Describes the scheduling, benefits, range of presentations, and problems involved in sustaining a weekly faculty seminar that has run for 25 years.

1064. Harrington, Dick. "Writing about General Apache." *TETYC* 16 (October 1989): 190–192.

A Vietnam veteran gives his teacher material for the teacher's own poem.

1065. Herbst, Jurgen. *And Sadly Teach: Teacher Education and Professionalization in American Culture*. Madison: University of Wisconsin Press, 1989. 231 pages

Argues that the refusal to educate and value public school teachers as professionals and to grant them the independence of professional status in their classrooms is the chief and most persistent cause underlying the recurrent complaints about American public education.

1066. Herndon, Kathleen M. "The Generating of Writing Assignments and Planning of Writing Instruction by Secondary English Teachers." *DAI* 49 (February 1989): 2133A.

Examines the preparation practices of teachers and proposes a model for writing instruction.

1067. Hughes, Bradley T. "Balancing Enthusiasm with Skepticism: Training Writing Teachers in Computer-Aided Instruction." *CC* 7 (November 1989): 65–78.

Sets out principles to follow in training teachers to use computers in writing instruction, describes various categories of software, and explains how to choose among them.

1068. Hussein, Yehia Ismail. "The Relationship between Attitudes of English Teachers in Egypt toward Methods of Teaching English

and Selected Demographic Characteristics."
DAI 50 (November 1989): 1199A.

Studies the relationship between teachers' attitudes toward three methods of teaching English and selected demographic characteristics.

1069. Infantino, Bob. "The CTC Raises the Hoop." *CalE* 25 (May–June 1989): 26–27.

Argues that new standards issued by the [California] Commission for Teacher Credentialing are too stringent.

1070. Infantino, Bob. "What Do Teachers Know about Teaching?" *CalE* 25 (March–April 1989): 22–23.

Argues that teaching candidates should be exposed to issues in testing.

1071. Isensee, Elizabeth, and Roger Johnson, Jr. *Handbook for Writing Coaches*. Hattiesburg, Miss.: University of Southern Mississippi, 1988. ERIC ED 304 693. 14 pages

Answers 26 questions about writing coaches' duties, qualifications, and other aspects of their work.

1072. Kelsay, Karla L. "The Process of Reflection in Teaching as Utilized by Enablers: A Micro-Ethnographic Study of Teachers of the Gifted." *DAI* 49 (April 1989): 2913A.

Studies three teachers and focuses on teaching as "thinking about teaching and thinking while teaching."

1073. Lape, Sue V. "Janice Gohm Webster on Inexperienced TAs [response to Webster, *BADE* 92 (Spring 1989)]." *BADE* 94 (Winter 1989): 59.

Faults Webster for suggesting that tenured faculty members should teach freshman composition. Describes a program at Ohio State University that prepares teaching assistants.

1074. Lytle, Susan, and Marilyn Cochran-Smith. "Teacher Research: Toward Clarifying the Concept." *CSWQ* 11 (April 1989): 1–3, 22–27.

Reviews the literature on teacher research, giving examples of systematic inquiry and suggestions for approaches.

1075. Moss, Barbara Gae. "Teacher Change as Experienced through the Implementation of a Process Writing Approach." *DAI* 50 (December 1989): 1546A.

Studies the attitude changes of four elementary school teachers introduced to the process writing approach and institutional impediments to its implementation.

1076. Nakadate, Neil. "Discourse Communities, Rites of Passage, and the Teaching of English: South Africa and the U.S." Paper presented at the CCCC Convention, St. Louis, March 1988. ERIC ED 303 800. 13 pages

Describes two teaching experiences, conducting a developmental writing course for American minority students and leading a seminar on American literature for ESL teachers at black schools in South Africa.

1077. Nyquist, Jody D., Robert D. Abbott, and Donald H. Wulff, eds. *Teaching Assistant Training in the 1990s*. New Directions for Teaching and Learning, no. 39. San Francisco: Jossey-Bass, 1989. 137 pages

A guide to implementing effective training programs for teaching assistants. Presents successful models and techniques for helping teaching assistants improve their teaching.

1078. Policastro, Margaret. *A Training Manual for Adult Reading and Writing Tutors*. Chicago: Roosevelt University College of Education, 1989. ERIC ED 301 850. 67 pages

Provides a training manual for tutors. A self-paced, workbook format includes 12 exercises.

1079. Pytlik, Betty P. "Teaching Teachers of Writing: Workshops on Writing as a Collaborative Process." *CollT* 37 (Winter 1989): 12–14.

Reports on successful activities to introduce workshop participants to the process approach, including collaborative learning and peer-response groups.

1080. Rosenthal, Anne. "Knowing the Ropes: Women Professing." *Pre/Text* 9 (Fall-Winter 1988): 214–217.

Argues that women should shift from "strategic" to "tactical" modes, resisting modes as feminist scholars.

1081. Save, Edward L. "The Behaviors and Attitudes of Teachers of Academic Subjects at Dunwood High School towards the Teaching of Composition." *DAI* 49 (April 1989): 2918A.

Surveys teachers and students and finds the students seeing "extremely low use" of writing tasks and the teachers seeing "low use."

1082. Selfe, Cynthia L., Dawn Rodrigues, and William R. Oates, eds. *Computers in English and the Language Arts: The Challenge of Teacher Education.* Urbana, Ill.: NCTE, 1989. 299 pages

Prints 21 essays that discuss preparing English teachers to use computers effectively in the classroom. The first section describes 12 teacher preparation and in-service programs. The second section attempts to define components of model teacher education programs.

1083. Shapiro, Nancy Larson, and Ron Padget, eds. *The Point: Where Teaching and Writing Intersect.* Teachers and Writers Think/Ink Books. New York: Teachers and Writers Collaborative, 1983. ERIC ED 304 699. 149 pages

A collection of 25 poems, short fiction, and essays on teaching writing.

1084. Smith, Eugene, and Marilyn Smith. "A Graduate Internship in Teaching." *TETYC* 16 (October 1989): 197–200.

Describes a model program in which graduate students are paired with community college mentors.

1085. Smith, Philip E. "A Pedagogy of Critical and Cultural Empowerment: What We Talk about in Graduate Teaching Seminars." Paper presented at the CCCC Convention, Seattle, March 1989. ERIC ED 307 617. 11 pages

Describes a program at the University of Pittsburgh in which graduate teaching assistants and fellows discuss issues related to their teaching, writing, and research projects.

1086. Storms, Barbara Ann. "Teacher Training in Writing Instruction and Its Relationship to Student Achievement, Instructional Practices, and Teacher Attitudes." *DAI* 49 (April 1989): 2888A.

Finds that the mean scores of students' writing assessments increased as the teacher's level of training increased.

1087. Storms, C. Gilbert. "Preparing Business and Technical Writing Teachers: An Extended Program." *JBTC* 3 (September 1989): 53–63.

Describes a three-semester training program for graduate assistants that blends seminars with apprentice, guided, and independent teaching.

1088. Webster, Janice Gohm. "Composition Teachers: No Experience Necessary?" *BADE* 92 (Spring 1989): 41–42.

Argues against using new graduate students to teach composition. Advocates as a prerequisite a course in teaching composition and urges assigning tenured faculty to composition classes.

1089. Williams, James D. *Preparing to Teach Writing.* Belmont, Calif.: Wadsworth, 1989. 350 pages

Examines the implications of major research studies and theories for teaching writing. Findings from a variety of studies suggest methods for and examples of classroom practices.

1090. Wilson, David Edward. "Teacher Change and the Iowa Writing Project." *DAI* 50 (October 1989): 926A.

Finds that the program influenced teachers' beliefs and practices but that the context of schooling impeded incorporating new techniques.

See also 923, 930, 1105, 1116, 1151, 1630

3.2 ADMINISTRATION

1091. Benjet, Rosalind G., and Margaret Loweth. "A Perspective on the Academic Underclass, the Part-Timers." *TETYC* 16 (February 1989): 40–42.

Discusses unions for part-time faculty members.

1092. Bennett, James Louis. "The Effects of Instructional Methodology and Student Achievement Expectations on Writing Performance in Community College Composition Classes." *DAI* 49 (March 1989): 2512A.

Studies the effect of required writing center assignments on students. Makes future research recommendations for testing writing center assignments.

1093. Braune, Veriena May. "Reactions to Change: The Results of Implementing the Right-to-Read Program in One Rural Texas School." *DAI* 49 (April 1989): 2907A.

Reports on data collected over a 10-year period to study resistance to change.

1094. Campbell, Carolyn. "The Influence of Social Context: An Anthropological Study of Conflict Resolution among Teachers in Two Urban Schools." *DAI* 50 (August 1989): 475A.

A social, anthropological investigation focusing on how the social context can influence the relationship between actors.

1095. Cassebaum, Anne. "A Comment on 'The Wyoming Conference Resolution' [*CE* 49 (March 1987)]." *CE* 51 (October 1989): 636–638.

Urges teachers of English to support one another in bettering conditions for nontenured and part-time instructors.

1096. CCCC Committee on Professional Standards for Quality Education. "CCCC Initiatives on the Wyoming Conference Resolution: A Draft Report." *CCC* 40 (February 1989): 61–63.

Presents a draft "Statement of Principles and Standards for the Postsecondary Teaching of Writing" and discusses ways to support reform in writing instruction.

1097. CCCC Executive Committee. "Statement of Principles and Standards for the Postsecondary Teaching of Writing." *CCC* 40 (October 1989): 329–336.

Presents guidelines developed in response to "the conditions which undermine the quality of postsecondary writing instruction."

1098. Cobb, Loretta. "Addressing Professional Concerns." *WLN* 13 (March 1989): 11–12.

Encourages writing center directors to use Simpson's "Statement of Professional Concerns for Writing Center Directors" (1985) to support their positions in academia.

1099. Ellwein, Leon B., Mohamad Khachab, and Robert H. Waldman. "Assessing Productivity: Evaluating Journal Publication across Academic Departments." *AM* 64 (June 1989): 319–325.

Departmental productivity rankings are little influenced by the number of authors per article but are heavily influenced by the citation rankings of journals.

1100. Holden, Karen C., and W. Lee Hansen, eds. *The End of Mandatory Retirement: Effects on Higher Education.* New Directions for Higher Education, no. 68. San Francisco: Jossey-Bass, 1989. 116 pages

Eight essays use research conclusions to project how eliminating mandatory retirement will affect the average retirement age, the cost of benefits, the tenure system, and job openings for new Ph.D.s.

1101. Hollabaugh, Mark. "Clearing the Fog." *JCST* 18 (March–April 1989): 327–329.

Suggests using the Gunning Fog Index as one factor in textbook selection.

1102. Huber, Bettina J., Denise M. Pinney, David E. Laurence, and Denise Bourassa Knight. "MLA Surveys of Ph.D. Placement: Most Recent Findings and Decade-Long Trends." *BADE* 92 (Spring 1989): 43–50.

Reports on a longitudinal study of Ph.D. placement in English, foreign languages, and linguistics programs.

1103. Inghilleri, Moira. "Learning to Mean as a Symbolic and Social Process: The Story of Two ESL Writers." *DPr* 12 (July–September 1989): 391–411.

The results of conferences about student writing were not completely satisfactory since the aims of students and their tutors sometimes conflicted.

1104. Killingsworth, M. Jimmie, Thomas Langford, and Richard Crider. "Short-Term Faculty Members: A National Dilemma and a Local Solution." *BADE* 94 (Winter 1989): 33–39.

Reviews the literature on the topic, reports on a survey of department chairs, and explains an "idealist" solution adopted by Texas Tech University.

1105. Lucas, Ann F., ed. *The Department Chairperson's Role in Enhancing College Teaching.* New Directions for Teaching and Learning, no. 37. San Francisco: Jossey-Bass, 1989. 113 pages

Discusses how chairpersons can motivate faculty members and create a departmental environment to encourage good teaching.

1106. Malek, James S. "*Caveat Emptor;* or, How Not to Get Hired at DePaul." *BADE* 92 (Spring 1989): 33–36.

Argues that job candidates, Ph.D. institutions, and departments that are hiring have responsibilities, outlining what they are.

1107. McCleary, Bill. "Four C's Issues Final Draft of Standards for Fair Treatment of College Writing Teachers, Conversion of Part-Time and Temporary Jobs to Tenure Track." *CompC* 2 (November 1989): 1–3.

Summarizes the CCCC "Statement of Principles and Practices for the Postsecondary Teaching of Composition."

1108. McCleary, Bill. "MLA's Commission on Writing and Literature Ends Work In a Spirit of Cautious Optimism." *CompC* 2 (September 1989): 1–3.

The Commission's report draws mixed reactions.

1109. McCleary, Bill. " 'Nonregular' Faculty Members and the Wyoming Resolution." *CompC* 2 (May 1989): 7, 10.

Argues that the Wyoming Resolution should be expanded to include full-time, permanent, nonregular faculty.

1110. McLeod, Susan. "Jossey-Bass Publishes Book by Network Members on How to Keep Your Writing across the Curriculum Program Going." *CompC* 2 (May 1989): 8–9.

Describes nine essays in *Strengthening Programs for Writing across the Curriculum.* Includes an annotated bibliography of 20 books and articles.

1111. McLeod, Susan, ed. *Strengthening Programs for Writing across the Curriculum.* New Directions for Teaching and Learning, no. 36. San Francisco: Jossey-Bass, 1989. 138 pages

Includes essays on common problems administrators of writing across the curriculum programs face. Authors are not indexed separately in this volume.

1112. McLeod, Susan, and Kathy Jane Garretson. "The Disabled Student and the Writing Program: A Guide for Administrators." *WPA* 13 (Fall-Winter 1989): 45–52.

Discusses how to accommodate the physically, emotionally, and learning-disabled student in the writing classroom.

1113. Miller, Lewis H. "Bold, Imaginative Steps Are Needed to Link Teaching with Research." *CHE* 36 (13 September 1989): A52.

Changes in reward systems must first occur before faculty members can link research and teaching.

1114. Monaghan, Peter. "Feeling They Are Exploited, Writing Instructors Seek Better Treatment and Working Conditions." *CHE* 35 (5 April 1989): A13, A15.

Reports on the CCCC's draft of a statement defining how schools should treat their writing instructors, especially those who are untenured.

1115. Olson, Gary A., and Joseph M. Moxley. "Directing Freshman Composition: The Limits of Authority." *CCC* 40 (February 1989): 51–60.

Reports that writing program administrators are viewed by their chairs as exercising relatively little authority. Recommends that their authority be extended.

1116. Puccio, Paul M. "Graduate Instructor Representation in Writing Programs: Building Communities through Peer Support." Paper presented at the CCCC Convention, St. Louis, March 1988. ERIC ED 297 333. 12 pages

Argues that graduate students' involvement in writing program decisions, especially peer visitations and support groups, will strengthen graduate assistant teaching.

1117. Robertson, Linda R. "Alliances between Rhetoric and English: The Politics." *CompC* 2 (May 1989): 5–7.

Rhetoric faculty members should argue that "Freshman English is an intellectually bankrupt course" and design a course of rhetorical studies.

1118. Savage, Mary C. "Writing as a Neighborly Act: An Antidote for Academentia." *BADE* 92 (Spring 1989): 13–19.

Identifies the problems of over-specialization or academentia, discusses its effect on the status of writing teachers, and argues that writing teachers become models for countering academentia.

1119. Soven, Margot. "Critical Thinking: The Role of the Writing across the Curriculum Project Administrator." *CompC* 2 (October 1989): 8–9.

Describes how a program director at La-Salle University led the way in integrating critical thinking into the undergraduate curriculum.

1120. "Textbook Authors Association Continues Attack on Sales of Complimentary Copies and Other Unethical, Unprofessional Actions." *CompC* 2 (October 1989): 5.

Reports on the Association's response to unethical textbook adoption practices. Includes a sample resolution for faculty senates.

1121. Timmerman, John H. "Advice to Candidates." *CE* 50 (November 1988): 748–751.

Longs to hear unconventional responses to questions posed in hiring interviews. Offers four kinds of advice for job candidates, urging them to be themselves.

1122. Watkins, Beverly T. "Colleges Urged to Use Full-Time Professors in Writing Programs." *CHE* 36 (4 October 1989): A13, A15.

Colleges should replace part-time English teachers, who often lack facilities and time to be effective, with full-time teachers.

1123. Welp, Mary, Robert F. Sommer, Fred Reynolds, and Grant F. Scott. "Four Comments on 'Advice to Candidates' [*CE* 50 (November 1988)]." *CE* 51 (October 1989): 628–637.

Reacts to Timmerman's impatience with candidates' traditional approaches to teaching and interviewing.

1124. White, Edward M. *Developing Successful College Writing Programs*. Higher Education Series. San Francisco: Jossey-Bass, 1989. 256 pages

A guide to implementing a systematic, centrally coordinated writing program that is integrated into the entire undergraduate curriculum. Ten chapters grouped into three sections examine the current status of writing instruction, provide a basis for designing writing programs, and discuss organizational, staffing, and teacher development strategies.

See also 1198

3.3   SUPPORT SERVICES

1125. Aarons, Victoria, and Willis A. Salomon. "The Writing Center and Writing across the Curriculum: Some Observations on Theory and Practice." *Focuses* 2 (Fall 1989): 91–102.

Recognizes the writing center as being "where the university's methodological and ideological diversity is felt most acutely and most excitingly."

1126. Ballard, Kim, and Rick Anderson. "The *Writing Lab Newsletter:* A History of Collaboration." *CompC* 1 (January 1989): 5, 7–8.

The newsletter "is grounded in the collaborative nature of writing lab tutoring."

1127. Barnes, Linda Laube. "Why Is There a Text in This Class? Classroom Teachers' (Re-) Views of Computer-Assisted Composition Textbooks." *CC* 7 (November 1989): 28–36.

Six teachers agree that no print textbook is particularly useful in computer-assisted composition classrooms. Software and manuals encouraging creativity would be better.

1128. Bartholomae, David. "Freshman English, Composition, and CCCC." *CCC* 40 (February 1989): 38–50.

Reprints the Chair's Address to the 1988 CCCC Annual Convention. Discusses the founding and future of CCCC.

1129. Behm, Richard. "Ethical Issues in Peer Tutoring: A Defense of Collaborative Learning." *WCJ* 10 (Fall Winter 1989): 3–12.

Focuses on the conflict between education defined as certification or as self-discovery. Concludes that collaborative learning is ethical and reflects actual writing situations.

1130. Bell, Jim. "What Are We Talking About?: A Content Analysis of the *Writing Lab Newsletter,* April 1985–October 1988." *WLN* 13 (March 1989): 1–5.

Finds that most articles cover philosophy and practice. Encourages articles based on other modes of inquiry: history, criticism, controlled experimentation, clinical studies, formal models, and ethnography.

1131. Benson, Kirsten. "Who Will Staff the Writing Center?" *WLN* 14 (October 1989): 13–16.

Suggests that writing centers can increase their staffs and services by soliciting funds from departments whose students use the center and by providing noncredit workshops.

1132. Bernhardt, Stephen A. "Designing a Microcomputer Classroom for Teaching Composition." *CC* 7 (November 1989): 93–110.

Explains how to set up a college computer writing lab-classroom. Discusses layout, space, selecting hardware and software, and funding.

1133. Bishop, Wendy. "We're All Basic Writers: Tutors Talking about Writing Apprehension." *WCJ* 9 (Spring-Summer 1989): 31–42.

Apprehensive writers are ineffective tutors. Training helps tutors understand their own apprehension, gives them methods of overcoming it, and increases their effectiveness as writers and tutors.

1134. Bishop, Wendy. "The Writing Center through Writers' Eyes." *WLN* 14 (November 1989): 3–7.

Students' narratives about the writing center reveal their anxieties about criticism, convey their perceptions of tutors, and provide helpful insights into their worlds.

1135. Boswell, Rebecca. "Tutors' Column: Leaders Making Leaders." *WLN* 13 (January 1989): 9–10.

Describes the anguish, fear, and anger student writers initially experience during tutorials, but concludes that the process makes stronger, more assertive writers.

1136. Brockmann, R. John. "A Technical Communication Society Revives in Australia." *TC* 36 (February 1989): 43–46.

Draws parallels and contrasts between technical communication in Australia and in the U.S.

1137. Cake, Leslie J. "EAS: An Electronic Advising System." *CollM* 7 (May 1989): 141–145.

Describes a word-processing system that supplements the university's calendar by searching for the extensive information needed for a faculty-student advising session.

1138. Carino, Peter. "Posing Questions for Collaborative Evaluation of Audiotaped Tutorials." *WLN* 14 (September 1989): 11–13.

Suggests that audiotaping is less threatening and equally informative as videotaping. Includes instructions for implementation and 14 questions for evaluation.

1139. Chapman, David. "Requiem for a Writing Center." *WLN* 14 (December 1989): 7–8.

Presents a fantasy in which a writing center changes its emphasis from helping students discover and generate texts to ensuring that texts are flawlessly correct.

1140. Christenson, Michael D. "Tutors' Column: Pardon My Footprints on Your Brain." *WLN* 14 (December 1989): 9.

Suggests that tutors should be sensitive as they question, lead, and encourage students, for tutors are dealing with people, not just papers.

1141. Cosby, Wayne. "Unexpected Help from a Form." *WLN* 13 (May 1989): 5.

Presents eight guidelines for conducting tutorials.

1142. Cozzens, Christine S. "The Writing Center and the Senior Thesis: A Context for Writing as Teaching." *WLN* 13 (May 1989): 11–14.

Cites the role a tutor plays in assisting a writer to determine, develop, and execute a major writing project. Provides case studies.

1143. DeCiccio, Albert C. "Literacy and Authority as Threats to Peer Tutoring: A Commentary Inspired by the Fifth Annual Conference for Peer Tutors in Writing." *WLN* 13 (June 1989): 11–13.

Argues that peer tutoring increases literacy by empowering students and threatens professional authority by suggesting that alternative answers are possible.

1144. Ede, Lisa. "Writing as a Social Process: A Theoretical Foundation for Writing Centers?" *WCJ* 9 (Spring-Summer 1989): 3–13.

Writing centers are essential to discussions of social constructionism because their collaborative strategies challenge traditional concepts of authorship, one reason why centers are marginalized.

1145. Einerson, Allen. "Writing Center Workshops for High Risk Students." *WLN* 13 (February 1989): 1–5.

Describes writing strategies designed to help students solve math problems, think critically, and write essay examinations.

1146. Enos, Theresa. "Gender and Journals: Conservers or Innovators?" *Pre/Text* 9 (Fall-Winter 1988): 209–214.

Reviews 12 composition journals from 1982 on to ascertain the gender of authors. Finds that male authors continue to dominate scholarly publishing.

1147. Fanning, Patricia J. "Posing Questions: The Student-Centered Tutorial Session." *WLN* 14 (December 1989): 1–2, 11.

Provides questions tutors can use at different stages of writing to ensure a student-produced text.

1148. Farrell, Pamela B., ed. *The High School Writing Center: Establishing and Maintaining One.* Urbana, Ill.: NCTE, 1989. 178 pages

Twenty-two articles offer information on establishing a writing center and monitoring its daily operation.

1149. Fishbain, Janet. "Write with Confidence: A Writing Lab Workshop for Returning Adult Students." *WLN* 13 (May 1989): 1–4, 10.

Describes five, 75-minute sessions that present strategies for meeting various writing tasks and for incorporating students' experiences. Outlines optional sessions on the library and on computers.

1150. Freed, Stacy. "Subjectivity in the Tutorial Session: How Far Can We Go?" *WCJ* 10 (Fall-Winter 1989): 40–43.

Concludes that tutors may interject a differing viewpoint, helping students scrutinize their writing but still maintaining an objective focus on the students' written work.

1151. Gadbow, Kate. "Teachers as Writing Center Tutors: Release from the Red Pen." *WLN* 14 (December 1989): 13–15.

Argues that experienced teachers who become tutors frequently change their teaching styles. Cites five changes teachers undergo.

1152. Gills, Paula. "The Troubleshooter." *WLN* 13 (April 1989): 4–5.

Discusses identifying, scheduling, and teaching dyslexic students. Cites articles and textbooks that provide "practical advice and educational strategies."

1153. Goldsmith, Marc, and Ann Robertson. *Mitchell College: Word Processing within the Freshman English Curriculum.* Bloomington, Ind.: ERIC/RCS, 1988. ERIC ED 301 276. 18 pages

Describes the development of a computer laboratory to serve the word-processing needs of basic writers at a private college.

1154. Haas, Teri. "Profiles: An Interview with Dr. Myra Kogen, Director of the Brooklyn College Writing Center." *WLN* 13 (April 1989): 11–15.

Discusses the origin, operation, funding, and staffing of the Brooklyn College Writing Center.

1155. Harris, Muriel. "A User's Guide to Writing Centers." *CompC* 1 (January 1989): 4–7.

Writing centers offer students feedback on their writing, answers to questions, diagnostic information about writing problems, and other specific services.

1156. Head, Susan D. "The Sweetwater Model for Writing Improvement." Paper presented at the Association for the Development of Computer-Based Instructional Systems, Philadelphia, November 1988. ERIC ED 301 887. 19 pages

Describes a computer-assisted writing laboratory project that integrates literature and writing for junior high and high school students.

1157. Healy, Dave. "Varieties of Apathetic Experience." *WLN* 14 (October 1989): 5–8.

Provides six questions that reveal reasons for apathy. Cites 12 kinds of apathetic situations and strategies for handling them.

1158. Herrington, Anne J. "The First 20 Years of *Research in the Teaching of English* and the Growth of a Research Community in Composition Studies." *RTE* 23 (May 1989): 117–138.

Traces the broadening of RTE's research community from researchers using uniformly quantitative models to include qualitative research and a greater variety of theoretical perspectives.

1159. Holbrook, Hilary Taylor. "Issues in the Writing Lab: An ERIC/RCS Report." *WCJ* 9 (Spring-Summer 1989): 67–72.

Cites ERIC documents that discuss the effective training of peer tutors, the use of computers as administrative and teaching tools, and outreach to university and community.

1160. Hynds, Susan. "Perspectives on Perspectives in the Writing Center Conference." *Focuses* 2 (Fall 1989): 77–90.

Suggests that tutors need to engage in "mutual exploration" with students and "learn to become comfortable being co-learners."

1161. Johnstone, Anne. "The Writing Tutorial as Ecology: A Case Study." *WCJ* 9 (Spring-Summer 1989): 51–56.

Studies the dialectic of resistance and response between tutors and clients, tutors and training courses, and texts and readers.

1162. King, Mabel T. "Software Security in the University Computer Laboratories." *CollM* 7 (May 1989): 131–132.

Explains computer virus threats and lists precautions for avoiding them.

1163. Kleist, David. "Tutors' Column: The *Weltschmerz* of Prescriptive Grammar." *WLN* 14 (September 1989): 9–10.

Attributes his ability to write well to extensive reading and writing. Suggests that student writers should read as well as study grammar.

1164. Krapohl, Cheryl. "Late Night at the Writing Center: Service Station or Oasis?" *WLN* 14 (October 1989): 9.

Encourages students to become independent thinkers and original writers rather than to settle for a quick fix of errors.

1165. Lavely, Marcia M. "Tutors' Column: The Fruits of Tutoring." *WLN* 13 (February 1989): 9–10.

Describes several tutorial situations, the challenges involved, and the sense of accomplishment gained.

1166. Leahy, Richard. "Rocky Mountain Diary." *WLN* 13 (April 1989): 1–3, 8.

Reports that sessions at the Rocky Mountain Writing Center Association meeting treated tutor training, computers and writing centers, "expectation conflict," and writing across the curriculum.

1167. Leahy, Rick. "Seven Myth-Understandings about the Writing Center." *WLN* 14 (September 1989): 7–8.

Describes information in a newsletter sent to all faculty members that counters misconceptions about the writing center's services and goals.

1168. Lochman, Daniel T. " 'A Dialogue of One': Orality and Literacy in the Writing Center." *WCJ* 10 (Fall-Winter 1989): 19–29.

Describes the counselor-student relationship as two voices collaborating to produce a third, moving the student from a highly oral to a more literate academic discourse.

1169. Maid, Barry, Sally Crisp, and Suzanne Norton. "On Gaining Insight into Ourselves as Writers and as Tutors: Our Use of the Myers-Briggs Type Indicator." *WLN* 13 (June 1989): 1–5.

Cites the characteristics of four personality types: introversion/extroversion; sensing/intuition; feeling/thinking; judging/perceiving. Discusses strategies each type may use to write effectively.

1170. McCleary, Bill. "Upgrading 'Bizcom': Business and Management Communications Professors Seek to Increase Clout." *CompC* 2 (March 1989): 1–2.

To increase their professional status, teachers of business and management communications established *Management Communication Quarterly*. They also changed the format and raised the standards for the *Journal of Business Communication*.

1171. McKenzie, Lee. "The Union of a Writing Center with a Computer Center: What to Put in the Marriage Contract." *WLN* 14 (November 1989): 1–2, 8.

Notes that combining writing and computer centers necessitates decisions about supervision, sharing computers with other disciplines, teaching students to use machines, and defining the degree of integration desired.

1172. Mills, Nina. "Tutors' Column." *WLN* 13 (April 1989): 9–10.

A nontraditional student, Mills learns word processing and then becomes a tutor. She likes the "connected" way of knowing that writing centers encourage.

1173. Mink, JoAnna Stephens. "Developing a Writing Center Identity." *WLN* 13 (February 1989): 5–6.

Discusses methods for developing a logo, used on bookmarks and t-shirts to advertise a center's services.

1174. Mohr, Ellen. "Credit in the Writing Center." *WLN* 13 (June 1989): 13–16.

Provides descriptions of one-credit courses in sentence pattern skills, proofreading, composing, practical writing, and research skills.

1175. Morse, Philip S. "Using Communication Skills in the Writing Conference." *WLN* 14 (September 1989): 1–6.

Describes five attending skills and four influencing skills. Suggests a four-step conference format.

1176. Murphy, Christina. "Freud in the Writing Center: The Psychoanalytics of Tutoring Well." *WCJ* 10 (Fall-Winter 1989): 13–18.

Compares psychotherapy and tutoring as interventive processes based on empathetic bonds between a therapist-tutor and a client-student.

1177. Perkins, William. "Tutors' Column: Tutorin' Is like Torquein.' " *WLN* 14 (November 1989): 9–10.

Compares teaching students to recognize and manipulate sentence elements to teaching someone to recognize and manipulate engine parts.

1178. Popken, Randall L. "The Context-Sensitivity Problem in Models and Exercises for the Writing Lab." *WLN* 13 (February 1989): 11–13.

Argues that textbook exercises concerning creating thesis statements, topic sentences, and appropriate syntax frequently ignore real-life contexts.

1179. Puma, Vincent D. "The Write Staff: Identifying and Training Tutor-Candidates." *WLN* 14 (October 1989): 1–4.

Describes procedures for identifying, selecting, screening, training, and staffing writing centers.

1180. Reynolds, Robert L. "Collaboration and Community Formation in English Microcomputer Labs." Paper presented at the CCCC Convention, St. Louis, March 1988. ERIC ED 299 592. 8 pages

Suggests how the design features of writing centers can encourage productive student collaboration.

1181. Scharton, Maurice. "The Third Person: The Role of the Computer in Writing Centers." *CC* 7 (November 1989): 37–48.

Case studies illustrate four ways in which computers affect tutoring writers. Sees computers as a humanizing force.

1182. Smith, Janet. "Tutors' Column: The Seduction of a Schoolmarm." *WLN* 13 (May 1989): 9–10.

Relates her conversion from being a "pompous pontificator" of truth and beauty to becoming a tutor who values the collaborative process.

1183. Smulyan, Lisa, and Kristin Bolton. "Classroom and Writing Center Collaborations: Peers as Authorities." *WCJ* 9 (Spring-Summer 1989): 43–49.

Differentiates collaborative situations according to the authority inherent in the social context. Using data from high school students, examines their pleasures in classroom collaboration and their difficulties in tutoring.

1184. Spilman, Isabel B. "Tutors' Column: Tutoring Five on Five." *WLN* 13 (June 1989): 9–10.

Argues that collaborative learning in small groups can work. Students draft papers; discuss main ideas, supporting evidence, and stylistics; and thus create a real audience.

1185. Taylor, David. "Peer Tutoring's Hidden World: The Emotional and Social Issues." *WLN* 13 (January 1989): 1–5.

In learning to meet the writing needs of others, tutors reinforce their own writing, encourage and empower students, and assume control over the educational process.

1186. Thaiss, Christopher J. "An Introduction to the National Network of Writing across the Curriculum." *CompC* 2 (March 1989): 9–10.

Describes the purpose, structure, and activities of the Network.

1187. Towns, Cheryl Hofstetter. "Serving the Disabled in the Writing Center." *WLN* 14 (November 1989): 14–16.

Suggests six ways to assist the disabled student. Cites several resources for training tutors.

1188. Upcraft, M. Lee, and John N. Gardner, eds. *The Freshman Year Experience: Helping Students Survive and Succeed in College*. Higher Education Series. San Francisco: Jossey-Bass, 1989. 605 pages

A guide to the policies, strategies, programs, and services designed to ensure students' retention and academic success, especially in the first year of college. Contains 29 discussions treating the freshman population, model programs, and ways to build campus support for them.

1189. Upton, James. "A 'WALK' in the Writing Center." *WLN* 13 (May 1989): 15–16.

Presents a nine-point worksheet designed to enhance a student's understanding of an assignment and to aid the tutor in assisting the student.

1190. Wolcott, Willa. "Talking It Over: A Qualitative Study of Writing Center Conferencing." *WCJ* 9 (Spring-Summer 1989): 15–29.

Data from observations, interviews, and questionnaires are used to compare a writing center and teacher-student conferences and to determine the focus and effectiveness of tutorials.

See also 26, 33, 1078, 1098, 1598, 1615

3.4   ROLE IN SOCIETY

1191. Auerbach, Leslie Ann. "Censorship and East European and Soviet Theater and Film, 1963–1980: The Censor's Game." *DAI* 49 (April 1989): 3043A.

Studies how censorship in the Eastern block created an ambience of diminishing imaginative freedom. The study concludes that censorship works.

1192. Brodkey, Linda. "Transvaluing Difference." *CE* 51 (October 1989): 597–601.

Calls for respecting differences in response to accounts of the November 1988 meeting of the National Association of Scholars.

1193. Coughlin, Ellen K. "Scholars in the Humanities Are Disheartened by the Course of Debate over Their Disciplines." *CHE* 36 (13 September 1989): A1, A14-A15.

Humanist scholars debate methods of responding to charges that their work is politicized, trivialized, and preoccupied with irrelevancies.

1194. Fowler, Judy, and Stefan Martin. "School-College Partnerships and Their Impact on Writing Programs." *WPA* 12 (Spring 1989): 43–56.

Describes the setbacks and successes of a University of Maryland–Baltimore program in cooperation with city schools to establish a writing program in the high schools.

1195. Lloyd-Jones, Richard, and Andrea A. Lunsford. *The English Coalition Conference: Democracy through Language*. Urbana, Ill.: NCTE and Modern Language Association, 1989. 87 pages

Presents and comments on position papers from a 1987 conference involving eight major professional organizations and treating every level of English education. Participants stressed "the education of citizens" of democracies and emphasized "the specific value of English studies" in fostering students' abilities to articulate their own and others' views of a culturally diverse society. Includes several bibliographies and a foreword by Wayne Booth.

1196. Marzano, Robert J. *Policy Constraints to the Teaching of Thinking*. Aurora, Colo.: Mid-Continent Regional Educational Laboratory, 1988. ERIC ED 303 772. 15 pages

Notes growing national recognition that direct instruction in higher order thinking skills should be a high priority. Discusses barriers to implementing thinking skills instruction.

1197. McCleary, Bill. "Active Learners, Interactive Classrooms, Integration of 'Language Arts' at All Levels Advocated in English Coalition Conference Report." *CompC* 2 (October 1989): 1–3.

Summarizes the Conference's report and its recommendations for elementary, secondary, and college instruction.

1198. *NCTE Forum*. Urbana, Ill.: NCTE, 1989. 95 pages

A compilation with commentary of NCTE position statements, resolutions, and short documents issued since 1988.

1199. Parsons, Gerald. "Why I Don't Believe in the 'Real World' Anymore." *TWT* 16 (Winter 1989): 42–51.

Argues for discontinuing the use of "real world" because of its implications about the profession and about the relevance of technical writing teachers' work.

1200. Speck, Bruce W., and Thomas J. Pabst. "A Cooperative Model for English Composition." *IlEB* 76 (Spring 1989): 16–28.

Discusses the need for and describes a model for cooperation between secondary school and college composition programs.

1201. Watkins, Beverly T. "English Departments Urged to Emphasize Speaking and Writing Skills." *CHE* 35 (29 March 1989): A15.

Reports on a conference of 60 teachers representing every level of education. They recommend that English departments balance literature offerings with speaking and writing classes.

See also 1065

4

Curriculum

4.1 GENERAL DISCUSSIONS

1202. Albars, Randall K. "The Pedagogy of Voice: Putting Theory into Practice in a Story Workshop Composition Class." Paper presented at the CCCC Convention, St. Louis, March 1988. ERIC ED 301 881. 23 pages

Identifies the theoretical principles behind the story workshop format and discusses the role of voice.

1203. Andersen, Wallis May. "Computer Invention Programs Today: Accessible and Authorable." Paper presented at the CCCC Convention, St. Louis, March 1988. ERIC ED 301 875. 24 pages

Classifies and analyzes software for prompting or planning writing.

1204. Barbieri, Edmund L. "A Unified Series of Essays and Articles on the Teaching of Thinking." *DAI* 50 (November 1989): 1194A.

Focuses on the teaching of thinking from a historical, civic, social, philosophical, psychological, and pedagogical point of view.

1205. Barnes, Douglas, James Britton, and Mike Torbe. *Language, the Learner, and the School*. 4th ed. Portsmouth, N.H.: Boynton/Cook, 1989. 166 pages

Reissues Barnes's study of how language use in the secondary school limits learning. Britton and Torbe discuss the results of the study.

1206. Benson, Kirsten F. "The Writer First: Using Computers to Make One-to-One Conferencing More Successful." *CAC* 3 (Winter 1989): 51–55.

In a computer-based conferencing classroom, students retain physical and symbolic control over their texts while the recursive nature of writing is reinforced.

1207. Berlin, James. "James Berlin Responds [to Scriven, Flower, and Schlib, *CE* 51 (November 1989)]." *CE* 51 (November 1989): 770–777.

Clarifies his position that proponents of cognitive psychology avoid social critique and thus unprofitably isolate the task environment.

1208. Berry, Eleanor. "Speech Synthesizers as Aids to Revision." *CC* 6 (August 1989): 82–92.

Shows how speech synthesizers can be used as revision aids.

1209. Blanchard, Lydia. "Writing-Thinking: The Historical Perspective for an Electronic World." Paper presented at the CCCC Convention, St. Louis, March 1988. ERIC ED 298 509. 13 pages

Argues that students should be taught how media affect thought and how to use one media to challenge another.

1210. Bleich, David. "Genders of Writing." *JAC* 9 (1989): 10–25.

Questions the belief that we should continue to teach expository prose or academic discourse. Both are distorted by ideology, including an unenlightened view of gender.

1211. Boothby, Samuel Young. "The Influence of Computer-Mediated Writing Conferences on Revision: Case Studies of College Students." *DAI* 49 (March 1989): 2566A.

Examines computer-mediated writing conferences via electronic mail to determine the influence of peer and teacher comments on two students' revisions.

1212. Bowen, Betsy A. "Talking about Writing: Collaborative Revision in the Peer Writing Conference." *DAI* 49 (April 1989): 2953A.

Describes cognitive strategies that participants in conferences use.

1213. Brooke, Robert, and John Hendricks. *Audience Expectations and Teacher Demands*. Studies in Writing and Rhetoric. Carbondale, Ill.: Southern Illinois University Press, 1989. 148 pages

Examines the task of teaching writing for an audience when students know that the teacher, not the audience addressed, assigns the grade.

1214. Butler, Sydney, and Roy Bentley. "Lifewriting: Surfacing What Students Really Want to Write About." Paper presented at the NCTE Convention, Los Angeles, November 1987. ERIC ED 298 515. 16 pages

Reports on a study that showed that students who were free to choose their topics struggled to find one important to them.

1215. Cannon, Sally Irene. "Reader-Response: From Literature to Student Writing." *DAI* 49 (June 1989): 3643A.

Argues that the same skills students acquire in responding to literature can be used in responding to students' texts.

1216. Cheney, Lynne V. "Text of the Foreword, Introduction, and Core-Course Descriptions from the Model Curriculum Proposed in Humanities Fund Report." *CHE* 36 (11 October 1989): A16-A20.

A long excerpt from the NEH chair's report on suggested changes in the curriculum of U.S. colleges.

1217. Christenbury, Leila. "Reactivating the Learning Process: A Short History, A Brief Rationale." *Leaflet* 88 (Winter 1989): 5–9.

Advocates inductive teaching to free students from passive roles in learning.

1218. Clifford, Geraldine Joncich. *A Sisyphean Task: Historical Perspectives on the Relationship between Writing and Reading Instruction*. Washington, D.C.: Office of Educational Research and Improvement, 1987. ERIC ED 297 318. 51 pages

Favors integrating reading and writing after showing how reading has dominated and how reading and writing have been treated separately.

1219. Colatrella, Carol, Joseph M. Lapetina, and Varant Najarian. "Teaching Writing as a Liberal Art." *FEN* 18 (Fall 1989): 23–26.

Discusses the problems of writing taught as a component of humanities core courses. Suggests roles for tutors.

1220. Collins, James L., ed. *Vital Signs 1: Bringing Together Reading and Writing*. Portsmouth, N.H.: Boynton/Cook, 1989. 176 pages

The first volume in an announced annual addressed to English teachers from junior high school through the first year of college. Fifteen essays discuss the range of literature and writing activities that reflect the student's role as a maker of meaning.

1221. Comley, Nancy R. "Critical Thinking-Critical Teaching." *CE* 51 (October 1989): 623–627.

Reviews five books that discuss both theory and methods of developing critical thinking skills.

1222. Cronin, Frank C. "Textuality, Reader-Response Theory, and the English Classroom." *EngR* 40 (1989): 29–31.

Poststructuralism, in contrast to New Criticism, helps students control texts to avoid being manipulated by the texts of their everyday lives.

1223. Crow, Linda W. "The Nature of Critical Thinking." *JCST* 19 (November 1989): 114–116.

Summarizes and illustrates five major areas of teaching critical thinking. Suggests reinforcements through writing activities.

1224. D'Arcy, Pat. *Making Sense, Shaping Meaning: Writing in the Context of a Capacity-Based Approach to Learning*. Portsmouth, N.H.: Boynton/Cook, 1989. 180 pages

Draws upon D'Arcy's work of 20 years with James Britton and Nancy Martin. Demonstrates how teachers can use writing to increase their students' powers of perception and understanding.

1225. Donahue, Patricia, and Ellen Quandahl, eds. *Reclaiming Pedagogy: The Rhetoric of*

the Classroom. Carbondale, Ill.: Southern Illinois University Press, 1989. 179 pages

Twelve essays comment on the intersection of contemporary critical theory and composition teaching. Uses theory to read the classroom in its institutional context, the language of teaching, student essays, and the content and assignments of composition courses.

1226. Easley, Alexis. "Learning through Writing." *JDEd* 10 (Fall 1989): 10–12.

Discusses students' "frequent failure to produce meaningful essays" and suggests instructional approaches and sample assignments to promote writing as a learning process.

1227. Edwards, Derek, and Neil Mercer. "Reconstructing Context: The Conventionalization of Classroom Knowledge." *DPr* 12 (January–March 1989): 91–104.

Conceptions shared by teachers and students provide the context for future teaching and learning.

1228. Erickson, Barbara Griffiths. "We Can Do—22 Percent Better: Computers and the Writing Process." *IlEB* 76 (Spring 1989): 35–38.

Briefly describes the implementing of a high school computers-and-writing program based on college research.

1229. Feichtl, Nancy. "Using Proverbs to Facilitate Metaphorical Language Comprehension." *DAI* 49 (April 1989): 2910A.

Section I finds higher test scores for students taught with proverbs; Section II is a collection of "high interest" proverbs.

1230. Fleckenstein, Kristie S. "Progress Logs: Teaching Writing Process Awareness." *TETYC* 16 (May 1989): 106–112.

Students keep journals to log progress on specific assignments.

1231. Flower, Linda. "Three Comments on 'Rhetoric and Ideology in the Writing Class' and 'Problem Solving Reconsidered' [*CE* 50

(September 1988)]." *CE* 51 (November 1989): 765–769.

Claims that Berlin creates a false dichotomy between cognitive and social dimensions and that Carter constructs an "oddly rigid" definition of *goal*.

1232. Forman, Sid. "Computing Your 'Overhead.' " *CalE* 25 (January–February 1989): 18–19.

Combining an overhead projector with a liquid crystal display projector and a computer can help in teaching composition.

1233. Franklin, Sharon, and Jon Madian, eds. *The Writing Notebook: Creative Word Processing in the Classroom—November/December 1986, January/February 1987, and April/May 1987.* Eugene, Oreg.: The Writing Notebook, 1986–1987. ERIC ED 301 883. 137 pages

Three journals present approximately 40 articles related to word processing in the classroom.

1234. Frisch, Adam. "The Proposal to a Small Group: Learning to See Otherwise." Paper presented at the CCCC Convention, Seattle, March 1989. ERIC ED 303 796. 6 pages

Provides an assignment asking students to write to a peer audience rather than to the teacher as examiner.

1235. Goodman, Marcia Renee. "Teaching Writing and Thinking." *V&R* 1 (Spring 1989): 3–14.

Reviews Sommers's research on revision and discusses classroom applications.

1236. Gose, Michael. "Making Small Groups Work." *CalE* 25 (November–December 1989): 10–11, 19, 21.

Offers advice on planning effective group discussions.

1237. Gradwohl, Jane M., and Gary M. Schumacher. "The Relationship between Content Knowledge and Topic Choice in Writing." *WC* 6 (April 1989): 181–195.

Demonstrates that 37 sixth graders had significantly more knowledge about topics they wanted to read about than "don't want" or teacher-chosen topics.

1238. Graves, Donald H., Jerome C. Harste, Ken Macrorie, and P. David Pearson. *When Bad Things Happen to Good Ideas.* Urbana, Ill.: NCTE, 1988.

Each speaker discusses "Whatever Happened to . . ." four concepts in the teaching of writing: process pedagogy, the reading-writing connection, journal keeping, and testing. A cassette recorded during the 1988 NCTE Convention in St. Louis.

1239. Green, Matthew James. "The Computer and Revision Strategies in Academic Writing." *DAI* 50 (September 1989): 612A.

Students developed positive attitudes toward computers, but revisions did not correlate with writing quality.

1240. Greenwood, Claudia M. "Factors Which Influence Reentry Women in College Composition." Paper presented at the CCCC Convention, St. Louis, March 1988. ERIC ED 297 326. 13 pages

Argues that the greatest support comes from instructors who are resource persons, facilitators, and collaborators and who reduce women's fear of failure.

1241. Haas, Christina. "How the Writing Medium Shapes the Writing Process: Effects of Word Processing on Planning." *RTE* 23 (May 1989): 181–207.

Finds that writers using word processors did less planning overall, less planning before beginning to write, and more "local or sequential" planning than writers using pen and paper.

1242. Hahn, Jim. " 'You Know What I Mean'—Or Do They? Writer-Based Prose Is Halfway Home." *V&R* 1 (Spring 1989): 15–23.

Reviews Flower's study of egocentric writing and discusses its implications for teaching.

1243. Harris, Jeanette, Diana George, Christine Hult, and M. Jimmie Killingsworth. "Computers in the Curriculum: Looking Ahead." *WPA* 13 (Fall-Winter 1989): 35–44.

Discusses the present role computers play in college writing programs and makes predictions and recommendations concerning their future.

1244. Harris, Joseph. "Discourse and Community." Paper presented at the CCCC Convention, Seattle, March 1989. ERIC ED 304 689. 15 pages

Suggests that teachers engage in ongoing criticism of discourses that are contested in the classroom.

1245. Hartnett, Carolyn G. "Clues to Mode of Discourse." Paper presented at the International Systemic Congress, East Lansing, August 1988. ERIC ED 301 876. 35 pages

Describes a pilot study for teaching students to write "thoughtfully" and for programming computers to recognize linguistic expressions that indicate such writing.

1246. Holmes, Stewart. "Sound Bite Virus and General Semantics Immunology." *ETC* 46 (Spring 1989): 43–46.

Describes ways to teach relationships between words and things by using meditation and by reading and writing haiku.

1247. Holt, Mara. "Toward a Democratic Rhetoric: Self and Society in Collaborative Theory and Practice." *JTW* 8 (Spring-Summer 1989): 99–112.

Argues that Gere in *Writing Groups* and LeFevre in *Invention as a Social Act* see collaboration as pluralistic, "equalizing power relations" so that individuals may be heard.

1248. Huber, Bettina J., and David Laurence. "Report on the 1984–1985 Survey of the English Sample: General Education Requirements in English and the English Major." *BADE* 93 (Fall 1989): 30–43.

Reports on general education requirements in writing and literature, including courses added or dropped and areas of concentration in the major.

1249. Hunter, Susan. "Oral Negotiations in a Textual Community: A Case for Pedagogy and Theory." *WI* 8 (Spring 1989): 105–110.

Reviews current theory about the relationship between oral and literate discourse to make a case for the necessity of talk in composition classes.

1250. Hurlbert, C. Mark. "Toward Collectivist Composition: Transforming Social Relations through Classroom Practices." *WI* 8 (Summer 1989): 166–176.

Composing is seen as an individual act emphasizing competition. Advocates practices grounded in Marx, Petrovsky, and collective class writing projects.

1251. Hynds, Susan. "Love and Power in the Profession: Reflections on a Gender-Free English." *EngR* 40 (1989): 11–16.

Male and female dichotomies of "objective and subjective," "intuition and intellect," and "love and power" affect how we define knowledge in the teaching of English.

1252. Janangelo, Joseph. "Fighting Baptism with a Hose: Understanding Student Resistance to Liberation Pedagogy." *EEd* 21 (December 1989): 219–229.

Discusses three major areas of student resistance to liberation pedagogy. Students dislike open-ended problem-solving assignments, see education as a commodity, and regard teachers as authority figures.

1253. Johnson, Frederick L. "Educating Underprepared Students in Community Colleges: An Analysis of Terms, Metaphors, and Concepts." *DAI* 50 (November 1989): 1190A.

Reconceptualizes programs for underprepared community college students by suggesting an alternative metaphor and term.

1254. Kirsch, Max, Michael Ribaudo, and Harvey Wiener. "National Project on Computers and College Writing Coordinating Research on Computers in the Writing Class." *CompC* 2 (October 1989): 6–7.

Discusses a three-year project to assess computer-based writing programs at 15 campuses.

1255. Knudson, Ruth E. "Effects of Instructional Strategies on Student Writing." *DAI* 49 (April 1989): 2955A.

Tests the effectiveness of models, process-focused questions, both models and questions, and free writing as instructional strategies. Concludes that models were most effective.

1256. Kraemer, Kristi. "Revising Responding: One View of *Sharing Writing: Using Peer Response Groups in the English Classroom.*" *V&R* 1 (Spring 1989): 33–40.

Discusses how Spear's findings can be used to improve collaboration and peer critiques.

1257. Lawrence, Sandra Marie. "Journal Writing as a Tool for Learning in College Classrooms." *DAI* 49 (March 1989): 2568A.

Investigates how two community college teachers used journal writing to assist their students with learning. Only a few students benefited.

1258. Lemon, Hallie. "On the Trail of Character X: A Successful Collaborative Writing Project." *IlEB* 76 (Winter 1989): 63–70.

Discusses methods of using peer criticism and peer tutoring to encourage a sense of teamwork in the classroom.

1259. Logan, Shirley Wilson. "An Ethnographic Study of Computer Writers in an Undergraduate Composition Class." *DAI* 49 (January 1989): 1721A.

Researches the implications of computer assistance in an upper-level writing class of 15 students, comparing the role of revision to previous findings.

1260. Mack, Nancy. "The Social Nature of Words: Voices, Dialogues, Quarrels." *WI* 8 (Summer 1989): 157–165.

Draws on Bakhtin to argue that the academy can "adopt useful features of street language" to encourage active and engaged student writing.

1261. MacNealy, Mary Sue. "Commenting on Student Writing: Some Effects of Computer-Assisted Delivery." *DAI* 50 (November 1989): 1238A.

Results indicate that a significant advantage exists when students edit on-line with computer-delivered advice.

1262. Marx, Michael Steven. " 'Windows' on the Composing Process." *CC* 6 (August 1989): 63–79.

Asserts that windows or split screens encourage writing as discovery by enabling students to see various parts of a work being written on a computer.

1263. Mason, Jana W. *Reading and Writing Connections*. Needham Heights, Mass.: Allyn & Bacon, 1989. 310 pages

Prints 12 papers presented at a 1986 University of Illinois conference that documented connections between reading and writing. Describes how writing can take place in the classroom in conjunction with reading.

1264. Matalene, Carolyn B., Robert L. Oakman, and Robert L. Cannon. "LiveWriter in the Composition Classroom." *CompC* 2 (April 1989): 4–8.

This Macintosh communications program allows teacher and student to interact as the student writes.

1265. Mayher, John S. *Uncommon Sense: Theoretical Practice in Language Education*. Portsmouth, N.H.: Boynton/Cook, 1989. 320 pages

Studies the unfounded assumptions or "common" sense that underlies many unproductive classroom practices. Discusses the clear thinking or "uncommon" sense upon which sound teaching should be based.

1266. McCleary, Bill. "Ninth Edition of Popular Text Thrives by Combining the Old and the New." *CompC* 2 (February 1989): 1–3.

Traces the history and influence of McCrimmon's *Writing with a Purpose*.

1267. Minot, Walter S. "Personality and Persona: Developing the Self." *RR* 7 (Spring 1989): 352–362.

Proposes assignments to enhance a writer's self-esteem and composing skill.

1268. Misegadis, Mary Helen. "A Comparative Study of the Self-Paced English Composition I and Traditional English Composition I Curriculum at Barton County Community College." *DAI* 49 (January 1989): 1722A.

Compares instructional procedures for English composition as they are implemented in a self-paced and in a traditional writing classroom. Finds no significant differences.

1269. Moberg, Goran George. *Merging Computer Writing and Collaborative Learning: The Role of Space in Room N779*. Alexandria, Va.: EDRS, 1988. ERIC ED 302 849. 11 pages

Describes the positive effects that room design can have on collaborative learning and computer-assisted writing.

1270. Mulvaney, Maureen Keefe. "The Effects of the Process Approach and Prewriting Strategies on the Writing Performance and Apprehension of Students with Different Learning Styles." *DAI* 49 (June 1989): 3606A.

Studies effects of the process approach and selected prewriting strategies on the writing anxiety of students with different learning styles.

1271. Murphey, Tim. "Sociocognitive Conflict: Confused? Don't Worry, You May Be Learning!" *ETC* 46 (Winter 1989): 312–315.

Analyzes productive ways to help students resolve cognitive confusion. Productive ways result from assuming that other viewpoints possibly may be right.

1272. Murray, Donald M. *Expecting the Unexpected: Teaching Myself—and Others—to Read and Write*. Portsmouth, N.H.: Boynton/Cook, 1989. 288 pages

Collects 24 articles on writing and its teaching, written by Murray since 1982.

1273. Neilsen, Allan R. *Critical Thinking and Reading: Empowering Learners to Think and Act*. Monographs on Teaching Critical Thinking. Urbana, Ill.: NCTE and ERIC/RCS, 1989. 54 pages

Criticizes attitudes toward critical thinking that see it as a form of knowledge rather than a method of creating knowledge. Provides guidelines for teachers to help students move from "transmission pedagogy" to "transactional pedagogy." Includes an ERIC bibliography.

1274. Newbold, W. Webster. "Beyond Our Silicon Daze: Toward an Integrated Computer Environment in the Composition Classroom." *CAC* 3 (Summer 1989): 15–21.

Discusses the advantages of a computer classroom, especially one with networked computers.

1275. New Jersey Basic Skills Council. *Teaching Reading and Writing: In College, in High School, in Every Subject*. Trenton: New Jersey State Department of Higher Education, 1984. ERIC ED 303 788. 35 pages

Offers a booklet responding to the results of the New Jersey College Basic Skills Placement Test.

1276. Newkirk, Thomas, ed. *To Compose: Teaching Writing in High School and College*. 2d ed. Portsmouth, N.H.: Heinemann, 1989. 336 pages

Nineteen essays on creating a classroom in which students are treated as writers.

1277. Novak, John A., and Janet M. Dettloff. "Developing Critical Thinking Skills in Community College Students." *JCST* 19 (September–October 1989): 22–25.

Illustrates and analyzes task-analysis methods for developing critical thinking skills.

1278. Oliver, Eileen I. "Effects of Assignment on Writing Quality at Four Grade Levels." *EQ* 21 (1989): 224–232.

Finds that three assignment variables— topic, purpose, and audience—affected the writing of students differently at different stages of development.

1279. O'Reilley, Mary Rose. " 'Exterminate . . . the Brutes'—And Other Things That Go Wrong in Student-Centered Teaching." *CE* 51 (February 1989): 142–146.

Reassesses the student-centered class-room's being predicated on a diffusion of power. Argues that teachers' abdicating their power is dangerous and confusing to students.

1280. Paine, Charles. "Relativism, Radical Pedagogy, and the Ideology of Paralysis." *CE* 51 (October 1989): 557–570.

Calls on teachers to change both their methods and the content of courses to avoid bringing students to "an ideology of relativism-equals-despair."

1281. Parsons, Les. *Response Journals*. Portsmouth, N.H.: Heinemann, 1989. 96 pages

A practical guide for journal-based writing programs. Argues that the effectiveness of response journals depends on a system of formative and summative evaluation.

1282. Partridge, Susan. *Students, Their Writing, and the Word Processor*. Bloomington, Ind.: ERIC/RCS, 1987. ERIC ED 301 169. 18 pages

Surveys the attitudes of 25 undergraduates about using word processing.

1283. Phelan, Patricia, and NCTE Committee on Classroom Practices, eds. *Talking to Learn*. Classroom Practices in Teaching English, vol. 24. Urbana, Ill.: NCTE, 1989. 146 pages

Twenty-four essays discuss ways of developing students' abilities to speak and listen effectively. Focuses on using oral communication to help students understand litera-ture and gain self-confidence in various kinds of communication.

1284. Posey, Evelyn. "Micro Style: Using a Word Processor to Enhance Prewriting." *WLN* 14 (December 1989): 12–13.

Explains two techniques that make use of word processors. Invisible writing helps students concentrate on ideas, and cooperating writing allows readers to respond during text production.

1285. Posey, Evelyn. "Micro Style: Which One Should I Buy?" *WLN* 13 (February 1989): 7–8.

Provides guidelines for purchasing computers and printers to meet students' needs.

1286. Prince, Michael B. "Literacy and Genre: Towards a Pedagogy of Mediation." *CE* 51 (November 1989): 730–749.

Positions the pedagogical practice of generic substitution historically, cognitively, and theoretically. Illustrates with a sample syllabus.

1287. Rafoth, Bennett A. "Speaking-Writing Courses: A Survey of Writing Program Administrators." Paper presented at the CCCC Convention, Seattle, March 1989. ERIC ED 303 830. 18 pages

Reports on approximately 250 survey responses. Forty percent of the respondents indicated that 10 percent of instructional activities integrated speaking and writing; 45 percent reported no such integration.

1288. Reither, James A., and Douglas Vipond. "Writing as Collaboration." *CE* 51 (December 1989): 855–867.

Collaborative writing involves coauthoring, workshopping, and knowledge making. Illustrates the process with a case study and guidelines for designing courses.

1289. Reynolds, John Frederick. "Classical Rhetoric and Computer-Assisted Composition: Extra-Textual Features as 'Delivery.' " *CAC* 3 (Spring 1989): 101–107.

Word processing and desktop publishing allow for a reconceptualization of delivery as presentation.

1290. Rittenhouse, Wayne Randall. "The Dialectical Nature of Success in College: Identifying Motives and Confronting Contradictions." *DAI* 50 (July 1989): 70A.

Advocates incorporating motives into the curriculum and using language activities to gain control over one's life.

1291. Rodrigues, Dawn, and Raymond Rodrigues. "How Word Processing Is Changing Our Teaching: New Technologies, New Approaches, New Challenges." *CC* 7 (November 1989): 13–25.

Argues that teachers have learned to teach writing in new ways when they use computers in classrooms.

1292. Ronald, Kate, and Hephzibah Roskelly, eds. *Farther Along: Transforming Dichotomies in Rhetoric and Composition*. Portsmouth, N.H.: Boynton/Cook, 1989. 224 pages

In a collection of 12 essays writing teachers consider ways of overcoming the damaging splits in composition theory and practice.

1293. Rust, Richard D. "Composition Instruction with a Videobeam Projection of the Computer Screen." *CAC* 3 (Spring 1989): 108–115.

Describes using Microsoft Word, vertical split screens, and videobeam projection to teach composition, especially revision.

1294. Safford, Dan. "Revision Revisited." *ExEx* 34 (Spring 1989): 30–35.

Explains how teachers can use drafts of their own writing as a model in the classroom.

1295. Scharton, Maurice. "Models of Competence: Responses to a Scenario Writing Assignment." *RTE* 23 (May 1989): 163–180.

Investigates "disparities between writers' and teachers' interpretations of an assign-

ment." Writers whose interpretations matched the teachers' scored higher.

1296. Schilb, John. "Three Comments on 'Rhetoric and Ideology in the Writing Class' and 'Problem Solving Reconsidered' [*CE* 50 (September 1988)]." *CE* 51 (November 1989): 769–770.

Critiques Berlin's method of analysis as blurring differences and lacking detail regarding the various ways a world view can be realized or utilized.

1297. Schriver, Karen Ann. "Teaching Writers to Anticipate the Reader's Needs: Empirically Based Instruction." *DAI* 50 (July 1989): 90A.

Writers first evaluated poorly written texts and then considered reader feedback in the form of think-aloud protocols.

1298. Scriven, Karen. "Actively Teaching the Passive Voice." *TETYC* 16 (May 1989): 89–93.

Believes that passive constructions have been unfairly and indirectly devalued in textbooks.

1299. Scriven, Karen. "Three Comments on 'Rhetoric and Ideology in the Writing Class' and 'Problem Solving Reconsidered' [*CE* 50 (September 1988)]." *CE* 51 (November 1989): 764–765.

Claims that both Carter and Berlin fail to distinguish between cognitive psychology and cognitive rhetoric and, as a result, deprecate empirical research as limiting.

1300. Sears, Richard. "Computer Sessions within the Composition Classroom: A Report from a Berea College Computer Workshop." *CAC* 3 (Winter 1989): 62–67.

Describes the programs and processes that participants in a computer seminar regarded as valuable for composition instruction.

1301. Sheirer, John. "An Assignment to Promote Awareness of Nonsexist Language." *ExEx* 34 (Spring 1989): 27–29.

Provides sample sentences and suggestions for revision.

1302. Simpson, Michele L., Norman A. Stahl, and Christopher C. Hayer. "PORPE: A Research Validation." *JR* 33 (October 1989): 22–28.

This study reports that, when secondary pupils were taught an integrative reading-writing strategy called PORPE, student learning increased.

1303. Sloane, Thomas O. "Reinventing *Inventio*." *CE* 51 (September 1989): 461–473.

Calls for a return to methods of classical rhetoric that emphasize Ciceronian *states* and *inventio,* which he defines as pro and con reasoning.

1304. Smit, David W. "Some Difficulties with Collaborative Learning." *JAC* 9 (1989): 45–58.

Examines theory and research supporting collaborative pedagogy for composition. Concludes that most research is flawed, failing to show that collaborative teaching improves writing.

1305. Smith, Charles R. "Text Analysis: The State of the Art." *CAC* 3 (Winter 1989): 68–78.

Evaluates "Chunkers, Checkers, Counters, and Parsers" currently being used in writing instruction.

1306. Smith, Leslie. "Writers Who Are Gay and Lesbian Adolescents: The Impact of Social Context." Paper presented at the CCCC Convention, Seattle, March 1989. ERIC ED 304 695. 10 pages

Suggests that writing teachers inspire a change in classroom communication and behavior to create more positive experiences for homosexual students.

1307. Soles, Derek A. J. "Two Approaches to Teaching College Writing: A Comparative Study." *DAI* 50 (November 1989): 1239A.

Findings indicate that the current-traditional approach and the new rhetorical approach were equally effective.

1308. Stewart, Donald C. "What Is an English Major, and What Should It Be?" *CCC* 40 (May 1989): 188–202.

Surveys 194 undergraduate programs for English majors. Proposes reforms in the literature major and new options in other areas.

1309. Stokes, Laura. "How Linda Flower Teaches My Students—and Me—about Writing and Thinking." *V&R* 1 (Spring 1989): 24–32.

Uses Flower's article on writer-based prose to argue against teaching five-paragraph essays.

1310. Strenski, Ellen. "Disciplines and Communities: 'Armies' and 'Monasteries' and the Teaching of Composition." *RR* 8 (Fall 1989): 137–145.

Analyzes metaphors of writing instruction and their implications.

1311. Strickland, James. "Computer Strategies for Teaching Revision: It May Be Convenient, but Its Not Easy." Paper presented at the NCTE Convention, St. Louis, November 1988. ERIC ED 301 890. 20 pages

Describes six revision strategies that use the computer.

1312. Stroble, Elizabeth J. "Use of Electronic Mail to Facilitiate Peer Group Response during the Writing Process." *DAI* 50 (November 1989): 1284A.

Suggests using electronic mail as a tool for students learning to write.

1313. *Student Writing Groups.* Tacoma, Wash.: Wordshop Productions

A 35-minute interactive videotape that demonstrates a method for reading and responding to writing within groups. A 26-page instructional booklet explains the process, presents a teacher's guide and instructions for students, and reprints the paper used in the demonstration.

1314. Suhor, Charles. *Beyond Trends in English and Language Arts Instruction*. Alexandria, Va.: EDRS, 1988. ERIC ED 302 852. 21 pages

Analyzes contemporary movements in composition, reading, literature, and oral language, especially as related to public school instruction.

1315. Suhor, Charles. "Beyond 'Trends' in English and Language Arts Instruction." *EngR* 40 (1989): 1–10.

Briefly describes recent movements and countermovements in composition, reading, literature, and guided oral discourses. Cites studies from 1986 to 1989.

1316. Suhor, Charles. "Beyond 'Trends' in English and Language Arts Instruction." *IlEB* 76 (Spring 1989): 2–15.

Introduces to English instructors the "new wrinkles in the trends that are now well-established in the professional literature" of English departments. Describes movements such as "guided oral discourse," "English first," and so on.

1317. Tebo-Messina, Margaret. "Authority and Models of the Writing Workshop: All Collaborative Writing Is Not Equal." *WI* 8 (Winter 1989): 86–92.

Contrasts models developed by Bruffee, Elbow, and Moffett on an "authority continuum," ultimately favoring Moffett's shifting the balance of authority from teachers to student groups.

1318. Thompson, Isabelle K., Warren W. Werner, and Joyce Rothschild. "A Survey of Writing Instruction in Colleges and Universities, 1975–1976 to 1985–1986." *BADE* 94 (Winter 1989): 29–32.

Reports on writing instruction at a sample of graduate institutions, finding that types of writing courses and enrollments have increased.

1319. Tilly, Anthony, and Peter Myers. *Influence of Word Processing on the Attitudes and Writing of Postsecondary Students*. Toronto: Ontario Department of Education, 1988. ERIC ED 298 536. 147 pages

Reports on a study of 650 students. Finds that they enjoyed, valued, and used word processors.

1320. Trimbur, John. "Consensus and Difference in Collaborative Learning." *CE* 51 (October 1989): 602–616.

Examines criticisms of collaborative learning and explores the meaning of consensus.

1321. Ulichny, Polly, and Karen Watson-Gegeo. "Interactions and Authority: The Dominant Interpretive Framework in Writing Conferences." *DPr* 12 (July–September 1989): 309–328.

Teachers may dominate conferences in such a way as to undermine the aims of process writing approaches.

1322. Usteyee, Carol H. "The Effects of Teaching Style on Student Writing about Field Trips with Concrete Experiences." *DAI* 49 (April 1989): 2916A.

Collects both observational and quantitative data. Questions the use of tests to measure teaching style.

1323. Willis, Wayne. "Liberating the Liberal Arts: An Interpretation of Aristotle." *JGE* 39 (1988): 193–205.

Argues for a return to an Aristotelian form of liberal education, one that promotes both "liberal" (transcendent) and "illiberal" (utilitarian) studies.

1324. Wilson, Martena G. "The Role of Teacher-Student Interaction in the Production of Written Compositions." *DAI* 50 (October 1989): 860A.

Results suggest that smooth teacher-student interactions helped students incorporate academic rhetorical styles.

1325. *Writing Processes*. Chico, Calif.: California State University—Chico.

A 38-minute videotape introduces students to writing processes by interviewing seven writers: a poet, a novelist, a playwright, a journalist, two technical writers, and a published student writer.

1326. Yagelski, Robert P. "Written Commentaries as a Way of Learning about Writing." *JTW* 8 (Fall-Winter 1989): 39–48.

Students' written comments about their own writing are a risk-free opportunity to record concerns, a discovery tool for teachers, and an analytical way to "learn about writing through writing."

See also 117, 129, 157, 269, 278, 413, 514, 546, 722, 819, 865, 922, 932, 938, 1060, 1124, 1143, 1183, 1198, 1201, 1640, 1767, 1773

4.2   HIGHER EDUCATION

4.2.1 DEVELOPMENTAL WRITING

1327. Anstendig, Linda L. "Toward Critical Literacy: An Integrated Skills Reinforcement Program for Basic Writers." *DAI* 50 (August 1989): 376A.

A case study reporting on a basic writing class that used a content-rich curriculum, sequenced assignments, and an integrated approach to reading, speaking, writing, and listening.

1328. Armstrong, Cheryl. "Basic Writers' Problems Are Problems Basic to Writing." Paper presented at the CCCC Convention, St. Louis, March 1988. ERIC ED 298 512. 13 pages

Reports that the problems of basic writers are like those of any writer confronted with an unfamiliar or difficult writing situation.

1329. Beyersdorfer, Janet M., and David K. Schauer. "Semantic Analysis to Writing: Connecting Words, Books, and Writing." *JR* 32 (March 1989): 500–508.

Describes how an integrative approach that connects vocabulary analysis, literature

study, and writing can promote reading comprehension.

1330. Bolman, David Laurence. "Preposition Errors in the Compositions of Mexican-American Basic Writing Students." *DAI* 50 (December 1989): 1583A.

Analyzes written preposition errors in 370 themes of Anglo, African-American, and Mexican college students to identify factors contributing to these errors.

1331. Buley-Meissner, Mary Louise. " 'Am I really that bad?': Writing Apprehension and Basic Writers." *JBW* 8 (Fall 1989): 3–20.

Advocates using the Daly-Miller measure of writing apprehension to help students assess their strengths and weaknesses in composing. Includes seven case studies.

1332. Buley-Meissner, Mary Louise. "The Reluctant Writer." *ArEB* 31 (Spring 1989): 14–21.

Students in a basic writing class use autobiographical writing to work through their negative attitudes toward writing.

1333. Cheney, Donna Ragon. "Teaching Basic Writing: Synthesizing Divergent Elements of Who Can Teach." *DAI* 49 (June 1989): 3644A.

Synthesizes components of the basic writing discipline so that theory, research, and practice come together to provide teaching strategies.

1334. Collins, James L. "Writing Partnerships Offer Help for Basic Writers." *CompC* 2 (November 1989): 9–10.

Collaborative writing helps basic writers understand successful writing.

1335. Collins, Terence. "A Summary of the Learning-Disabled College Writers Project at the University of Minnesota General College." Paper presented at the CCCC Convention, Seattle, March 1989. ERIC ED 303 819. 32 pages

Examines the effect of word processing on learning-disabled writers. The three-year project examined 18 sections enrolling 57 students and taught by eight instructors.

1336. Davis, Judith. "The Morton Downey Jr. Model: Talk Show Influence on Classroom Discussion." *TETYC* 16 (October 1989): 156–164.

Presents exercises to improve students' discussion techniques.

1337. Etchison, Craig. "Word Processing: A Helpful Tool for Basic Writers." *CC* 6 (April 1989): 33–43.

Describes a study of two small classes of basic writers using computers. Although word processing increased the quantity of writing, the quality changed little.

1338. Fishman, Jerry. "Doodlefunking." Paper presented at the Western College Reading and Learning Association, Albuquerque, April 1987. ERIC ED 303 803. 10 pages

Describes an exercise to promote the creative use of written language.

1339. Fitzgerald, Sallyanne H. "Re-Uniting the Arts of Language: Assignments in the Basic Writing Class." *FEN* 18 (Fall 1989): 31–33.

Advocates employing whole language notions—reading, writing, speaking, listening—in creating writing assignments.

1340. Flammia, Madelyn J. "The Effect of the Word Processor on Basic Writers' Use of Revision Techniques in Freshman Composition." *DAI* 50 (October 1989): 933A.

Results reveal that revisions differed for both groups, but neither set of changes had significant effect upon the quality of written work.

1341. Gardner, Phillip. "Laugh and Let Learn." *Leaflet* 88 (Fall 1989): 19–20.

Presents options for having students write and test a process paper.

1342. Gates, Rosemary L. "Coherence and Contextuality: Linguistic Features of Register in the Text." *FEN* 18 (Fall 1989): 12–19.

Discusses the use of register—field, mode, and tenor—as part of coherence in developmental writers' texts.

1343. Gould, Christopher. "Teaching Literature to Basic Writers." *JBW* 8 (Spring 1989): 57–66.

Finds that articles relating literature and basic writers are theoretically "inconsistent, even contradictory." Concludes that students are being held back from "culturally enfranchising" coursework.

1344. Hamilton-Wieler, Sharon. "Awkward Compromises and Eloquent Achievements." *EEd* 21 (October 1989): 152–169.

Explores the influence of context upon the writing in six subject areas of 18-year-olds in South London.

1345. Harris, Muriel, and Katherine E. Rowan. "Explaining Grammatical Concepts." *JBW* 8 (Fall 1989): 21–41.

Aims "to show how insights and strategies from concept-learning literature can make the teaching of grammatical concepts efficient and effective."

1346. Hawisher, Gail E., and Ron Fortune. "Research into Word Processing and the Basic Writer." Paper presented at the AERA, New Orleans, April 1988. ERIC ED 298 943. 24 pages

Finds no significant difference in writing quality or thinking skills among students using word processing.

1347. Hawisher, Gail E., and Ron Fortune. "Word Processing and the Basic Writer." *CollM* 7 (August 1989): 275–281.

Finds no significant differences among 40 basic writers using and not using word processors.

1348. Krohn, Franklin B., and Dennis M. Perez. "Management of Classroom Stutterers." *ExEx* 35 (Fall 1989): 12–13.

Offers 10 suggestions.

1349. Lagatta, Jill Reed. "The Effect of the Writing Conference on the Text Development of Basic Writers." *DAI* 49 (June 1989): 3646A.

Studies the effects of the writing conference on text development and on the writing processes of basic writers.

1350. LoPresti, Gene. "A Case Study of the Reading-Writing Models of a Basic Writing Student." *JTW* (Special Issue 1989): 205–226.

Offers an extensive analysis of a case study. Advocates broad reading for basic readers and writers, a focus on strengths in writing, and an awareness of students' intentions about literacy.

1351. Martinez, Joseph G. R., and Nancy C. Martinez. "Who Is Alien in the Developmental Classroom?: A Comparison of Some Student-Teacher Values." *JBW* 8 (Fall 1989): 99–112.

Advocates "finding a common ground of values, perceptions and knowledge" for successful teacher-student interaction. Surveys educational psychologists' research on teacher-student values.

1352. Murphy, Ann. "Transference and Resistance in the Basic Writing Classroom: Problematics and *Praxis*." *CCC* 40 (May 1989): 175–187.

Questions the appropriateness of the analogy between composition teaching and Lacanian models of psychoanalysis, arguing that the analogy ignores issues of power and authority in the classroom.

1353. Otte, George. "The Deference Due the Oracle: Computerized Text Analysis in a Basic Writing Class." *JBW* 8 (Spring 1989): 46–56.

Error Extractor and Macroworks Analyst programs were used to identify patterns of error and to reduce the number of errors. Found "tabulating and quantifying" helpful to low-level students.

1354. Popken, Randall L. "Language-for-Special-Purposes Theory and Basic Writing." Paper presented at the CCCC Convention, St. Louis, March 1988. ERIC ED 297 340. 23 pages

Argues that basic writers need to be taught the rules and rituals of college life, not grammar exercises or artificial topics.

1355. Rafoth, Bennett A. "Students as Theorists: Developing Personal Theories of Composing." *JTW* (Special Issue 1989): 193–204.

Describes a course for basic writers who, in researching their own writing processes, participated in meaning making as responsible authorities. Includes course outline.

1356. Robinson, Jill. "Cliches: Finding Fresh Language." *ExEx* 34 (Spring 1989): 16–20.

Students read a cliche-filled poem and then translate the cliches.

1357. Sager, Mollee B. "Exploiting the Reading-Writing Connection to Engage Students in Text." *JR* 33 (October 1989): 40.

Describes a reading-writing strategy that provides a context within which students can use language in the ways of a writer, expand their background knowledge, and assess their comprehension.

1358. Schultz, John. "The Power of Acceptance of Mixed Diction—of the Student's Voice— in the Teaching of Composition." Paper presented at the CCCC Convention, Atlanta, March 1987. ERIC ED 300 809. 27 pages

Weak students developed a capacity for internal listening and reading and wrote better when they used their own voice to develop a mixed diction.

1359. Schwalm, David. "Teaching Basic Writing: The Community College on the University Campus." *WPA* 13 (Fall-Winter 1989): 15–24.

Discusses an experiment at Arizona State University, where community college faculty members teach basic writing courses.

1360. Scriven, Karen. "Validating the Deaf Experience: Group-Directed Context for the Hearing Impaired." *WI* 8 (Winter 1989): 76–82.

Provides ideas for assignments that can be used in a two-semester reading- and writing-intensive composition course for hearing-impaired students.

1361. Sedgwick, Ellery. "Alternatives to Teaching Formal, Analytical Grammar." *JDEd* 12 (Spring 1989): 8–10, 12, 14, 20.

Reviews the place of grammar in writing instruction. Reinforces 80 years of research indicating that teaching formal grammar is ineffective and offers alternatives for improving student writing.

1362. Sudol, David. "Basic Rhetoric: Selling English 100." *TETYC* 16 (February 1989): 23–28.

A teacher explains to students why they need basic writing.

1363. Svacina, Jean Marie. "The Computer as a Tool in Teaching Basic Writing to College Freshmen." *DAI* 50 (August 1989): 303A.

Finds that the writing skills of 60 students using computers in composition classes did not improve, although the students thought that they did.

See also 29, 404, 854, 1076, 1364, 1379, 1412, 1439, 1442, 1717, 1727, 1771, 1848

4.2.2 FRESHMAN COMPOSITION

1364. Anderson, Vivienne, and Karen Fitts. "Awakening Students to Rhetorical Process: Audience, *Ethos,* and Anonymity in Journal Correspondence." *JTW* (Special Issue 1989): 175–192.

Journals exchanged between classes increased students' awareness of rhetorical situations, helped them construct an identity, awakened resistance, and employed metalanguage.

1365. Baer, Eugene Michael. "Reading in the Composition Course: Instructional Strategies and Student Traits." *DAI* 50 (November 1989): 1237A.

Shows the effects of reading upon writing when they are combined to enhance interactions.

1366. Bailey, Steven. "The Interviewer and the Millionaire: Teaching Students How to Gather Information through Interviews." *ExEx* 35 (Fall 1989): 14–16.

Students roleplay mock interviews, write what they learn, and then compare papers to learn about point of view.

1367. Beers, Terry. "The Knack for Art: The Why and the Wherefore of Combining Strategies of Invention." *FEN* 17 (Spring 1989): 25–29.

Presents an approach to the teaching of invention that stresses the interdependence of different strategies by considering the question of value in each.

1368. Bishop, Wendy. "Using Postcards for Invention." *ExEx* 35 (Fall 1989): 27–31.

Presents four writing exercises to encourage descriptive writing.

1369. Blythe, Joan Heiges. "Law as Focus." *CEAF* 19 (1989): 13–15.

Studying and writing about legal issues and language invigorated a freshman writing and literature class.

1370. Brooke, Robert, Tom O'Connor, and Ruth Mirtz. "Leadership Negotiation in College Writing Groups." *WE* 1 (Fall 1989): 66–85.

A case study of two writing groups using conflict and negotiation theory.

1371. Brown, Thomas H. "Maintaining an 'Ethical Center' in the Composition Course." *CEAF* 19 (1989): 1–3.

Reports that a dull composition course was saved by student-selected topics and collaborative workshops for prewriting, revising, and editing.

1372. Buckland, Bonnie Vick. "Faculty Perceptions of the Role, Goals, and Outcomes of Freshman Composition at Private Colleges." *DAI* 50 (December 1989): 1574A.

Descriptively analyzes the roles and goals of freshman composition at five small private colleges in Appalachia and corresponding faculty perceptions.

1373. Byrd, Margie. "Summarizing Strategies of Junior College Students." *DAI* 50 (December 1989): 1613A.

Uses protocol analysis to describe the summarizing strategies of 12 junior college freshmen.

1374. Comprone, Joseph J. "Textual Perspectives on Collaborative Learning: Dialogic Literacy and Written Texts in Composition Classrooms." *WI* 8 (Spring 1989): 119–128.

Discusses heteroglossia in science essays by Stephen Jay Gould, Lewis Thomas, and Oliver Sacks. Suggests strategies for moving "collaborative pedagogies back into texts themselves."

1375. Cypert, Rick. "A Return to the 'Treasure-House of Invention': Memory in the Composition Classroom." *FEN* 17 (Spring 1989): 35–38.

Discusses contemporary uses of memory and style to generate information for student writers.

1376. Dean, Terry. "Multicultural Classrooms, Monocultural Teachers." *CCC* 40 (February 1989): 23–37.

Discusses the problem of cultural dissonance in education and describes six ways of including the study of cultural diversity in the composition classroom.

1377. Demmrich, Ingrid. "A Bridge to Academic Discourse: Social Science Research Strategies in the Freshman Composition Course." *CCC* 40 (October 1989): 343–348.

Writing based on research strategies adopted from the social sciences initiates freshmen into academic discourse.

1378. Desjardins, Linda A. *Is a Picture Really Worth a Thousand Words?* Bloomington, Ind.: ERIC/RCS, 1987. ERIC ED 304 696. 13 pages

Finds that using stories and films in a composition class was more effective when accompanied by specific writing assignments and teacher guidance.

1379. Dobie, Ann B. "Strategies for Teaching Spelling." Paper presented at the CCCC Convention, Seattle, March 1989. ERIC ED 304 692. 16 pages

Advocates encouraging students to assume responsibility for solving inductively their own spelling problems. Offers techniques for students to use.

1380. Dodson, Charles B. "Perceiving and Using Slanting Devices: Two Assignments." *ExEx* 34 (Spring 1989): 10–15.

Students analyze the language in a periodical in one assignment and then write a speech displaying the characteristics they have learned.

1381. Downing, Crystal, Marie Foley, Lee Anne Kryder, and Jeffrey Segall. "Birthing a Student Publication: Confessions of Four Midwives." *BADE* 94 (Winter 1989): 40–41.

Describes the development of an annual anthology of freshman essays, explains how it is used in the classroom, and outlines how to produce similar volumes.

1382. Eddy, Gary. "A Poet Teaches Composition." Paper presented at the CCCC Convention, St. Louis, March 1988. ERIC ED 297 347. 13 pages

Proposes Freire's critical literacy as a guide for both poetry writing and college composition.

1383. Feehan, Michael. "Conferencing, Culture, and Common Sense." *FEN* 17 (Spring 1989): 17–19.

Warns writing instructors about communication problems that occur as they intervene in students' writing. Suggests attention to sociolinguistics.

1384. Foley, Marie. "Unteaching the Five-Paragraph Essay." *TETYC* 16 (December 1989): 231–235.

Proposes teaching the essay as a journey.

1385. Foster, Bill R., Jr. "Classical Imitation and Reading-Writing Connections: Analysis and Genesis Enter the Twentieth Century." Paper presented at the CCCC Convention, Seattle, March 1989. ERIC ED 307 619. 21 pages

Claims that the classical concept of imitation as analysis followed by genesis connects classical imitation to the recent reading-writing connections proposed for composition instruction.

1386. Frye, Bob. "Artful Compositions, Corder's 'Laws of Composition,' and the Weekly Letter: Two Approaches to Teaching Invention and Arrangement in Freshman English." *JTW* 8 (Fall-Winter 1989): 1–14.

Using shared symbols in different genres and writing letters between students and teachers emphasizes the complementary nature of invention and structure. Includes letter excerpts.

1387. Fulkerson, Tahita. "Rhetoric Lessons in Film Reviews." *TETYC* 16 (May 1989): 84–88.

Students compare professional reviews of a film, then write their own reviews of another film.

1388. Gates, Rosemary L. "Defining and Teaching Voice in Writing: The Phonological Dimension." *FEN* 17 (Spring 1989): 11–17.

Reviews linguistic research on the sound, shape, and meaning of phrases. Presents a pedagogy to help students become aware of phonological rules and so develop a written voice.

1389. Greene, Wendy Tibbetts, and Lynn Veach Sadler. "Combining Software for Ease, Accuracy, and Idea Generation." *CollM* 7 (May 1989): 127–130.

Describes a freshman composition course using combined original and standard software in a computer-assisted composition laboratory.

1390. Haeger, Cherie Ann. "Greeting Cards for Teacher Appreciation Day: An Exercise in Selecting Vocabulary for a Specific Audience." *ExEx* 34 (Spring 1989): 21–23.

A case assignment in which students also prepare a rhetorical outline.

1391. Hashimoto, I. "Razzle-Dazzle in the Classroom; or, Where Do We Go While the Band Plays On." *FEN* 18 (Fall 1989): 2–4.

A humorous review of common, contemporary notions about teaching writing. Suggests that they have nothing to do with how people learn to write. Offers a model.

1392. Herzer, Scott, and Jill Robinson. "Your Writing Is Unique." *ExEx* 35 (Fall 1989): 43–45.

An activity reveals how voice in writing is individual, even when the writer has collaborated with others.

1393. Hill, Carolyn. "Beyond the Enthymeme: *Sorites,* Critical Thinking, and the Composing Process." Paper presented at the CCCC Convention, Seattle, March 1989. ERIC ED 307 612. 12 pages

Describes a writing assignment intended to promote audience-directed critical thinking during the composing process.

1394. Hood, Mike. "Designing an Idea-Centered Freshman Composition Program to Empower Student Writers." Paper presented at the CCCC Convention, Seattle, March 1989. ERIC ED 303 828. 18 pages

Describes the freshman composition sequence at Belmont Abbey College. Discusses its focus on critical thinking and reports on measures used to assess the program.

1395. Hurst, Mary Jane. "A Final Assignment for a Composition Course." *ArEB* 31 (Spring 1989): 29–31.

Students write an in-class essay in which they describe the characteristics of good writing.

1396. Kiedaisch, Jean, and Sue Dinitz. "Persuasion from the Student's Perspective: Perry and Piaget." Paper presented at the CCCC Convention, Seattle, March 1989. ERIC ED 307 615. 12 pages

Claims that Perry's and Piaget's theories of cognitive development can help explain students' choices and behaviors in writing persuasive papers.

1397. Kinkead, Joyce. *"Tack Sa Mychket:* Teaching in Stockholm." *UEJ* (1989): 7–9.

A Fulbright Scholar describes her teaching of freshman composition at the University of Stockholm.

1398. Kline, Nancy. "Intertextual Trips: Teaching the Essay in the Composition Class." *JTW* 8 (Fall-Winter 1989): 15–38.

Offers a close reading of three professional and three student texts to emphasize pleasure for writer and reader. Sets a goal of sensing "the essay as a living document."

1399. Kraemer, Don. "Enthymemes and Feminist Discourse: Mediating Public and Private Identity." *FEN* 18 (Fall 1989): 37–40.

Discusses the enthymeme from a feminist perspective, giving an example of its use in class.

1400. Kremers, Carolyn. "Through the Eyes and Ears of Another Culture: Invention Activities and a Writers' Workshop." *ExEx* 35 (Fall 1989): 3–11.

A series of freewriting exercises and group work enables students to explore other cultures.

1401. Laib, Nevin K. "Good Writing Cannot Be Taught Effectively as an Empty Collection of Rules." *CHE* 35 (5 July 1989): A36.

Debunks the folklore on how to teach writing and decries prejudice from the academic community toward composition teachers and writing programs.

1402. Laib, Nevin K. "Good Writing Cannot Be Taught Effectively as an Empty Collection of Rules." *CompC* 2 (September 1989): 4–5

Current criticism of freshman composition reveals a "misunderstanding of the nature of rhetoric." Reprinted from *CHE* 35 (5 July 1989).

1403. Lofty, John. "Bridging High School and College Writing." *FEN* 18 (Fall 1989): 26–27, 30–31.

Describes a questionnaire given to freshmen to help them probe high school writing experiences before writing an initial course essay on the topic.

1404. Lotto, Edward. "Utterance and Text in Freshman English." *CE* 51 (November 1989): 677–687.

Argues that metalinguistic awareness is essential to fostering attention to text. Gives practical suggestions.

1405. Magistrale, Tony. "Tracing the Narrative 'I': Using a Prose Model as a Guide to Student Writing." *CEAF* 19 (1989): 2–3.

Defends the use of prose models that novice writers study while composing their own pieces.

1406. MaHood, James. "Motivating Writing through Experiences of Creativity." *DAI* 50 (September 1989): 651A.

Reports more positive attitudes, improved writing, and increased self-esteem when creativity theory and writing were combined in a freshman composition class.

1407. Majied, Mahasin Halima. "The Language Content in Selected College English Textbooks." *DAI* 50 (September 1989): 691A.

Attempts to provide objective standards for assessing language and linguistic content in textbooks and courses of study.

1408. McCarthy, John Augustine. "Freshman Writers and Word Processors: Case Studies in the Revision Practices of College Composition Students." *DAI* 50 (December 1989): 1584A.

Explores the role of computers in altering the revising practices and writing strategies of 11 freshman composition students.

1409. McCotter, Kathryn. "Creative Spelling Exercise." *ExEx* 34 (Spring 1989): 6–7.

Offers three writing assignments in which students create new spellings in advertisements, poetry, and dialogue.

1410. McGinnis, Jo K. D. "Computers in Composition at the University of Arizona." *DAI* 50 (November 1989): 1128A.

Demonstrates how one composition program has successfully integrated computers into the curriculum.

1411. Merrifield, Susan Ruth. "Readin' and Writin' for the Hard-Hat Crowd: The Introductory English Curriculum at the University of Massachusetts at Boston, 1965–1985." *DAI* 50 (October 1989): 866A.

Examines the evolution of the introductory English curriculum, which evolved from a four-semester introduction to classic literature to two semesters of writing practice.

1412. Meyer, Charles. "Functional Grammar and Its Application in the Composition Classroom." *JTW* 8 (Fall-Winter 1989): 147–168.

Advocates using basic rules as well as syntactic, semantic, and prosodic principles in teaching punctuation. Suggests operational tests for punctuation marks.

1413. Moore, Ellen E. "Writing for an Audience." *ExEx* 35 (Fall 1989): 25–26.

Explains an assignment that requires students to write an article modeling a popular periodical style.

1414. Neil, Lynn Riley. "Teacher-Student Writing Conferences as an Intervention in the Revision Practices of College Freshmen." *DAI* 50 (December 1989): 1547A.

Assesses the impact of teacher-student conferences on the revision practices of six college freshmen of average English ability.

1415. Nelson, Jennie Lee. "Examining the Practices That Shape Student Writing: Two Studies of College Freshmen Writing across the Disciplines." *DAI* 49 (June 1989): 3638A.

One study examines how freshmen interpret writing assignments; a second study, how they responded to an extended writing-to-learn task.

1416. O'Hearn, Carolyn. "Recognizing the Learning-Disabled College Writer." *CE* 51 (March 1989): 294–304.

Discusses how college composition teachers may recognize learning disabilities through students' writing.

1417. Olson, Lyle D. "The Effect of Newswriting Instruction in English Composition I on the Writing Performance and Attitudes of Students." *DAI* 50 (July 1989): 89A.

Examines the effects of one-half semester's newswriting instruction compared to traditional composition instruction.

1418. Palmer, William Worden. "Awareness of Writing/Thinking/Learning: Interconnections for College Freshmen." *DAI* 50 (September 1989): 640A.

Analyzes ways of developing, using, and teaching awareness.

1419. Parmeter, Sarah-Hope. "Writing in the Real World: Homophobia Versus Community in the Composition Classroom." Paper presented at the CCCC Convention, Seattle, March 1989. ERIC ED 303 824. 8 pages

Reports on assignments eliciting first-person narratives from gay, lesbian, and minority students.

1420. Pebworth, Ted-Larry. "*Paradise Lost* and Freshman Composition." *CEAF* 19 (1989): 10–12.

Describes a writing course with Milton as a text.

1421. Peoples, Peg. "Developing a Position Statement in the Collaborative Classroom." *ExEx* 34 (Spring 1989): 3–5.

Explains a group exercise that prepares students to see both sides of an issue when writing argumentative essays.

1422. Pitts, Mary Ellen. "Discovery of the Self through the Writing Process: Autobiography as a Heuristic Identity." Paper presented at the CCCC Convention, St. Louis, March 1988. ERIC ED 297 362. 16 pages

Proposes approaching autobiography in Barthes's sense of textuality so that it can provide a model for discovering one's identity.

1423. Raign, Kathryn Rosser. "*Stasis* Theory Revisited: An Inventional *Techne* for Empowering Students." *Focuses* 2 (Spring 1989): 19–26.

Suggests that classical *stasis* questions are useful for students' prewriting explorations.

1424. Raymond, Richard C. "Teaching Students to Revise: Theories and Practice." *TETYC* 16 (February 1989): 49–58.

Offers advice and sample assignments for helping students move from rewriting to revision.

1425. Redd-Boyd, Theresa M., and Wayne H. Slater. "The Effects of Audience Specification on Undergraduates' Attitudes, Strategies, and Writing." *RTE* 23 (February 1989): 77–108.

Finds that assigning a specific audience significantly enhances writers' "interest, effort, and use of audience-based strategies," but not the persuasiveness of their writing.

1426. Rice, H. William. "Computers in Freshman English." *TETYC* 16 (February 1989): 29–34.

Describes a course structure for using computers to help teach revision.

1427. Ritchie, Joy S. "Beginning Writers: Diverse Voices and Individual Identity." *CCC* 40 (May 1989): 152–174.

Describes five factors contributing to dialogic writing workshops.

1428. Rose, Shirley K. "The Voice of Authority: Developing a Fully Rhetorical Definition of Voice in Writing." *WI* 8 (Spring 1989): 111–118.

Attempts a "rhetorically elaborate explanation" of assignment sequences based on cognitive development. Describes writing tasks in terms of how writers negotiate authority.

1429. Rosu, Anca. "Pragmatics and the Teaching of Writing." Paper presented at the CCCC Convention, St. Louis, March 1988. ERIC ED 297 322. 10 pages

Argues that writing teachers need to accept as much as offer. They need to become more receptive readers, allowing the student's identity to grow.

1430. Schriner, Delores K. "Theory into Practice: A Critical Literacy Curriculum for NAU." *ArEB* 31 (Spring 1989): 6–10.

Describes a funded project to restructure freshman composition around critical literacy.

1431. Schriner, Delores K., and William C. Rice. "Computer Conferencing and Collaborative Learning: A Discourse Community at Work." *CCC* 40 (December 1989): 472–479.

Reports that computer conferencing promotes collaborative learning and the formation of communities of writers.

1432. Shedletsky, Len. *Meaning and Mind: An Interpersonal Approach to Human Communication.* Annandale, Va.: SCA, 1989. 117 pages

Discusses the role the mind plays in communication. Designed to help students explore their thought processes and gain greater insight into their communications.

1433. Shen, Fan. "The Classroom and the Wider Culture: Identity as a Key to Learning English Composition." *CCC* 40 (December 1989): 459–465.

Examines ideological and logical clashes between Chinese identity and an identity "dictated by the rules of English composition."

1434. Sirc, Geoffrey. "Gender and 'Writing Formations' in First-Year Narratives." *FEN* 18 (Fall 1989): 4–11.

Analyzes male and female writing in freshman narratives, constructing a sociological-psychological explanation.

1435. Smelcer, John E. "A Round-Robin Creative Writing Exercise." *ExEx* 34 (Spring 1989): 8–9.

Three student groups write respectively the beginning, middle, and end for a story, each section having been started by the reader.

1436. Spaulding, Cheryl L. "The Effects of Ownership Opportunities and Instructional Support on High School Students' Writing Task Engagement." *RTE* 23 (May 1989): 139–162.

Investigates how two factors—ownership opportunities and instructional support—affect student writers' sense of engagement with the writing task. Instructional support wins.

1437. Spellmeyer, Kurt. "A Common Ground: The Essay in the Academy." *CE* 51 (March 1989): 262–276.

Argues that, both by studying essay conventions and by allowing the self to emerge in their texts, students will write better and learn more.

1438. Spellmeyer, Kurt. "Foucault and the Freshman Writer: Considering the Self in Discourse." *CE* 51 (November 1989): 715–729.

Represents Foucault as emphasizing discontinuity rather than coherence. Illustrates with two contrasting students' texts.

1439. Stanley, Linda C. "Misreading Students' Journals for Their Views of Self and Society." *JBW* 8 (Spring 1989): 21–31.

Explains how deconstructive "misreading" helps students "confront . . . oppositions with which we all live and . . . work toward a moral language that will begin to dissolve them."

1440. Stone, Judy. "The Good-Bye Paper: A Dip into the Rain Barrel." *ExEx* 35 (Fall 1989): 32–35.

Presents a guided memory writing assignment about a time when the student had to say good-bye to someone.

1441. Sunstein, Bonnie, and Philip M. Anderson. "Metaphor, Science, and the Spectator Role: An Approach for Nonscientists." *TETYC* 16 (February 1989): 9–16.

Students read the work of science writers and learn to write metaphorically. Includes sample assignments.

1442. Thompson, Diane P. "Using a Local Area Network to Teach Computer Revision Skills." *JTW* 8 (Fall-Winter 1989): 77–86.

Students detect textual problems, negotiate revisions, and learn computer commands for revision. Examines partial texts for revisions that add, delete, substitute, and reorder.

1443. Thomson, Lynn M. "Mythomanics: A Painless Dictionary and Vocabulary Skills Builder." *ExEx* 34 (Spring 1989): 36–38.

Explains a variation on the Balderdash game in which groups of students submit and later vote on the definitions of unusual words.

1444. Tobin, Lad. "Bridging Gaps: Analyzing Our Students' Metaphors for Composing." *CCC* 40 (December 1989): 444–458.

Suggests that metaphor can be used to help students and teachers describe and communicate their experience of the writing process.

1445. Tremmel, Robert. "Investigating Productivity and Other Factors in the Writer's Practice." *FEN* 17 (Spring 1989): 19–25.

Reports on initial research into the impact of regular writing practice in writing courses.

1446. Tritt, Michael, and Nick J. Aversa. "Reclaiming the Essay: A Tentative Voice in Student Writing." *Focuses* 2 (Fall 1989): 67–76.

Offers approaches for shifting students away from "simplistic solutions," a "dogmatic tone," and a "self-satisfied voice" in essay writing.

1447. Vatalaro, Paul A. "Blending Shelley with Shor: A Romanticist Finds Harmony in Composition." *ArEB* 31 (Spring 1989): 11–13.

Describes the "idiosyncratic" Rhetoric 101 class taught by a Shelley specialist.

1448. Vipond, Dianne. "Activating the Visual Imagination through Guided Imagery." *ExEx* 35 (Fall 1989): 39–42.

Explains a prewriting exercise.

1449. York, Lamar. "In Defense of the Five-Paragraph Essay." *CEAF* 19 (1989): 16–17.

Expresses appreciation for the traditional formula.

See also 34, 52, 188, 1092, 1348, 1361, 1717, 1742, 1840

4.2.3 ADVANCED COMPOSITION

1450. Dickerson, Mary Jane. " 'Shades of Deeper Meaning': On Writing Autobiography." *JAC* 9 (1989): 135–150.

Because autobiography is a sophisticated genre involving the social creation of the self, dialogic interaction, and self-knowledge, the genre is particularly appropriate for advanced composition.

1451. Hilligoss, Susan. "Preoccupations: Private Writing and Advanced Composition." *JAC* 9 (1989): 124–134.

Describes an advanced writing course in which students studied and wrote about their past private writings.

1452. Reagan, Sally Barr. "Less Is More: Engaging Students in Learning." *JTW* 8 (Spring-Summer 1989): 41–50.

Describes assignments to foster decentered classrooms. Results are less apprehension, more fluency, and changed attitudes and processes.

See also 195, 196, 1398, 1735

4.2.4 BUSINESS COMMUNICATION

1453. Abrate, Jayne. "Techniques of Teaching Business Correspondence in French." Paper presented at the Eastern Michigan University Conference on Languages for Business and the Professions, Ann Arbor, April 1988. ERIC ED 304 929. 17 pages

Describes a method that introduces students to the functions of various formats for French letters. Discusses the cultural ramifications of style, word choice, and tone.

1454. Andera, Frank. "Voice Input to Computers: How Will It Affect the Teaching of Business Communication?" *BABC* 52 (December 1989): 18–20.

Explains why business communication instructors should introduce students to dictation skills as they work on writing projects.

1455. Arnold, Vanessa Dean. "A 25-Year Perspective on the Pedagogy of Business Communication." *BABC* 52 (September 1989): 3–6.

Reviews trends in business communication as seen in publications of the ABC since 1963.

1456. Barbour, Dennis H. "The Practice Assignment." *BABC* 52 (March 1989): 23–24.

Describes a case used as a first assignment in a business writing course.

1457. Becker, Susan. "My Favorite Assignment: Feedback." *BABC* 52 (September 1989): 22–24.

Describes a business communication assignment in which students give the instructor feedback through memos.

1458. Beebee, David D. "Type Rites: Rhetoric and Reality in an Introductory Typewriting Classroom within a Context of Ritual." *DAI* 49 (April 1989): 2902A.

A narrative on the typewriting class as ritual.

1459. Bowman, Joel P., Bernadine P. Branchaw, and Thomas J. Welsh. "The Application of Behavioral Techniques to Business Communication Instruction." *JBC* 26 (Fall 1989): 323–346.

Evaluates common methods of teaching writing. Proposes a course built on behavioral strategies using clearly defined objectives. Pre- and posttesting showed the course to be effective.

1460. Brownell, Judi. "The Radial Model: An Integrated Approach to In-House Communication Training." *BABC* 52 (March 1989): 3–10.

Describes a model for training in organizational communication, including business writing skills.

1461. Burgar, Maria. "No Footnotes Necessary." *BABC* 52 (March 1989): 32–35.

Discusses reasons for community college students' difficulties in writing courses. Suggests strategies for motivating them through assignments relevant to their careers.

1462. Caprio, Anthony. "Translation Training for the Professions: A Model for Program Development and Administration." Paper presented at the Eastern Michigan University Conference on Languages for Business and the Professions, Ann Arbor, April 1988. ERIC ED 304 921. 13 pages

Describes a model program for training translators for the professions offered at the American University. Provides suggestions for adapting the model.

1463. Cortese, Joanne G. "Computer Applications in Teaching Business and Professional Writing Courses in Four-Year Colleges: Research Suggesting Curricular Changes." *BABC* 52 (December 1989): 3–5.

Reviews literature covering general and specific uses for computers in business communication courses.

1464. Cross, Geoffrey A. "Conflict and Capitulation: A Bakhtinian Analysis of a Failed Collaboration." Paper presented at the CCCC Convention, Seattle, March 1989. ERIC ED 307 623. 24 pages

Finds that the interaction and changing alignment of various socially rooted forces may determine the outcome of a collaborative writing project in business.

1465. DuFrene, Debbie D., and Beverly H. Nelson. "Selecting Word-Processing Software for Business Communication Classes." *BABC* 52 (December 1989): 6–8.

Presents a decision model with six criteria to help instructors choose appropriate software.

1466. Dukes, Thomas. "Business Writing and the Loss of the University." *CEAF* 19 (1989): 3–5.

Argues that business and technical writing courses can be liberating if they teach students to investigate and analyze their chosen careers.

1467. Dukes, Thomas. "I Uphold the Patriarchy in My Business Communication Classes—Why Can't I Stop?" *BABC* 52 (March 1989): 38–41.

Discusses three areas in which ingrained cultural sexism is found in business communication classes.

1468. Ewald, Helen Rothschild, and Virginia McCallum. "The Performance Appraisal: A Crucial Business Process and Product." *BABC* 52 (September 1989): 39–47.

Discusses the need for instruction in writing performance appraisals. Presents strategies for writing these documents.

1469. Flatley, Marie E. "Finding Experts Online." *BABC* 52 (December 1989): 16.

Explains the benefits of students' using database searches for their writing projects.

1470. Freed, Richard C., and David D. Roberts. "The Nature, Classification, and Generic

Structure of Proposals." *JTWC* 19 (1989): 317–351.

Posits functional systems for classifying all proposals. Suggests a generic structure for proposals to eliminate current confusion about how to teach proposal writing.

1471. Gates, Rosemary L. "An Academic and Industrial Collaboration on Course Design." *JBTC* 3 (September 1989): 78–87.

This flexible community-based course was taught by both university and business professionals.

1472. Gengler, Barb, and Cindy Johanek. "Munchkin Madness: Creating a Real Discourse Community." *WLN* 14 (December 1989): 3–6.

Cites nine writing skills, seven behavioral skills, and eight business-related skills acquired by participants in creating an enterprise. Lists 20 possible enterprises.

1473. Gieselman, Robert D. "Business Communication as an Academic Discipline." *Issues* 2 (Fall-Winter 1989): 20–35.

Seeks to define a "more precise domain" for business communication as a separate academic unit outside of English departments and business schools.

1474. Hagge, John. "The Spurious Paternity of Business Communication Principles." *JBC* 26 (Winter 1989): 33–55.

Rejects the view that business communication principles date from about 1910. Identifies similar principles in books published in 1876 as well as in the 2,000-year-old epistolographic tradition.

1475. Hagge, John. "Ties That Bind: Ancient Epistolography and Modern Business Communication." *JAC* 9 (1989): 26–44.

Major principles of business communication—including audience adaptation, clarity, conciseness, and genres—have striking parallels in Greek and Roman epistolography.

1476. Hall, John D. "Communication Apprehension and Learning." *BABC* 52 (June 1989): 6–7.

Presents the results of a study of the relationship between learning and students' communication apprehension in report writing classes.

1477. Harris, Hilda. "Teaching Dictation Skills." *BABC* 52 (December 1989): 17.

Describes an assignment in dictation that helps students sharpen writing skills.

1478. Insley, Robert G. "Integrating Style-Analysis Software into the Basic Business Communication Course." *BABC* 52 (December 1989): 8–11.

Discusses the advantages, disadvantages, and pedagogical implications of software that checks style and grammar.

1479. Irvine, Christine M. "Integration of Microcomputers in Collegiate Written Business Communication Courses." *DAI* 49 (April 1989): 2903A.

Finds no relationship between the age of teachers and their use of available microcomputers or between the numbers of students and their use of available microcomputers.

1480. Jarboe, Susan. "Teaching Communication Consulting and Training; or, Reminiscences of a Trainer." *SCJ* 55 (Fall 1989): 22–41.

Presents a course structure and major assignments. Discusses ethical considerations.

1481. Kallendorf, Craig, and Carol Kallendorf. "Aristotle and the Ethics of Business Communication." *JBTC* 3 (January 1989): 54–69.

Extends the *ethos-logos-pathos* paradigm into an "indeterminate" world where ethical strategies are problematical but where rhetorical scrutiny can advance discourse toward probable truth and responsible action.

1482. Kogen, Myra, ed. *Writing in the Business Professions*. Urbana, Ill.: NCTE and ABC, 1989. ERIC ED 303 816. 313 pages

Fourteen articles trace changes in the field of business communication over the past 20 years. Four sections: Process in Professional Writing; Writing in Corporations, Government, the Law, and Academia; Teaching Professional Writing; and Surveying Professional Writing Programs.

1483. Kostelnick, Charles. "Training in Context: Using Participants' Writing in Short-Term Seminars." *BABC* 52 (March 1989): 14–16.

Discusses methods for using students' writing to provide rhetorical contexts in a one-day writing seminar for state employees.

1484. Long, Jay E. "A Study of the Effect of Individually Guided Instruction and Traditional Instruction on Achievement of College Level Business Communication Students in the Basic Writing Skills." *DAI* 50 (October 1989): 857A.

Results indicate a positive relationship between posttest scores and English placement scores. The method of instruction was not a significant factor in writing skills achievement.

1485. Mehaffy, Robert, and Constance Warloe. "Corporate Communications: Next Step for the Community Colleges?" *TWT* 16 (Winter 1989): 1–11.

Outlines a process for community involvement in the design of professional writing courses within a community college curriculum.

1486. Miller, Mary L. "A Comparison of Fourth-Generation Language Usage in Fortune 500 Companies and Collegiate Information System Curricula." *DAI* 49 (April 1989): 2904A.

Finds that companies use vendor-supplied training in fourth-generation language more often than university training.

1487. Moore, Patrick. "Using the Front Page of *The Wall Street Journal* to Teach Document Design and Audience Analysis." *BABC* 52 (March 1989): 25–26.

Describes a business writing course assignment comparing *The Wall Street Journal* and the students' local daily newspaper.

1488. Pearce, C. Glenn, Wallace R. Johnston, and Donald W. Myers. "Communicating Truthfully and Positively in Appraising Work Performance." *BABC* 52 (September 1989): 48–51.

Presents a model for managers to use in communicating positively when evaluating employees' work.

1489. Reep, Diana C. "Report Writing for Social Workers: Special Needs in the Business Communication Course." *BABC* 52 (March 1989): 29–31.

Describes how report writing projects and special style considerations help prepare students to write court reports.

1490. Rockwood, Heidi M. "Teaching Business Letter Skills in a Business German Course on the Second-Year Level." Paper presented at the Eastern Michigan University Conference on Languages for Business and the Professions, Ann Arbor, April 1988. ERIC ED 304 935. 18 pages

Describes an approach to teaching business letter writing skills in German to second-year students with limited German language skills.

1491. Rogers, Priscilla S. "Choice-Based Writing in Managerial Contexts: The Case of the Dealer Contact Report." *JBC* 26 (Summer 1989): 197–216.

A study of 45 dealer contact reports for an auto company indicates that authors often ignored company rules about format and employed a situationally based narrative structure.

1492. Scheiber, H. J., and Peter J. Hager. "Strategic Planning in the Business Communication Classroom: A Model for Collaborative

Analytical Report Writing." *Issues* 1 (Spring 1989): 134–148.

Describes a classroom simulation of "corporate strategic planning" in which teams of students perform varied business-oriented transactional writing activities.

1493. Sheppard, Sharon. "The Informational Interview as a Tool for Sharpening Oral, Written, and Interviewing Skills." *BABC* 52 (June 1989): 19–20.

Describes an interview assignment and related oral and written follow-up assignments.

1494. Shipley, Margaret F. "Evaluating a Writing across the Curriculum Model Applied to Production/Operations Management in a University School of Business." *BABC* 52 (September 1989): 32–38.

Describes a group project that simulates the problem-solving method used by production/operations management analysts. Evaluating the project is also discussed.

1495. Southard, Sherry. "Institutional Politics: The Rhetoric of the Upward Bound." Paper presented at the CCCC Convention, Seattle, March 1989. ERIC ED 303 829. 14 pages

Discusses the need to inform students in business writing courses of the protocol of corporate culture.

1496. Speck, Bruce W. "Ethics: A Bridge for Studying the Social Contexts of Professional Communication." *JBTC* 3 (January 1989): 70–88.

Shows how teachers of professional communication can use Kohlberg's hierarchical model of moral development in a unit on business ethics based on case studies and simulations.

1497. Spinrad, Phoebe S. "The In-Basket: Real-World Teaching for a Real-World Task." *JBTC* 3 (January 1989): 89–99.

Argues for and illustrates a whole-environment approach to teaching the in-basket assignment.

1498. Stitt, Wanda L. "Dealing with Bias in Business Communication." *BABC* 52 (March 1989): 36–38.

Discusses six forms of bias and how they affect instruction in business communication.

1499. Sturges, David L. "Business Communication Writing and Computer-Aided Small Group Interaction." *BABC* 52 (December 1989): 12–15.

Explains the advantages of having students work collaboratively in using computers in business communication classes.

1500. Waltman, John L., and Steven P. Golen. "Effective Managerial Communication through Employee Newsletters." *JBTC* 3 (January 1989): 100–107.

Focuses on both the needs and roles of management and editors in development and production.

1501. Walzer, Arthur E. "The Ethics of False Implicature in Technical and Professional Writing Courses." *JTWC* 19 (1989): 149–160.

Through an analysis of a hypothetical proposal intended to mislead, argues that the ethical implications of particular rhetorical techniques should be addressed in the writing center.

1502. Weiss, Timothy. "A Process of Composing with Computers." *CC* 6 (April 1989): 45–59.

Describes an adaptation of computers to composing in a business and technical writing course.

1503. Wiegand, Richard. "Negative Adult Student Behavior in Consulting Classes in Business." *BABC* 52 (March 1989): 10–13.

Discusses problems in motivating employees to take business communication training classes in their organizations.

1504. Wong, Irene F. H., and Dorothy Cheung. "Improving Communication Skills through a Call Grammar Program." *BABC* 52 (December 1989): 22–28.

Describes Gramskil, a computer program designed to help business communication students improve their grammar.

1505. Zorn, Theodore E. "The Professor as Entrepreneur: The Challenges of Teaching the Organizational Communication Assessment Class." *BABC* 52 (September 1989): 16–21.

Identifies problems in teaching organizational communication assessment courses and offers strategies to meet these problems.

See also 4, 9, 14, 30, 32, 112, 465, 466, 791, 1536, 1537, 1541, 1553, 1641, 1653, 1699, 1797, 1804, 1820, 1844

4.2.5 SCIENTIFIC AND TECHNICAL COMMUNICATION

1506. Alexander, Lori L. "Cicero's Arrangement in Scientific Writing." *Issues* 2 (Fall-Winter 1989): 72–91.

Argues that classical rhetoric can help scientific writers write more persuasively and can be more useful in training students in technical and scientific communication.

1507. Allen, Jo. "The Question Isn't 'Could' but 'Should': The Case against Using Fiction in the Introductory Technical Writing Case." *TWT* 16 (Fall 1989): 210–219.

Argues that using literary examples in the technical writing class shortchanges both technical and literary genres, not legitimately presenting either.

1508. Allen, Jo. "The Student-Industry Link: Publicizing New Programs in Technical Communication." *TETYC* 16 (December 1989): 242–249.

Offers ideas for advertising new programs and encouraging student professionalism.

1509. Barker, Thomas T. "Word Processors and Invention in Technical Writing." *TWT* 16 (Spring 1989): 126–135.

Argues that word processors are more than revising tools. Suggests that collaborative writing, templates, and on-screen outlining capabilities enhance invention.

1510. Benson, Philippa J. "The Expanding Scope of Document Design." *TC* 36 (November 1989): 352–355.

Describes changes that have occurred in defining document design and anticipates future changes.

1511. Bishop, Wendy. "Revising the Technical Writing Class: Peer Critiques, Self-Evaluation, and Portfolio Grading." *TWT* 16 (Winter 1989): 13–25.

Advocates adding peer critiques, self-evaluation, and portfolio grading to technical writing classes as methods for enhancing writers' personal growth and focusing on content as well as form.

1512. Braine, George. "Writing in Science and Technology: An Analysis of Assignments from 10 Undergraduate Courses." *ESP* 8 (1989): 3–15.

Reports on a study of 61 writing assignments from 10 undergraduate science and technology courses. Classifies the assignments according to task and audience specifications, giving pedagogical recommendations.

1513. Carr, Janet H. "Technology and the English Teacher." *Leaflet* 88 (Fall 1989): 16–18.

Describes a program in which engineering students engaged in process writing for lab reports and for an extensive paper satisfying the third-year writing requirement.

1514. Charney, Davida H., and Jack R. Rayman. "The Role of Writing Quality in Effective Student Resumes." *JBTC* 3 (January 1989): 36–53.

Eighteen recruiters' ratings of 72 fictitious mechanical engineering resumes suggest that rhetorical sophistication and writing quality can be more important than job experience.

1515. Chytil, Helena. "The Final Step: Perfecting a Document." *TC* 36 (February 1989): 53–56.

Describes a systematic approach to eliminating errors.

1516. Curry, Jerome. "Introducing Realism into the Technical Definition Assignment." *TWT* 16 (Spring 1989): 123–125.

Outlines a process for teaching effective definitions by using writing groups and professionally written documents in which definitions of technical terms have been deleted.

1517. Curry, Jerome. "Teaching Technical Writing Students to Define." *TC* 36 (April 1989): 157–159.

Describes assignments intended to teach students how to write brief and extended definitions for both general and specialized audiences.

1518. Duin, Ann Hill. "Factors That Influence How Readers Learn from Text: Guidelines for Structuring Technical Documents." *TC* 36 (April 1989): 97–101.

Analyzes the complex act of reading and offers research-based advice to help technical writers design better documents.

1519. Dukes, Thomas. "Notes from a Technical Writing Institute: Preparing Technical Writers for the 'Real World'—and Other Nonsense." *TWT* 16 (Spring 1989): 153–154.

Argues that a broad general background is a primary ingredient for success as a technical writer. Technical writing courses are not sufficient by themselves.

1520. Durfee, Patricia B. "Writing to Learn in Technical Writing." *CollT* 37 (Winter 1989): 8–11.

Describes a course to increase students' practice in critical thinking. A structured journal helped students respond to, analyze, and organize writing assignments.

1521. Estrin, Herman A. "An American Technical Writing Teacher at the University of Paris." *TETYC* 16 (October 1989): 202–205.

A teacher spends two weeks teaching physics and chemical engineering students in France.

1522. Fearing, Bertie E., and W. Keats Sparrow, eds. *Technical Writing: Theory and Practice*. New York: MLA, 1989. 170 pages

A collection of essays examines current issues in the field. Focuses on the history and theory of technical writing, its process, its product, and its teaching. Compares technical writing in the academy and in industry. Authors are not indexed separately in this volume.

1523. Floreak, Michael J. "Designing for the Real World: Using Research to Turn a 'Target Audience' into Real People." *TC* 36 (November 1989): 373–381.

Describes a communication design project that used audience feedback methods throughout the process of planning, writing, and revising.

1524. Garay, Mary Sue. "Clinic Case: A Case to Elicit Point-Making during Revision of Survey-Based Reports." *TWT* 16 (Spring 1989): 155–168.

Argues that this case study helps students learn the necessity of using their own experience to give meaning to the numerical data in the assignment.

1525. Harmon, Joseph E. "Development of the Modern Technical Article." *TC* 36 (February 1989): 33–38.

Discusses the origins and evolution of the format, style, and content of the contemporary research paper.

1526. Haselkorn, Mark P. "From On-Line Documentation to Intuitive Interfaces: Technical Communicators Join the Design Team." *JTWC* 19 (1989): 357–370.

"As user advocate, usability tester, screen designer, and on-line documentation specialist," the technical communicator now plays a role in all phases of software and hardware development.

1527. Hilbert, Betsy. "A Response to Turpin's 'New Lamps for Old' [*WE* 1 (Fall 1989)]." *WE* 1 (Fall 1989): 97–98.

Praises Turpin's essay as a valuable corrective to narrow academic prejudice.

1528. Horowitz, Renee B. "Decision Analysis: A Foolproof Way to Avoid Research Regurgitation." *TWT* 16 (Spring 1989): 115–118.

Outlines an instructional method for analyzing audience needs and developing recommendations to management that are audience-centered.

1529. Karis, William M. "Using Literature to Focus Attention: Rhetorical Models and Case Studies." *TWT* 16 (Fall 1989): 187–194.

Argues that literature offers models for students to emulate and that case studies, a standard technical writing course pedagogy, are variant forms of fiction.

1530. Keeler, Heather. "A Writer's Readers: Who Are They and What Do They Want?" *TC* 36 (February 1989): 8–12.

Describes methods for classifying readers and identifying approaches that appeal to them.

1531. Killingsworth, M. Jimmie. "How to Talk about Professional Communication: Metalanguage and Heuristic Power." *JBTC* 3 (January 1989): 117–125.

Calls for a metalanguage based on grammatical, not moralistic or imported, terminology.

1532. Killingsworth, M. Jimmie, Michael K. Gilbertson, and Joe Chew. "Amplification in Technical Manuals: Theory and Practice." *JTWC* 19 (1989): 13–29.

"Drawing on the theory of classical and modern rhetoric, this article shows how amplification tends to increase and improve" various aspects of technical manuals.

1533. Kostelnick, Charles. "Visual Rhetoric: A Reader-Oriented Approach to Graphics and Design." *TWT* 16 (Winter 1989): 77–88.

Details a model of visual communication that provides design criteria for students to use when analyzing and designing technical documents.

1534. Lay, Mary M. "Interpersonal Conflict in Collaborative Writing: What We Can Learn from Gender Studies." *JBTC* 3 (September 1989): 5–28.

Discusses self-disclosure, control, trust, perceptions of groups and of conflict, congruence, and reward as keys to potentially androgynous interpersonal skills.

1535. Malone, Elizabeth L. "More Than One Way to Skin a Cat: Divergent Approaches to the Same Writing Case." *TWT* 16 (Winter 1989): 27–32.

Demonstrates the relative effectiveness of four different approaches to solving a single case study.

1536. McGuire, Peter, and Sara Putzell. "Defining Problems That Call for Innovation." *JTWC* 19 (1989): 255–265.

Describes ways in which technical writers can write persuasive definitions of problems that require innovative solutions.

1537. Mendelson, Michael. "The Rhetorical Case: Its Roman Precedent and the Current Debate." *JTWC* 19 (1989): 203–266.

Surveys the discussion on the possibilities and problems associated with using problem-solving rhetorical cases in business and technical writing classrooms.

1538. Merrill, Lynn L. "Notes from the Other Side: The Strange Profession of Technical Writing." *BADE* 92 (Spring 1989): 25–29.

Describes differences between the worlds of literature and of technical writing. Recommends a course of study for English majors intending to be technical writers.

1539. Miles, Thomas H. " 'Have Them Read a Good Book': Enriching the Scientific and Technical Writing Curriculum." *TWT* 16 (Fall 1989): 221–232.

Suggests that technical writing students read books by leading scientists and engineers for human and practical relevance as well as technical relevance.

1540. Norman, Rose. "Patent Writing as a Heuristic for Teaching Technical Description." *JBTC* 3 (September 1989): 64–77.

Explains how patent specification can be taught, adapted, and used to structure writing assignments according to rhetorical context.

1541. Phelps, Lonnie D., and Debbie D. DuFrene. "Improving Organizational Communication through Text." *JTWC* 19 (1989): 267–276.

"Defines organizational trust, discusses its usefulness in minimizing and eliminating common communication barriers, and explains how organizational trust can be developed and improved."

1542. Plunka, Gene A. "Teaching Technical Writing with News Releases." *TWT* 16 (Spring 1989): 95–101.

Outlines teaching strategies for writing news releases and argues for incorporating them within the traditional technical writing curriculum.

1543. *Proceedings of the Thirty-Sixth International Technical Communication Conference.* San Diego: Univelt, 1989. 750 pages

A collection of papers presented in Chicago, May 1989. Subjects include advanced technology applications; management and professional development; research, education, and training; visual communication; and writing and editing. Authors are not indexed separately in this volume.

1544. "A Professor Uses Tinkertoys to Teach Technical Writing." *CHE* 36 (27 September 1989): A19.

David Carson of Rensselaer Polytechnic Institute counters the fear of technical topics by asking students to write manuals for

and give oral presentations on toy machines the class has designed and built.

1545. Rentz, Kathryn C. "Literary Genre Theory and the Teaching of Professional Writing Forms." *TWT* 16 (Fall 1989): 196–208.

Analyzes the similarities and differences between the genre-oriented approach normally found in technical writing textbooks and the rhetorical orientation of much contemporary literary theory.

1546. Rowan, Katherine E. "Moving beyond the *What* to the *Why:* Differences in Professional and Popular Science Writing." *JTWC* 19 (1989): 161–179.

Understanding different goals of professional and popular science writers can help us develop criteria for "analyzing and evaluating different uses of organization, graphics, and language."

1547. Sides, Charles H. "What Does Jung Have to Do with Technical Communication?" *TC* 36 (April 1989): 119–126.

Explains Jung's theory of psychological types and the Myers-Briggs Type Indicator. Argues that knowledge of these types can be useful in technical writing contexts.

1548. Spilka, Rachel. "The 'Audience Continuum.' " *TWT* 16 (Spring 1989): 147–152.

Argues that technical writing teachers should use a variety of pedagogical approaches, including the "audience continuum" for teaching audience awareness and audience analysis.

1549. Spilka, Rachel. "Interacting with Multiple Readers: A Significant Component of Document Design in Corporate Environments." *TC* 36 (November 1989): 368–372.

Summarizes an ethnographic study of engineers. Emphasizes the importance of oral communication in corporate culture and the need to recognize diverse audiences.

1550. Stratton, Charles R. "Anatomy of a Style Analyzer." *JTWC* 19 (1989): 119–134.

Explains how computerized style analyzers work and describes methods for evaluating the effectiveness of such programs.

1551. Sullivan, Patricia. "What Computer Experience to Expect of Technical Writing Students Entering a Computer Classroom: The Case of Purdue Students." *JTWC* 19 (1989): 53–68.

"Presents the results of a survey of Purdue University students' knowledge of, use of, and attitudes toward computers as they enter the technical writing class."

1552. *Technical Communication and Ethics.* Washington, D.C.: Society for Technical Communication, 1989. 120 pages

Collects 16 essays about ethics for technical communicators and teachers of technical communication. Includes five codes of ethics, developed by the 1958 Society for Technical Writers and Editors as well as the most recent Society for Technical Communication Code for Communicators. Authors are not indexed separately in this volume.

1553. *Technical Writing Processes.* Chico, Calif.: California State University—Chico.

An 18-minute videotape introduces students to technical and business writing processes by interviewing two technical writers and a marketing specialist.

1554. Thompson, Isabelle Kramer. "Cultural Literacy and the Auto Mechanic: Teaching Reading and Writing to Technical Students." *TETYC* 16 (February 1989): 43–48.

Finds ideas about cultural literacy inappropriate for technical students.

1555. Turpin, Elizabeth R. "New Lamps for Old: A Reevaluation of Technical Communication in the Context of Classical Rhetoric." *WE* 1 (Fall 1989): 87–96.

Argues that classical rhetoric provides a sound foundation for the concerns of technical communication: organization, style, persuasion, and social roles.

1556. Vaughn, Jeanette. "Sexist Language—Still Flourishing." *TWT* 16 (Winter 1989): 33–40.

Explores the problem of sexist language and discusses several methods for dealing with it.

1557. Veiga, Nancy E. "Sexism, Sex Stereotyping, and the Technical Writer." *JTWC* 19 (1989): 277–283.

Argues that, while technical writers should avoid sex stereotyping, they can use male and female stylistic traits to "improve the quality of their documents."

1558. Werner, Warren W. "Models and the Teaching of Technical Writing." *JTWC* 19 (1989): 69–81.

Defines the concept of model, describes ways in which students misuse models in a writing class, and suggests ways to help students use models more effectively.

1559. Werner, Warren W. "An RFP for Research Reports." *TWT* 16 (Spring 1989): 120–122.

Advocates this instructional tool as a method for facilitating students' transition from writing in school to writing on the job.

1560. *Writing for Survival.* Chico, Calif.: California State University—Chico, 1988.

A 28-minute videotape featuring interviews with a student engineer, an employer, and five professionals. Respondents discuss the importance of writing in their work. VHS format.

1561. Zeidner, Martin A. "Experts: What Are They?" *JTWC* 19 (1989): 241–244.

Discusses some of the problems and dangers associated with relying in scientific work on seeming expertise rather than on evidence.

1562. Zhang, Zaixin. "Is Scientific Research Part of Prewriting in the Scientific Writing Process?" *JTWC* 19 (1989): 285–296.

Writing researchers "should reassess the notion of the prewriting stage in the scientific writing process" as well as the usefulness of traditional heuristic procedures.

See also 14, 19, 30, 32, 286, 340, 446, 474, 785, 1466, 1470, 1471, 1501, 1502, 1645, 1671, 1740, 1769

4.2.6 WRITING IN LITERATURE COURSES

1563. Beauvais, Paul J. "The Reporter's Reading Method: Classroom Applications of a Self-Directed Reading System." *ExEx* 35 (Fall 1989): 17–21.

Provides a model that encourages students to rank the questions they have about a text.

1564. Desjardins, Linda A. "Is a Picture Really Worth a Thousand Words?" *Leaflet* 88 (Spring 1989): 31–38.

Describes an approach to using film in a composition and literature class. Includes all assignments for one short story on film.

1565. Geisler, Cheryl, and David S. Kaufer. "Making Meaning in Literate Conversation: A Teachable Sequence for Reflective Writing." *RSQ* 19 (Summer 1989): 229–244.

Presents a reading-writing sequence to encourage reflective features in students' writing.

1566. Gere, Ann Ruggles. "Composition and Literature: The Continuing Conversation." *CE* 51 (October 1989): 617–622.

Reviews four books offering "new ways to teach" and tries to establish connections between reading and writing instruction.

1567. Giroux, Henry A., and Harvey J. Kaye. "The Liberal Arts Must Be Reformed to Serve Democratic Ends." *CHE* 35 (29 March 1989): A44.

The authors promote arguments about a literary "canon" because they encourage students to develop critical faculties and to realize democratic principles.

1568. Greenwood, Scott C. "Summarize, Compare, Contrast, and Critique: Encouraging Active Reading through the Use of Cinema." *ExEx* 35 (Fall 1989): 22–24.

Explains four writing assignments that require students both to read the book and view the film.

1569. Hart, Francis Russell. *Literature in the Classroom: Teaching Students to Learn.* Columbus, Ohio: Ohio State University Press, 1989. 166 pages

Reflects on teaching experiences and shares pedagogical and curricular experiments in the teaching of literary texts and contexts.

1570. Hesse, Douglas. "Some Alternatives to Plot, Theme, and Setting: Social Construction and Critical Thinking." *IlEB* 76 (Winter 1989): 12–22.

Addresses issues involved in the problematizing of literature, suggesting alternative ways of teaching students to read, think, and write about literature.

1571. Keroes, Jo. "Half Someone Else's: Theories, Stories, and the Conversation of Literature." Paper presented at the CCCC Convention, Seattle, March 1989. ERIC ED 307 614. 26 pages

Claims that students should be invited into the process of storytelling in literature, "the story" being central to readers' involvement with a work of fiction.

1572. Martin, Bruce K. "Teaching Literature as Experience." *CE* 51 (April 1989): 377–385.

Asserts that "we read the text . . . as we read experience." Encourages teachers to resist defining literary meaning, thereby freeing students to be "true readers."

1573. McNeil, Lynda D. "Logging the Interpretive Act: Dialogical Interaction in the Literature Classroom." Paper presented at the CCCC Convention, St. Louis, March 1988. ERIC ED 297 369. 21 pages

Proposes using a log in literature classes, allowing students to make meaning and to share in the dialogue with the text and with peers.

1574. Nugent, Susan Monroe, and Harold E. Nugent. "Learning through Writing: The Double-Entry Journal in Literature Classes." *EQ* 21 (1989): 258–263.

Argues that writing in journals, sharing responses in small groups, participating in class presentations, and synthesizing results in a second journal constitute "the coming to know" process.

1575. Price, Jody L. "Teaching the American Dream." *Leaflet* 88 (Winter 1989): 22–26.

Lists texts and describes procedures for a one-semester literature course focusing on varied conceptions of the American Dream.

1576. Ryan, Frank L. "The Teacher as Rhetor: A Note on Humanistic Humanization in the Classroom." *Leaflet* 88 (Fall 1989): 2–9.

Explicates the author's use of *ethos, pathos,* and *logos* in bringing students to a literary work.

1577. Schwartz, Helen J. "Literacy Theory in the Classroom: Computers in Literature and Writing." *CC* 7 (November 1989): 49–63.

Shows how current software and hardware help students understand new ways of learning, create community among readers, and promote shared explorations of cultural contexts.

1578. Scriven, Karen. "Writing about Literature: Interpretation through Exposition." *TETYC* 16 (December 1989): 280–283.

Finds summarizing literary texts a useful composition exercise.

1579. Segreto, Anna. "Teachers, Leave Those Kids Alone." *JTW* 8 (Spring-Summer 1989): 31–40.

Students' written imaging of Eliot's "Prufrock" and Pink Floyd's "The Wall" led to original poems. "I let my students instruct me in their own lives."

1580. Smith, Eugene. "Shaping Literacy Response through Collaborative Writing." Paper presented at the CCCC Convention, Seattle, March 1989. ERIC ED 303 820. 13 pages

Offers a collaborative writing assignment for a college literature classroom. Includes the evaluations of 29 students.

1581. Smith, Maggy, and Peggy Salome. "Poetry as a Springboard to Critical Thinking." *ExEx* 35 (Fall 1989): 36–38.

Students create a new character from an existing poem and write a description and interior monologue of this person.

1582. Soven, Margot, and William M. Sullivan. *Exploratory Writing as a Resource for Cultural Literacy.* Bloomington, Ind.: ERIC/RCS, 1988. ERIC ED 300 806. 24 pages

Provides a series of assignments for a course on the contemporary novel that emphasizes exploratory writing.

1583. Spanos, William V. "Theory in the Undergraduate English Curriculum: Towards an Interested Pedagogy." *Boundary* 16 (Winter-Spring 1989): 41–70.

Treats the importance of interpretation and its relationship to theory, as presented through the various discourses of postmodern literary criticism.

1584. Taylor, Joanne. "Drama in the Classroom: Lady Macbeth Comes to Life!" *ExEx* 34 (Spring 1989): 24–26.

Explains how performing scenes can enhance students' appreciation of drama.

1585. Thompson, Diane P. "Introducing Adult Students to Writing about Literature." *TETYC* 16 (February 1989): 37–39.

Adult students learn to appreciate literature by writing lies, rewriting published stories, and creating poems. Then they move to analysis.

1586. Vatalaro, Paul. "Not Minding 'Forged Manacles': Putting Anxiety in Place for Writing about Poetry." *Leaflet* 88 (Fall 1989): 10–15.

Describes a sequence of writing activities from freewriting about poetry to writing a short critical essay about a specific poem.

1587. Waggener, Joseph. "Important Media Classics: Filmstrips, Tape Recorders, and Record Players." *MM* 25 (January–February 1989): 16–19, 66–67.

Describes teaching techniques that make use of media for subjects such as writing and poetry appreciation.

See also 1640

4.2.7 COMMUNICATION IN OTHER DISCIPLINES

1588. Ambron, Joanna Theresa. "Implementing Writing across the Curriculum: Strategies in the Biological Sciences." *DAI* 50 (August 1989): 339A.

Reports on the success of strategies such as journal writing, freewriting, microthemes, and clustering, as used in biology classes.

1589. Andersen, Susan McKinney. "The Composing Process and Speech Communication: An Examination of the Strategies of Six Successful Student Speakers." *DAI* 50 (August 1989): 300A.

Studies the composing processes of students preparing public speeches.

1590. Bacon, SusanEllen Nielsen. "Factors Predictive of Listening Improvement in College Students Enrolled in a Course of Listening and Learning." *DAI* 49 (April 1989): 2861A.

A study of 342 freshmen to determine factors predicting which students would benefit from a program in instructional listening. Results were inconclusive.

1591. Barnett, Octo. "Information Technology and Undergraduate Medical Education." *AM* 64 (April 1989): 187–190.

Identifies 11 areas to consider when integrating a computer-based information system into a curriculum.

1592. Cain, Mary Ann. "Examining Our Own Lenses: An Ethnographic Study of an Economics Classroom." Paper presented at the CCCC Convention, Seattle, March 1989. ERIC ED 307 613. 14 pages

Finds that writing instructors must be willing to examine their assumptions about other disciplines when investigating practices in writing across the curriculum.

1593. Colomb, Gregory C. "Where Should Students Start Writing in the Disciplines." Paper presented at the CCCC Convention, St. Louis, March 1988. ERIC ED 297 341. 15 pages

Proposes that all writing teachers be located in the disciplines since English department writing is only appropriate in English departments.

1594. Contreras, Victoria Martinez. "A Rationale for the Teaching of Spanish Composition to the Native Speaker at the College Level." *DAI* 50 (December 1989): 1583A.

Present arguments compiled from a survey of current teaching practices for establishing a one-semester writing course in Spanish composition for Spanish native speakers.

1595. Couch, Ruth. "Dealing with Objections to Writing across the Curriculum." *TETYC* 16 (October 1989): 193–196.

Counters fears that time will be wasted, students will be overwhelmed, assignments will be useless, or faculty in other areas will be unable to evalute writing.

1596. DeVolder, M. L., and W. S. de Grave. "Approaches to Learning in a Problem-Based Medical Programme: A Developmental Study." *MEd* 23 (May 1989): 262–264.

Problem-based learning encourages individuals to develop different kinds of learning strategies, even if instruction in "how to learn" is not provided.

1597. Dickey, John S. "On Science Education." *JCST* 19 (December 1989): 132–133, 143.

Suggests innovative ways to teach science, including writing to learn and using videotexts.

1598. Dinitz, Susan, and Diane Howe. "Writing Centers and Writing across the Curriculum: An Evolving Partnership." *WCJ* 10 (Fall-Winter 1989): 41–51.

Discusses three possible models. Training tutors as facilitators for peer group critiques is an economically feasible and pedagogically sound model for a writing across the curriculum program.

1599. Durrant, Karen R., and Charles R. Duke. "Developing Sensitivity to Audience: Connecting Theory and Practice." *TETYC* 16 (October 1989): 165–173.

Students employ Kroll's three perspectives on audience—social, rhetorical, and informational—in a creative writing class.

1600. Fischler, Alan. "From the Inferno: Reflections on a Sojourn in a Communication Program." *CHE* 35 (2 August 1989): A28.

A critical review of college communication courses such as interpersonal communication, which the author views as classes without content.

1601. Frantzen, Diana. "The Effects of Grammar Supplementation of Written Accuracy in an Intermediate Spanish Content Course." *DAI* 49 (April 1989): 2954A.

Finds that students in a content course supplemented with grammar instruction scored higher on a grammar-focused test than the control group did.

1602. Freeman, Mary G. "Medical Documentation: A Composition Concern for Now and the Nineties." Paper presented at the Southeast Regional Conference on English in the Two-Year College, Louisville, February 1988. ERIC ED 300 832. 14 pages

Discusses the use of medical documentation drawn from clinical experience in teaching writing skills to practicing nurses in two-year colleges.

1603. Fulwiler, Toby. "Programs for Change: Computers and Writing across the Curriculum." *CompC* 2 (December 1989): 8–10.

The author's experience writing on a word processor suggests how students in writing across the curriculum programs can benefit from using computers.

1604. Fulwiler, Toby, and Art Young. *Programs That Work: Models and Methods for Writing across the Curriculum.* Portsmouth. N.H.: Boynton/Cook, 1989. 336 pages

Examines 14 successful writing across the curriculum programs in American colleges and universities. Contributors are not indexed separately in this volume.

1605. Ganguli, Aparna B. "Integrating Writing in Developmental Mathematics." *CollT* 37 (Fall 1989): 140–142.

Reports on a study. When writing assignments were integrated into instructions, underprepared students received higher grades than students taught conventionally.

1606. Garson, G. David. "Integrating Word Processing and Databases to Enhance Student and Scholarly Writing." *CAC* 3 (Spring 1989): 79–91.

Describes integrated software designed for managing ideas and especially suited for writing in the social sciences.

1607. Griffin, Barbara J. "Writing across the Curriculum Techniques in the Computer Classroom." *CAC* 4 (Summer 1989): 1–7.

Explains how the ideal classroom for many courses other than composition provides access to a word processor for every student.

1608. Hering, Paul, Linda K. Gunzburger, Thomas Loesch, and Mary Langbein. "An Experiment Involving Reading Assignments in a Medicine Clerkship." *AM* 64 (March 1989): 168–169.

Describes a method of teaching third-year medical students by restricting the amount of reading and by having them keep reading logs.

1609. Hoffmann, Gregg. "Abstracting in the Newsmaking Process." *ETC* 46 (Winter 1989): 324–327.

Discusses ways to teach students about the selectivity of newswriting. Suggests further research into the effects of abstracting on reporting.

1610. Hurlow, Marica L. "Role for Mass Communication in Writing across the Curriculum." *JourEd* 44 (Summer 1989): 56–58.

Discusses the role journalism professors can play in supporting writing across the curriculum and how such programs can assist journalism students in writing to learn content.

1611. Jordan, Diane Martin, and Michael Moorhead. "Writing across the Curriculum: The Mentor Project." *TETYC* 16 (May 1989): 99–103.

A writing across the curriculum program pairs English instructors with other faculty members.

1612. Joyce, John. "Anaphora and the Contemporary Creative Writer." *CEAF* 19 (1989): 18–19.

Argues that classical rhetorical schemes can enliven students' unassigned creative writing.

1613. Kirsch, Gesa, De Ann C. Finkel, and Alan W. France. "Three Comments on 'Only One of the Voices: Dialogic Writing across the Curriculum' [*CE* 50 (April 1988)]." *CE* 51 (January 1989): 99–106.

Three respondents believe that English departments contain expert writing teachers, not teachers whose expertise is limited to the teaching of English department writing.

1614. Law, Richard G. "Improving Student Writing: An Institutional Approach." *Issues* 1 (Spring 1989): 120–133.

Describes "comprehensive institutional policies" and "new pedagogical techniques" adopted at Washington State University to address the problem of students' poor writing skills.

1615. Leahy, Richard. "Writing Centers and Writing-for-Learning." *WCJ* 10 (Fall-Winter 1989): 31–37.

Compares two goals of writing across the curriculum: improving transactional writing abilities and fostering writing-for-learning through expressive writing. Offers four suggestions for increasing the emphasis on the latter goal.

1616. Lesher, Tina Rodgers. "The Writing Coach Movement: Teaching Composition in a New Context." *DAI* 49 (April 1989): 2851A.

Examines the use of outside professionals to provide continuing education for staff at newspapers. Offers recommendations for writing teachers.

1617. Livingston, James B. "Reading into the Subject of Science: Strategies for a More Literate Class." *ST* 56 (February 1989): 49–50.

Suggests lab journals, written reports, and research papers as three of seven methods for increasing literacy instruction in science courses.

1618. Lovejoy, Kim B. "A Model for the Analysis of Cohesion and Information Management in Publishing Writing in Three Disciplines." *DAI* 49 (January 1989): 1787A.

Compares professional writings in psychology, biology, and history and argues that the proposed analytical model will aid teachers of writing across the curriculum.

1619. Lund, Donna J. "A Structural Approach to Integrating Write to Learn in All Disciplines." Paper presented at the CCCC Convention, Seattle, March 1989. ERIC ED 304 698. 17 pages

Describes the Writing across the Business Disciplines Program at Robert Morris College.

1620. Mahala, Daniel. "Writing Utopias: Visions of the Uses of Literacy." *DAI* 49 (June 1989): 3605A.

Examines a writing across the curriculum program at SUNY—Albany in light of the author's experience and the theories of Freire, Jameson, and Foucault.

1621. Mauermeyer, Carol K. "Writing across the Curriculum Intervention at One Community College: A Case Study of the Innovation-Decision Process." *DAI* 49 (April 1989): 2904A.

Uses Roger's innovation-decision stage model to analyze the behavior of individuals as they confront writing across the curriculum.

1622. McLeod, Susan H. "Writing across the Curriculum: The Second Stage and Beyond." *CCC* 40 (October 1989): 337–342.

Describes how writing across the curriculum programs have survived and changed. Speculates about their future.

1623. Medhurst, Martin J. "Rhetorical Criticism: Forensic Communication in the Written Mode." *ComEd* 38 (July 1989): 205–213.

Describes a seven-assignment sequence for teaching undergraduates how to write argumentative prose in rhetorical criticism courses.

1624. Michalak, Stanley J., Jr. "Writing More, Learning Less?" *CollT* 37 (Spring 1989): 43–45.

Presents assignments for a political science course. Because students' grades did not improve significantly, calls for more research on effective strategies.

1625. Mitchell, Felicia, ed. *Writing-to-Learn Terminology: Sourcebook for Instructors*. Alexandria, Va.: EDRS, 1989. ERIC ED 301 882. 21 pages

Defines 96 writing-to-learn terms.

1626. Moxley, Joseph M., ed. *Creative Writing in America: Theory and Pedagogy*. Urbana, Ill.: NCTE, 1989. 272 pages

Collects 23 essays that discuss classroom methods. Treats the need for avid reading; presents prewriting, revising, and editing strategies; and examines the creative process as well as fundamental aspects of the craft. An appendix outlines course requirements for American M.F.A. programs.

1627. Mulcahy, Patricia Irene. "Improving Comprehensibility of Computer Instructions: The Effect of Different Text Structures on Success in Performing Procedures." *DAI* 50 (July 1989): 125A.

Shows that novice users need explicit task rules, a goal statement, and a clearly defined task sequence to comprehend computer instructions.

1628. Olson, Lyle D. "Technical Writing Methods Show Ways to Consider Audience." *JourEd* 44 (Summer 1989): 3–6.

Discusses audience analysis and awareness. Identifies five audience types and presents ways to differentiate among them.

1629. Ostrom, Hans. "Creative Writing: The Unexamined Subject." *WE* 1 (Fall 1989): 55–64.

Argues for the importance of creative writing as a writing course in the undergraduate curriculum.

1630. Partridge, Elizabeth. "Language Arts Is Not a Subject: An Integrated Approach to Teaching Language Arts Methods." *Leaflet* 88 (Spring 1989): 44–49.

Describes a team-taught, 10-semester-hour course combining instruction in language arts, social sciences, science, music, and physical education methods.

1631. Pearce, R. Charles. "Right Writing or Writing Right for Creativity in Advertising." *JourEd* 44 (Summer 1989): 7–12.

Discusses five techniques to help students focus on getting ideas onto the page: warm-ups, loop writing, sharing, revision, editing, and group sharing.

1632. Perkowitz, Sidney. "Can Scientists Learn to Write?" *JTWC* 19 (1989): 353–356.

Describes ways in which a substantial writing component in a senior physics class was valuable for both students and teacher.

1633. Popken, Randall L. "Essay Exams and Papers: A Contextual Comparison." *JTW* 8 (Spring-Summer 1989): 51–66.

Sees differences between essay examinations and history and sociology papers in their pedagogical function, prompts, rhetorical function, mechanics, style, and organization. Concludes that the genres are complementary.

1634. Porter, William C. "Teaching of Editorial Writing Uses Claims-Based Analysis." *JourEd* 43 (Winter 1989): 32–37.

Describes how claims-based analysis can assist readers and writers to understand the writing process. Gives examples and descriptions of five types of claims.

1635. Reynolds, Jim. *Teaching Writing in an Interdisciplinary Context: One Experiment*. Bloomington, Ind.: ERIC/RCS, 1985. ERIC ED 307 603. 18 pages

Describes an experimental program at East Texas State University that emphasizes writing across the curriculum.

1636. Rose, Barbara Joan. "Using Expressive Writing to Support the Learning of Mathematics." *DAI* 50 (October 1989): 867A.

Results indicate that expressive writing was a significant ancillary component of this calculus class.

1637. Ryan, Frank L. "No Gene Is an Island: Analogical Relations between Science and Literature." *Leaflet* 88 (Spring 1989): 12–20.

Presents a series of analogies between scientific facts and literary passages.

1638. Sady, Michael. "Changing Student Demographics Should Inspire Curricular Innovation." *JCST* 19 (September–October 1989): 38–40.

Outlines a CAI program for nontraditional students to supplement low faculty-student contact time.

1639. Salas, Floyd. "The Sorrow and the Glory: Publishing Student Work." *CalE* 25 (November–December 1989): 12–13.

Describes a project in which creative writing students from Foothill College put together an anthology of their work and that of professional writers.

1640. Schroeder, Eric James. "An Interview with Toby Fulwiler: 'The Mechanism Is the Writing.' " *WE* 1 (Fall 1989): 7–15.

Fulwiler discusses workshops with faculty members in other disciplines, writing in a literature class, and the development of student-centered pedagogy.

1641. Smith, Margaret Ann. "Classroom Community: A Study of Writing, Social Context, and Classroom Discourse." *DAI* 50 (August 1989): 330A.

Examines the teacher's persona, the student's sense of audience, and changing perceptions toward writing in an introductory management class.

1642. Soriano, Joseph R. "Thinking through Writing: Thought Experiments in Physics." *ST* 56 (March 1989): 70–73.

Discusses sequenced writing assignments that encourage critical thinking and analysis in science classes.

1643. Sperling, Jon A. "Let Me Tell You a Story." *JCST* 18 (May 1989): 361–364.

Illustrates uses of narratives and coconuts to facilitate learning in large lecture courses.

1644. Stegner, Wallace. *On the Teaching of Creative Writing*. Edited by Edward Connery Lathem. Hanover, N.H.: University Press of New England, 1989. 72 pages

Describes being a writer and the special attitude that writing teachers need in highly charged classrooms.

1645. Stewart, Barbara Y. "Merging Scientific Writing with the Investigative Laboratory." *JCST* 19 (November 1989): 94–95.

Describes Swarthmore's writing-intensive biology laboratory courses that are team taught by biologists and writing consultants.

1646. Strauss, Michael, and Toby Fulwiler. "Writing to Learn in Large Lecture Classes." *JCST* 19 (December 1989): 158–163.

Discusses methods such as visualizing informal thought, keeping chemistry logs, and holding laboratory workshops on writing about the subject.

1647. Trombulak, Steve, and Sallie Sheldon. "The Real Value of Writing to Learn in Biology." *JCST* 18 (May 1989): 384–388.

Writing increases students' appreciation of science as well as improves performance.

1648. Turner, Judith Axler. "Math Professors Turn to Writing to Help Students Master Concepts of Calculus and Combinatorics." *CHE* 35 (15 February 1989): A1, A14.

Describes the work of several math professors who use writing across the curriculum techniques to teach math theory.

1649. Vittum, Henry E., and Robert S. Miller. "Psychology and Literature: An Integrative Seminar." *Leaflet* 88 (Spring 1989): 2–11.

Describes the development of a general education course using psychoanalysis, behaviorism, and humanism to analyze selected literary works.

1650. Walton, H. J. "Problem-Based Learning." *MEd* 23 (November 1989): 479.

Problem-based learning clearly offers some advantages over traditional pedagogy but requires new types of evaluation involving writing and critical thinking.

1651. Woods, Donald R. "Developing Students' Problem-Solving Skills." *JCST* 19 (November 1989): 108–110.

Outlines six key questions for educators to use in incorporating problem solving

across the curriculum and in developing group skills in the classroom.

See also 2, 56, 184, 428, 1019, 1042, 1110, 1111, 1119, 1186, 1219, 1377, 1387, 1482, 1560, 1657, 1679, 1707, 1732, 1752, 1787, 1812

4.3   ADULT AND GRADUATE EDUCATION

1652. Aurelio, Santo Joseph. "Mnemonic Devices in the Teaching of Grammar." *DAI* 50 (November 1989): 1176A.

Concludes that mnemonic and conventional methods of instruction were equally efficacious in teaching word pairs.

1653. Canseco, Grace, and Patricia Byrd. "Writing Required in Graduate Courses in Business Administration." *TESOLQ* 23 (June 1989): 305–316.

Analyzes 55 course outlines from 48 graduate courses offered in one institution. Categorizes seven types of writing assignments. Discusses style requirements and pedagogical implications.

1654. Collins, Sheila D., Miriam Balmuth, and Priscilla Jean. "So We Can Use Our Own Names and Write the Laws by Which We Live: Educating the New U.S. Labor Force." *HER* 59 (November 1989): 454–469.

Describes a workplace literacy program begun in 1988 by two New York City trade unions. Includes four case studies.

1655. Cook, Marjorie Leona. "The Validity of the Contrastive Rhetoric Hypothesis as It Relates to Spanish-Speaking Advanced ESL Students." *DAI* 49 (March 1989): 2567A.

Studies 24 foreign graduate students by applying Kaplan's hypothesis that Spanish-speaking ESL learners transfer into English a disunified pattern of rhetorical organization.

1656. Enos, Theresa. "The Course in Classical Rhetoric: Definition, Development, Direction." *RSQ* 19 (Winter 1989): 45–48.

Discusses the courses in 38 doctoral programs surveyed by Chapman and Tate in *RR* 5 (Spring 1987).

1657. Feirn, Mary. "Writing in Health Science: A Short Course for Graduate Nursing Students." *WLN* 13 (January 1989): 5–8.

Describes nurses as writers, their needs, and the materials and teaching techniques used in a short course.

1658. Graybill, Donald Shelley. "Critical Pedagogy for the Non-Poor: A Case Study in Cross-Cultural Education for Transformation." *DAI* 50 (November 1989): 1178A.

Investigates the effects of a "transformation education" curriculum on four subjects in Cuernavaca, Mexico.

1659. Grossman, Janet L. "Journal Writing and Adult Learning: A Naturalistic Inquiry." *DAI* 50 (October 1989): 929A.

Results reveal favorable outcomes when students in a nontraditional graduate program kept journals.

1660. Handron, Dorothea Scott. "Developing Methods and Techniques for Fostering Media Literacy in Adults." *DAI* 50 (July 1989): 52A.

Promotes critically reflective viewing of public affairs television.

1661. Kenyon, Claudia. "Teaching Writing in Prison: A Personal Account." *ETC* 46 (Spring 1989): 3–6.

Discusses the conflicts encountered between a teacher's and student's expectations and ways to overcome them.

1662. Knudson-Fields, Barbara S. "A Study of Adult Literacy Providers in the State of Idaho." *DAI* 49 (April 1989): 2987A.

Surveys programs.

1663. Lunsford, Andrea, Helen Moglen, and James Slevin, eds. *The Future of Doctoral Studies in English*. New York: MLA, 1989. 170 pages

Examines the nature of the profession and the ways that graduate students are socialized into it. Concludes with the 1986 MLA survey of doctoral programs.

1664. McCormick, Gloria J. "The Effects of Using Print Media in Teaching Critical Thinking Skills to Adult Students." *DAI* 49 (April 1989): 2915A.

Students who participated in the critical thinking group did not show improvement over students who did not participate in the group.

1665. McLaughlin, Jane, and Kitty Turner, eds. *Leaves: Written by the Students of English as a Second Language*. Bloomington, Ind.: ERIC/RCS, 1988. ERIC ED 300 521. 48 pages

Shares a collection of stories written by adult ESL students in England. Authors are not indexed separately in this volume.

1666. Michigan State Board of Education. *Michigan Adult Literacy Initiative: A Five-Year Plan to Reduce Illiteracy in Michigan by 50 Percent*. Lansing: Michigan State Board of Education, 1984. ERIC ED 304 517. 62 pages

Describes the plan of action to reduce illiteracy.

1667. Pennsylvania State Department of Education. *A New Beginning: Pennsylvania. Department of Education Honors Outstanding Adult Students in Success Stories*. Harrisburg: Pennsylvania State Department of Education, 1989. ERIC ED 304 583. 55 pages

A booklet containing first-person narratives of 10 Pennsylvanians who discovered adult education programs that gave them the tools to create a new life.

1668. Popkin, Susan M. *Graduate Student Writing in Education: Education 310—Professional Communication for Students in Education*. Bloomington, Ind.: ERIC/RCS, 1988. ERIC ED 300 832. 24 pages

Discusses a writing course for graduate students.

1669. Rich, Rebecca Z. "The Effects of Training Adult Poor Readers to Use Text Comprehension Strategies." *DAI* 50 (November 1989): 1182A.

Concludes that strategy training improves the comprehension level of adult poor readers.

1670. Sommer, Robert F. *Teaching Writing to Adults: Strategies and Concepts for Improving Learner Performance*. Higher Education Series. San Francisco: Jossey-Bass, 1989. 265 pages

A guide to developing writing courses for adults in settings ranging from literacy courses to corporate training programs. Thirteen chapters grouped into three sections treat the distinctiveness of adult learners, adult-centered techniques for improving writing instruction, and delivering instruction in different settings.

1671. Stibravy, John, and John Muller. "Using Technical Writing to Enhance Adult Student Self-Esteem." Paper presented at the Conference on Teaching Adults: Myths and Realities, Cincinnati, October 1988. ERIC ED 300 655. 10 pages

Recommends task-oriented technical writing classes for reducing anxiety about writing among adult learners entering college.

1672. Stine, Linda J. "Computers and Commuters: A Computer-Intensive Writing Program for Adults." *CC* 6 (April 1989): 23–32.

Describes the development of a computer-assisted writing class for working adults that made writing easier and encouraged students' empowerment.

1673. Sullivan, Patricia A. "Writers' Conception of Audience in Graduate Literature Courses." *Reader* 19 (Spring 1989): 22–34.

Reports on a study of graduate students in English. Argues that dual audiences—readers of professional journals and professors or teachers—problematize writing for the students.

1674. Sutton, Peter. "Language Awareness for Adults." *AdEd* 61 (March 1989): 319–322.

Describes the development, aims, content, and methods of a course in language awareness.

1675. Tedick, Diane Jane. "The Effects of Topic Familiarity on the Writing Performance of Nonnative Writers of English at the Graduate Level." *DAI* 49 (March 1989): 2569A.

Finds that topics allowing writers to make use of their prior knowledge elicit more accurate representations of their writing proficiency than do general topics.

See also 27, 28, 112, 215, 402, 1046, 1084, 1460, 1483, 1485, 1503, 1616, 1681, 1727, 1818

4.4   ENGLISH AS A SECOND LANGUAGE

1676. Belcher, Lynne Renee. "ESL Composition: Analyzing Revision." *DAI* 50 (November 1989): 1237A.

Concludes that when ESL basic writers rewrite they make global changes instead of correcting only surface errors.

1677. Berkowitz, Diana, and Linda Watkins-Goffman. "Putting Grammar in Its Place in the Writing Curriculum." Paper presented at the TESOL Conference, Chicago, March 1988. ERIC ED 304 012. 12 pages

Suggests ways to integrate grammar instruction skills within a process approach to writing instruction.

1678. Bhatia, V. K. "Legislative Writing: A Case of Neglect in EA/OLP Courses." *ESP* 8 (1989): 223–238.

Because legal discourse deals with general abstract principles, EA/OLP courses should emphasize these principles in writing assignments.

1679. Braine, George. "Writing in the Natural Sciences and Engineering: Implications for ESL Composition Courses." Paper presented at the TESOL Conference, San Antonio, March 1989. ERIC ED 304 881. 7 pages

A study listing the types of writing assignments commonly found in undergraduate natural science and engineering courses.

1680. Budd, Roger. "Simulating Academic Research: One Approach to a Study Skills Course." *ELT* 43 (January 1989): 30–37.

Describes a simulation of an academic research project, undertaken to teach study skills to a class of mixed-level ESL students.

1681. Burnett, Donald F. "Towards a Taxonomy of Items for Listening Comprehension in English for Academic Purposes." *DAI* 49 (April 1989): 2861A.

Analyzes the academic listening situation by discussing learning-centered theories and classroom tasks.

1682. Charry, Myrna B. "Teaching ESL Students to Paraphrase What They Read." Paper presented at the New York College Learning Skills Association, New York, April 1988. ERIC ED 299 537. 6 pages

Advocates paraphrasing as an instructional as well as an assessment technique.

1683. Choi, Yeon Hee. "Textual Coherence of Argumentative Writing by American and Korean Students." *DAI* 50 (August 1989): 429A.

Suggests that native speakers of English and Korean have different notions of text coherence closely related to the writing conventions of their cultures.

1684. Christensen, Torkil. "Grammatical Overkill?" *EngT* 5 (October 1989): 38–41.

Foreign students, especially Japanese students, do not develop fluency in spoken English when taught by the grammar-translation method.

1685. Cummings, Anne. "Computer-Assisted Language Instruction." *MM* 26 (September-October 1989): 13.

Suggests computer applications and gives criteria for selecting software for foreign language learners.

1686. Cummings, Martha Clark. "What We Talk about When We Talk about Writing." *DAI* 49 (March 1989): 2567A.

Studies four, urban university students learning to compose in English. The two weaker writers were treated differently from the two stronger ones.

1687. DeCapua, Andrea. "An Analysis of Pragmatic Transfer in the Speech Act of Complaints as Produced by Native Speakers of German in English." *DAI* 50 (September 1989): 676A.

Partially because of pragmatic transfer, German speakers tend to be more direct in English than considered appropriate by native English speakers.

1688. Donato, Richard. "Beyond Group: A Psycholinguistic Rationale for Collective Activity in Second Language Learning." *DAI* 49 (June 1989): 3701A.

Finds that, if learning activities promote internalization of collective cognitive processes, student interaction can be a coherent mode of learning in itself.

1689. Dunkel, Patricia, and Sheryl Davy. "The Heuristic of Lecture Note Taking: Perceptions of American and International Students regarding the Value and Practice of Note Taking." *ESP* 8 (1989): 33–50.

Surveys attitudes of American and international students regarding note taking during lecture courses in the U.S.

1690. El-Dib, Mervat Abou Bakr. "Explorations into the Classroom Management of an Adult ESL Classroom." *DAI* 49 (March 1989): 2612A.

Concludes that classroom management is a "continuous process" without "specific and identifiable stages."

1691. Halio, Marcia P. "Writing for International Readers." *CollT* 37 (Fall 1989): 131–134.

Describes an ESL pedagogy that includes contrasting the syntax and style of American English with other languages and rewriting an essay aimed at an American audience for a first-language audience.

1692. Hudleson, Sarah. *Children's Writing in ESL.* Washington, D.C.: ERIC/FLL, 1988. ERIC ED 303 046. 3 pages

Discusses ways teachers can use writing in the classroom for ESL children.

1693. Kaewsanchai, Nisai. "A Proposed English as a Foreign Language Curriculum for Teachers' Colleges in Thailand." *DAI* 49 (April 1989): 2912A.

The program proposed focuses on business English for high school graduates and part-time students who need English for work.

1694. Kamel, Gehan W. "Argumentative Writing by Arab Learners of English as a Foreign and Second Language: An Empirical Investigation of Contrastive Rhetoric." *DAI* 50 (September 1989): 677A.

Shows that rhetorical ability in second language writing is attributable to experience and linguistic proficiency in the target language rather than to rhetorical transfer.

1695. Kilborn, Kerry. "Sentence Processing in a Second Language: The Timing of Transfer." *L&S* 32 (January–March 1989): 1–23.

Investigates how and when three different cues—word order, noun-verb agreement, and animacy relations—interact during comprehension.

1696. Laager, Dorothy M. "English, Made in U.S.A." *DAI* 50 (November 1989): 1294A.

An ESL reading text with activities and exercises in listening comprehension, grammar, speech, and writing.

1697. Lesikin, Joan. "The Social Consequences of Evaluating ESL Writing." Paper presented at the TESOL Conference, San Antonio, March 1989. ERIC ED 308 700. 17 pages

Discusses the social implications of evaluating ESL writing in the context of the hegemony theory, a radical view of schools as an agency for socialization.

1698. Lucas, Tamara. "Beyond Language and Culture: Individual Variation in Students' Engagement with a Written Genre." Paper presented at the TESOL Conference, Chicago, March 1988. ERIC ED 304 005. 29 pages

Examines journals written by nonnative speakers of English, exploring five text features: functions, content, audience, organization, and linguistic form.

1699. Martin, Ann V. "Bridging Language: Meeting the English Needs of International Professionals." Paper presented at the Eastern Michigan University Conference on Languages for Business and the Professions, Ann Arbor, April 1988. ERIC ED 304 908. 13 pages

Discusses the language problems professionals working overseas encounter and how to meet their English language needs.

1700. McDevitt, Damien. "How to Cope with Spaghetti Writing." *ELT* 43 (January 1989): 19–23.

Focuses on major errors in subordinating and coordinating constructions. Gives suggestions for recognizing and revising "spaghetti writing."

1701. McGinley, Kevin. "English for Special Purposes Materials Reflect the Lessons of Past Experience, Recent Thinking, and Aspects of the Local Situation." *DAI* 50 (October 1989): 1020A.

Examines how ESP materials are influenced by the past experience of materials writing, by recent thinking in the field, and by aspects of the local situation.

1702. Meyer, Robert E. "The Effect of Instructions on Aspects of Conversations between Native and Nonnative Speakers." *DAI* 49 (April 1989): 2952A.

Finds no significant differences between scores of nonnative speakers who were corrected by native speakers and those who were not.

1703. Mountainbird, Pauline. "Community College ESL Students Reflecting on Thoughts and Feelings about Writing and Themselves as Writers: An Exploratory Study in Metacognition." *DAI* 49 (June 1989): 3595A.

Explores metacognition in adult ESL learners in an advanced community college writing course. Students were asked about their attitudes toward writing, their writing identity, and their sense of self-direction.

1704. Peyton, Joy Kreeft, and Mulugetta Seyoum. *The Effect of Teacher Strategies on Students' Interactive Writing: The Case for Dialogue Journals.* Los Angeles: UCLA Center for Language Education and Research, 1988. ERIC ED 298 763. 36 pages

Finds that student-initiated topics and teachers' statements or opinions were the best way to develop dialogue journals.

1705. Powell, William W. "Compensatory Processing Strategies in Second Language Reading: An Investigation of the Effect of Thematic Context on the Cloze Task Performance of ESL Students." *DAI* 49 (April 1989): 2952A.

Suggests that cloze tests may limit the ability to apply top-down processing.

1706. Quigley, Martin. "Colleges Should Switch to the Immersion Method to Make Immigrant Students Fluent in English." *CHE* 35 (19 July 1989): B1.

Argues that current methods for teaching non-English speakers fail. Instead, students should be isolated in English-only "saturation" classes until they can communicate.

1707. Ramaglia, Judith. "Writing (ESL) in Accounting." Paper presented at the Eastern Michigan University Conference on Languages for Business and the Professions, Ann Arbor, April 1988. ERIC ED 304 905. 23 pages

Describes a technique that helped students develop expertise in accounting and improve their writing skills.

1708. Rapp, Linda Chan. "Proofreading Skills and Writing Proficiency: Error Detection, Editing Accuracy, and Linguistic Competence." Paper presented at the TESOL Conference, Chicago, March 1988. ERIC ED 307 802. 23 pages

Finds that more proficient ESL writers were better able to detect errors but not better able to treat errors accurately.

1709. Reid, Joy Maurine. "Quantitative Differences in English Prose Written by Arabic, Chinese, and English Students." *DAI* 50 (September 1989): 672A.

Analyzes differences in discourse fluency, lexical choice, and cohesion devices.

1710. Roach, William L. "Incorporating American Literature into the English as a Second Language College Composition Classroom." *DAI* 49 (April 1989): 2955A.

At the end of a course with a literature component, students showed no improvement on a test of writing skills but did improve in reading scores.

1711. Rodby, Judith. "A Polyphony of Voices: The Dialectics of Social Interaction and ESL Literacy Practices." *DAI* 50 (November 1989): 1239A.

Critiques the cognitive/individual view and argues for the social view of ESL literacy practices.

1712. Roy, Alice M. "Developing Second Language Literacy: A Vygotskyan Perspective." *JTW* 8 (Spring-Summer 1989): 91–98.

Discusses Vygotskyan principles of meditation, "higher mental functions," the interaction of psychological and social forces, internalization through dialogic action, "zone of proximal development," and problem solving.

1713. Schlumberger, Ann, and Diane Clymer. "Tailoring Composition Classes to ESL Students' Needs." *TETYC* 16 (May 1989): 121–128.

Argues that ESL students should be placed by holistically graded essays, that their courses should be organized thematically, and that they should write fewer papers and practice all language skills.

1714. Schlumberger, Ann, and Kate Mangelsdorf. "Reading the Context." Paper presented at the TESOL Conference, San Antonio, March 1989. ERIC ED 304 945. 23 pages

Reports on a study that investigates the effects of exposure to contrastive rhetoric.

1715. Siripham, Salakjit. "An Investigation of Syntax, Semantics, and Rhetoric in the English Writing of 15 Thai Graduate Students." *DAI* 50 (October 1989): 941A.

The Thai students made errors in syntax and semantics and were unaware of English rhetorical style.

1716. Spolsky, Bernard. *Conditions for Second Language Learning.* Language Education. Edited by Frances Christie. New York: Oxford University Press, 1989. 100 pages

Examines the conditions under which languages are learned and how learning relates to teaching.

1717. Sternglass, Marilyn S. "The Need for Conceptualizing at All Levels of Writing Instruction." *JBW* 8 (Fall 1989): 87–98.

Argues that "conceptual as well as linguistic activities need to be practiced" by students in ESL, remedial, and traditional courses.

1718. Tien, Hsia-fen Jen. "The Effects of Textual Styles on Reading Comprehension of EFL College Students in Taiwan." *DAI* 49 (February 1989): 2096A.

Examines the effects of text types—descriptive, narrative, expository, and persuasive—on second language learners.

1719. Villamil, Olga, and Angela Carrasquillo. *Assessing Writing in the ESL Classroom.*

Bloomington, Ind.: ERIC/RCS, 1988. ERIC ED 301 032. 14 pages

Discusses current theoretical goals about language learning and composition for the ESL writing teacher in Puerto Rico.

1720. Wallace, Ray. "Teaching English for the Professionals: English for Specific Purposes in ESL Undergraduate Composition Courses." Paper presented at the Eastern Michigan University Conference on Languages for Business and the Professions, Ann Arbor, April 1988. ERIC ED 304 904. 19 pages

Describes a course that modifies the British model of teaching English for specific purposes.

1721. Walsleben, Marjorie C. "The Effect of Integrative/Instrumental Motivation on the Expository Writing of Unskilled English as a Second Language Writers." *DAI* 49 (February 1989): 2098A.

Examines types of motivation and their effects on enhancing writing instruction.

1722. Watkins, Beverly T. "Discussion and Writing in Class Called Necessities for Students with a Limited Proficiency in English." *CHE* 36 (29 November 1989): A17-A18.

Students weak in English cannot take good notes and generally will not ask questions, but they learn more in courses supported by writing across the curriculum.

1723. Xu, George Q. *Helping ESL Students Improve Un-English Sentences in One-to-One Conferences.* Washington, D.C.: ERIC/FLL, 1989. ERIC ED 304 003. 9 pages

Suggests ways to analyze the causes of the writing errors of nonnative speakers, using tutorial conferences to suggest improvements.

1724. Xu, George Q. *Instruction of EFL Composition in China.* Washington, D.C.: ERIC/FLL, 1989. ERIC ED 304 019. 19 pages

Discusses the state of writing instruction in English in China. Notes a general devaluing of writing instruction and a predominant emphasis on form.

1725. Yorio, Carlos. "The Other Side of the Looking Glass." *JBW* 8 (Spring 1989): 32–45.

> Argues for "principled compromise" in dealing with ESL and other students' frustrations. Emphasizes that teachers should be attentive and responsive to students' perceptions of coursework.

See also 772, 791, 808, 1068, 1330, 1521, 1655, 1665, 1726, 1763, 1818, 1821

4.5 RESEARCH AND STUDY SKILLS

1726. Ahmadi, Hassan. "Reactions of International Students to Academic Library Services and Resources: Problems and Difficulties Encountered by International Students in Terms of Using Library Services and Resources at Two Sample American Universities (USC and UCLA)." *DAI* 49 (January 1989): 1608A.

> Finds particular problems for international students using electronic reference equipment and recommends special instruction.

1727. Barton, Ellen, and Ruth Ray. "Changing Perspectives on Summary through Teacher Research." *JTW* (Special Issue 1989): 165–174.

> An analysis of summaries by basic writers and graduate students reveals that summaries are not objective but interpretative.

1728. Betenbough, T. J., and Shirley A. Biggs, eds. *Innovative Learning Strategies, 1987–1988: Eighth Yearbook of the College Reading Improvement Special Interest Group*. Newark, Del.: IRA, 1988. ERIC ED 303 776. 126 pages

> Offers 12 articles grouped under two headings, program models and instructional strategies.

1729. Brookes, Gerry H. "Exploring Plagiarism in the Composition Classroom." *FEN* 17 (Spring 1989): 31–35.

> Presents an approach to the subject of plagiarism that includes discussing student research on plagiarism.

1730. Brown, Alan S., and Dana R. Murphy. "Cryptomnesia: Delineating Inadvertent Plagiarism." *JEPL* 15 (May 1989): 432–442.

> "Supports [the] existence of unconscious plagiarism," showing that "it is persistent across a variety of tasks, contexts, materials, and generation conditions."

1731. Cohen, Andrew D. *The Role of Instruction in Testing Summarizing Ability*. Washington, D.C.: ERIC/FLL, 1989. ERIC ED 308 691. 21 pages

> Finds that instructions on how to read texts and write summaries were helpful in identifying main ideas but were detrimental in blurring details.

1732. Donnelly, Patrick. "A Term Paper Project in Large Survey Courses." *HT* 22 (February 1989): 117–124.

> Advocates assigning papers in introductory humanities courses so that students do not "compartmentalize" writing.

1733. Egan, Philip J. "Frequent Short Writing: Motivating the Passive Reader." *CollT* 37 (Winter 1989): 15–16.

> Advocates improving adult students' reading and comprehension skills by having them write about texts, using short responses or micro-themes in all disciplines.

1734. Hilbert, Betsy. "Elegy for Excursus: The Descent of the Footnote." *CE* 51 (April 1989): 400–404.

> Discusses the increasing rarity with which footnotes are used, citing their usefulness.

1735. Hult, Christine. "Advanced Composition and the Computerized Library." *JAC* 9 (1989): 175–180.

> Discusses some pros and cons of four types of library computerized access systems. Advocates teaching them to advanced composition students.

1736. Kotler, Janet. "Reading for Pleasure: The Research Paper Reconsidered." *FEN* 18 (Fall 1989): 33–37.

Describes with examples a research paper writing assignment that engages students and produces responsible writing.

1737. Langer, Judith A. *Writing to Study and Learn*. Washington, D.C.: NIE, 1986. ERIC ED 297 316. 58 pages

Reports on two studies of ninth and eleventh graders. Analytical writing led to more and longer learning than answering questions or taking notes.

1738. Lawson, V. Lonnie. "Using a Computer-Assisted Instruction Program as an Alternative to the Traditional Library Orientation/Instruction Tour: An Evaluative Study." *DAI* 49 (June 1989): 3539A.

Students in the CAI group showed higher mean scores on a posttest than did students in a traditional program.

1739. Lechner, Judith V. "Bibliographic Instruction Evaluation: A Study Testing the Correlations among Five Measures of the Impact of a Bibliographic Instruction Program on Undergraduates' Information Searching Behavior in Libraries." *DAI* 50 (November 1989): 1124A.

Measures 301 freshmen, using four instruments (a fifth measure had to be abandoned). Concludes that no significant effects were attributable to the search strategy course.

1740. Little, Sherry Burgus. "The Research and Development Process and Its Relationship to the Evolution of Scientific and Technical Literature: A Model for Teaching Research." *TWT* 16 (Winter 1989): 68–76.

Advocates using a model of the research and development process as a framework for teaching research strategies to technical communicators.

1741. Madden-Simpson, Janet. "A Collaborative Approach to the Research Paper." *TETYC* 16 (May 1989): 113–115.

Discusses group work as preparation for individual research papers.

1742. Martin, Celest. "Who Is the General Audience and What Does It Want?: A Sequence for Teaching Informative Writing." *JTW* 8 (Fall-Winter 1989): 115–132.

Discusses six elements of informative writing: "significance, background, features, good/bad, procedures, and applications."

1743. McCleary, Bill. "How Plagiarism at Harvard Became Local News in Rochester." *CompC* 1 (January 1989): 9–10.

An account of Paul Scatena's discovering Shervert Frazier's plagiarism of medical articles.

1744. McCormick, Frank. "*The Plagiario* and the Professor in Our Peculiar Institution." *JTW* 8 (Fall-Winter 1989): 133–146.

Contends that definitions of plagiarism differ widely, that students often plagiarize inadvertently, that more instruction in documentation is needed, and that documentation is routinely ignored.

1745. Nairn, Lyndall. "A Workshop on Note Taking: How to Manage Information." *WLN* 13 (March 1989): 7–8.

Describes strategies used in four one-hour sessions focusing on improving listening skills, taking notes, practicing, and reviewing notes for examinations.

1746. Nelson, Jennie, and John R. Hayes. *How the Writing Context Shapes College Students' Strategies for Writing from Sources*. Pittsburgh: CSW, 1988. ERIC ED 297 374. 26 pages

Reports that the most effective writing from sources resulted from supplying intermediate feedback, from focusing on high-level goals, and from providing an audience other than the teacher as examiner.

1747. Nystrom, Christine. "On Abstracting . . . Etc." *ETC* 46 (Winter 1989): 364–367.

Describes two classroom exercises designed to acquaint students with one another and with the process of abstracting.

1748. Reiff, John, and Judith Kirscht. "Inquiry as a Human Process: Interviews with Researchers across the Disciplines." Paper presented at the CCCC Convention, Seattle, March 1989. ERIC ED 307 618. 18 pages

Interviews 14 college professors about their research projects. Ideas emerged and developed in research in the same way that ideas emerge and develop in composing.

1749. Sheets, Rick A., and Sally Rings. "Ideas in Practice: Tailor-Made Study Strategies: A Success Story!" *JDEd* 12 (Spring 1989): 22–24.

Examines the drawbacks of isolated study-skills programs and argues for customized, instructor-assisted workshops to reinforce study strategies within content areas.

1750. Stein, Mark. "Teaching Plagiarism." Paper presented at the CCCC Convention, New Orleans, March 1986. ERIC ED 298 482. 15 pages

Argues that the problem of plagiarism is really a problem of finding the proper mix between the speaker and those who have preceded the speaker.

1751. Strauss, Michael J., and John H. Clarke. "Fear and Trembling in the Examination Hour." *JCST* 18 (February 1989): 233–235.

Suggests writing-based strategies to help students prepare more effectively for examinations.

1752. Streepey, Janet, Nancy Totten, Gabrielle Carr, and Teresa Reynolds. *Writing and Research across the Curriculum: A Proposal for a New Course*. Alexandria, EDRS, 1987. ERIC ED 300 807. 22 pages

Outlines a term paper writing course taught in conjunction with a content course.

1753. Woods, Donald R. "Novice Versus Expert Research." *JCST* 18 (December 1988–January 1989): 193–195.

Finds correlations between knowledge structure and learning and suggests their relevance in classroom teaching.

See also 128, 1525, 1689

4.6   OTHER

1754. Collins, Terence. "University of Minnesota Research Confirms the Impact of Computers on the Writing of Learning-Disabled Students." *CompC* 2 (May 1989): 4.

Researchers studied two groups of 17 to 20 learning-disabled students using microcomputers in freshman writing courses.

1755. Gills, Paula. "The Troubleshooter." *WLN* 14 (November 1989): 12–13.

Cites 13 sources that discuss writing and the learning-disabled student. Argues that emotional as well as physical factors should be recognized. Lists nine common writing problems.

1756. Lazarus, Belinda D. "Serving Learning-Disabled Students in Postsecondary Settings." *JDEd* 12 (Spring 1989): 2–4, 6.

Addresses the challenges of educating learning-disabled students in postsecondary institutions. Differentiates between learning-disabled and developmental students and suggests accommodations to ensure equal access to all curricula.

1757. Long, Maxine. "Colleges and Universities Find Growing Numbers of Learning-Disabled Students Seeking Admission." *CompC* 2 (May 1989): 1–3.

Effectively teaching the growing number of learning-disabled college writing students requires instruction in learning strategies, a bi-modal approach, and a positive student-teacher relationship.

1758. Morelli, M. Eileen, and Heidi Farra. "Word Processing for College-Level Learning-Disabled Students: Practical and Technical Considerations." *CAC* 4 (Summer 1989): 8–14.

Teaching word processing to learning-disabled students gives them motivation and skills for success.

1759. Peyton, Joy Kreeft. "Cross-Age Tutoring on a Local Area Computer Network: Moving from Informal Interaction to Formal Academic Writing." *WI* 8 (Winter 1989): 57–67.

Advocates the interactive use of computers among deaf students as a more "natural" approach to language acquisition. Describes results of a project at Gallaudet University.

1760. Sivan, Eva D. "Integrating Psychological Principles of Motivation with Cognition Strategy Instruction." *DAI* 49 (April 1989): 2978A.

Reexamines, in terms of motivation, the Teacher Explanation Project, which demonstrated improvement when mental strategies were explained to poor readers.

1761. Wepner, Shelley B., Joan T. Feeley, and Sara Wilde. "Using Computers in College Reading Courses?" *JDEd* 13 (Fall 1989): 6–8, 24.

A study of a college reading course. Reports increased motivation in computer-based versus traditional approaches but finds no statistical gains in students' standardized test performance.

See also 435, 732, 1335, 1416

5

Testing, Measurement, and Evaluation

5.1 EVALUATION OF STUDENTS

1762. Allard, Lee R. "Analysis of Narrative and Procedural Discourse Written by Children." *DAI* 49 (February 1989): 2195A.

Examines word-, sentence-, and text-level properties to determine communicative effectiveness and individual performance across genres.

1763. Allen, Kathleen O'Brien. "The Development of a Test of Communicative Competence for Speakers of English as a Second Language in Zimbabwe." *DAI* 49 (April 1989): 2951A.

Describes the development of a test of communicative competence to replace the national examination, the Zimbabwe Junior Certificate.

1764. Anson, Chris M., ed. *Writing and Response: Theory, Practice, and Research.* Urbana, Ill.: NCTE, 1989. ERIC ED 303 826. 373 pages

Offers 16 essays describing theories of response, types of response, and research on the instructional context.

1765. Bamberg, Betty, and Karen Greenberg. *Postsecondary Writing Assessment: An Update on Practices and Procedures.* Bloomington, Ind.: ERIC/RCS, 1988. ERIC ED 300 822. 12 pages

Finds broad but variable acceptance of the CCCC Committee on Assessment's Resolution on Testing among a sample of member institutions.

1766. Barcelow-Hill, Georgina. "The Effect of Peer Critique Groups on Students' Critiquing and Writing Ability." *DAI* 50 (September 1989): 639A.

Finds that students became more proficient at critiquing but not in writing.

1767. Barker, E. Ellen. "The When, Where, How, and Why of Conferencing: A Summary and Interpretation of a Teacher Survey." Paper presented at the CCCC Convention, St. Louis, March 1988. ERIC ED 297 327. 16 pages

Reports on a survey of 100 faculty members who believe that conferencing is more valuable than written comments but who do not use it as their major instructional strategy.

1768. Beach, Daniel A. "Identifying the Random Responder." *JPsy* 123 (January 1989): 101–103.

Addresses the problem of students who respond "randomly or carelessly" on standardized tests.

1769. Beard, John D., Jone Rymer, and David L. Williams. "An Assessment System for Collaborative-Writing Groups: Theory and Empirical Evaluation." *JBTC* 3 (September 1989): 29–51.

Both group products and individual contributions are accounted for in a complex system validated by a survey of 136 students.

1770. Bishop, Wendy. "Qualitative Evaluation and the Conversational Writing Classroom." *JTW* (Special Issue 1989): 267–285.

Describes formative, summative, and dialogic uses for five kinds of classroom evaluation measures. Lists five positive outcomes of qualitative classroom evaluation.

1771. Buley-Meissner, Mary Louise. "Error Analysis in Basic Writing." *JTW* 8 (Spring-Summer 1989): 85–90.

Five principles address the writer's intention, parallels between the priorities of analysis and teaching, general intelligibility, reasonableness and encouragement, and reading aloud.

1772. Cannon, Sally I. "The Reading of Literature and Responding to Student Writing." *JTW* (Special Issue 1989): 239–254.

A descriptive research project. Confirms that practice in responding to literary texts strengthens students' responses to peers' texts.

1773. Capossela, Toni-Lee. "Improving Peer Response." *IIEB* 76 (Winter 1989): 30–39.

Discusses ways in which theoretical interest in the social nature of writing has a direct influence on teaching.

1774. Cherry, Roger D. "Fictional Scenarios and Rhetorical Specification in Writing Tasks: A Cautionary Note." *JAC* 9 (1989): 151–161.

Examines a single topic used in a large assessment. Its problematic fictional scenario and lack of rhetorical specification made it disastrous.

1775. Clark, Renee Smith. *Age Cohort Performance on the College-Level Examination Program General Examination in English Composition*. Bloomington, Ind.: ERIC/RCS, 1988. ERIC ED 300 390. 27 pages

Finds no significant difference among the performances of seven age cohort groups at a community college.

1776. Coffman, William E. "Research in Writing Assessment." Paper presented at the AERA, San Francisco, April 1986. ERIC ED 299 323. 9 pages

Argues that NAEP results are valid and reliable.

1777. Curran, Paul. "The Portfolio Approach to Assessing Student Writing: An Interim Report." *CompC* 2 (March 1989): 6–8.

Reports on a pilot portfolio project at SUNY—Brockport that has been successful with students and teachers.

1778. Curry, Boykin, ed. *Essays That Worked for Law Schools: 35 Essays from Successful Applications to the Nation's Top Law Schools with Comments from Admissions Officers*. New Haven, Conn.: Mustang, 1988. ERIC ED 302 113. 112 pages

Prints 35 application essays arranged in eight categories. Admissions officers rated them highly as working because they revealed the writer's personality.

1779. Curry, Boykin, and Brian Kasbar, eds. *Essays That Worked for Business Schools: 35 Essays from Successful Applications to the Nation's Top Business Schools with Com-*

ments from Admissions Officers. New Haven, Conn.: Mustang, 1987. ERIC ED 302 112. 128 pages

Prints 35 application essays arranged in seven categories. Admissions officers rated them highly because they revealed the writer's personality.

1780. Daiker, Donald A., and Nedra Grogan. *The Selection and Use of Sample Papers in Holistic Evaluation.* Washington, D.C.: ERIC/AIR, 1985. ERIC ED 305 391. 33 pages

Describes procedures for sample selection used by ETS for readers of AP examinations.

1781. Eidman-Andahl, Elyse. "Cracking through the Shell: Classroom Inquiry and Educational Policy." *JTW* (Special Issue 1989): 131–150.

Special assistance students studied prompts and standards of the Maryland Functional Writing Test. The test promoted "elaboration as emasculation," "the big lie," and "class antagonism."

1782. Faigley, Lester. "Judging Writing, Judging Selves." *CCC* 40 (December 1989): 395–413.

Examines assumptions made about student selves in writing evaluation. Suggests that teachers privilege writing that assembles familiar, unified "subject positions."

1783. Ferrara, Steven F. "Effects of Essay Order on Raters' Score Assignments in a Large Scale Writing Assignment." Paper presented at the AERA, Washington, D.C., April 1987. ERIC ED 302 573. 14 pages

In a study of how 38 raters scored 957 pairs of essays, the placement order of essays in scoring packets affected the scores for narrative essay prompts.

1784. Garrow, John R. "Assessing and Improving the Adequacy of College Composition Placement." *DAI* 50 (December 1989): 1639A.

Evaluates direct and indirect assessments and combinations of these measures, discussing their ability to place students adequately.

1785. Gavin, Carole Anne. "The Strategies of Native and Limited English Proficient Test-Takers as Revealed by Think-Aloud Protocols." *DAI* 50 (September 1989): 640A.

Strategies included intuition, analysis, and guessing.

1786. Gentile, Claudia Ann. "Defining College Juniors' Writing Abilities: Using Linguistic Cues to Explore Cognitive Constructs." *DAI* 50 (July 1989): 88A.

Offers descriptive profiles of how college juniors structure narrative and comparison-contrast papers to develop a means of assessing their writing abilities.

1787. Gerrard, Lisa. "Composition Pedagogy for Spanish Courses." *CompC* 2 (February 1989): 8–9.

Reports on a project that helped Spanish instructors evalute writing on the basis of organization, style, and content rather than errors alone.

1788. Greenberg, Karen L. "Writing Placement Testing." *CompC* 2 (February 1989): 4–6.

Argues that placement tests should measure writing ability as defined by composition teachers. Testers should consider validity and reliability.

1789. Grogan, Nedra, and Donald A. Daiker. "Team-Grading in College Composition." *WPA* 13 (Fall-Winter 1989): 25–34.

Describes successful team-grading experiences at Miami University of Ohio and recommends collaborative grading as part of an effective writing program.

1790. Guastello, Stephen J., Denise D. Guastello, and Larry L. Craft. "Assessment of the Barnum Effect in Computer-Based Test Interpretations." *JPsy* 123 (September 1989): 477–484.

Evaluates the validity of computer-based test interpretations in personality testing.

1791. Gurman, Ernest B. "The Effect of Prior Test Exposure on Performance in Two Instructional Settings." *JPsy* 123 (May 1989): 275–278.

This study indicates that students' test-taking performances improved when one teacher, rather than various members of the teaching team, prepared tests throughout the school term.

1792. Hadden, Craig. "The Placement Process at Colorado Mountain College: Placement Testing and the Advising Matrix." Paper presented at the Freshman Year Experience Conference, Columbia, S.C., December 1988. ERIC ED 32 298. 42 pages

Describes the interaction between placement testing and an advising matrix built from instructor-provided course information.

1793. Hayward, Malcom. "Choosing an Essay Test Question: It's Worse Than What You Know." *TETYC* 16 (October 1989): 174–178.

A research study of students' reactions to rhetorical aspects of essay questions. Prompts are more likely to be chosen when they are more readable and longer, when students think they see what is looked for, when answers seem easy to organize, and when questions rather than directions are given.

1794. Heller, Dana A. "Silencing the Soundtrack: An Alternative to Marginal Comments." *CCC* 40 (May 1989): 210–215.

Presents a strategy for commenting on student writing based on poststructuralist theory.

1795. Heller, Scott. "More Than Half of Students in Survey Flunk History and Literature Test." *CHE* 36 (11 October 1989): A15.

Commissioned by NEH, a Gallup survey of 696 college seniors indicated that colleges failed to teach general knowledge adequately.

1796. Hoetker, James, and Gordon Brossell. "The Effects of Systematic Variations in Essay Topics on the Writing Performance of College Freshmen." *CCC* 40 (December 1989): 414–421.

The amount of rhetorical specification and the kind of voice invited in a topic did not affect holistic scores of high- or low-ability writers.

1797. Hoffman, Robert, and Marcella Kocar. "Introducing Objectivity in Evaluating Writing Assignments." *BABC* 52 (September 1989): 25–26.

Describes a method for evaluating writing in business communication courses.

1798. Hunt, Alan J. "Taped Comments and Student Writing." *TETYC* 16 (December 1989): 269–273.

Finds responding to students' writing on audiocassettes fast and effective.

1799. Janopoulos, Michael. "Reader Comprehension and Holistic Assessment of Second Language Writing Proficiency." *WC* 6 (April 1989): 218–237.

Native-speaker holistic raters of compositions written by nonnative speakers attended to meaning.

1800. Keimowitz, Robert M. "Rx: Writing (I)." *AM* 64 (November 1989): 662–663.

Reflects on incorporating an essay into the MCAT. Encourages more emphasis on writing at all levels of school and beyond.

1801. Lawson, Bruce, Susan Sterr Ryan, and W. Ross Winterowd, eds. *Encountering Student Texts: Interpretive Issues in Reading Student Writing*. Urbana, Ill.: NCTE, 1989. 242 pages

Eighteen essays address the question, how do writing teachers read student papers? Four sections treat the ways teachers read student writing, the conflicts they encounter between theory and practice, the ethical responsibilities they recognize, and the reflections they make on their own responses.

1802. Lombard, Juliana V. *An Empirical Comparison of a Direct and Indirect Method of Assessing Writing Proficiency*. Pretoria, South Africa: Human Sciences Research Council, 1988. ERIC ED 303 519. 62 pages

Finds high correlations between objective multiple-choice and subjective essay assessments of 300 junior high school ESL students.

1803. Low, Graham D. "Testing Reader-Writer Relations in Academic Text: Some Preliminary Considerations." Paper presented at the International Association of Teachers of English as a Foreign Language, Edinburgh, Scotland, 1987. ERIC ED 299 572. 42 pages

Discusses the design and evaluation of a test to measure ESL students' ability to manipulate texts.

1804. Luse, Donna W., Beverly H. Nelson, and Debbie D. DuFrene. "The Grading Policies and Procedures Used in ABC Members' Introductory Business Communication Courses." *BABC* 52 (September 1989): 27–31.

Presents the results of a survey of ABC members concerning grading in business communication courses.

1805. Matalene, Carolyn B., and Nancy Barendse. "Transaction in Holistic Scoring: Using a Computer to Understand the Process." *JTW* 8 (Fall-Winter 1989): 87–108.

Two studies support holistic scoring for placement but not exit. Seven tables explain statistical profiles, vocabulary averages, vocabulary usage, factors, clusters, word pools, and organizational strategies.

1806. McAlexander, Patricia J., and Noel Gregg. "The Roles of English Teachers and Learning-Disabled Specialists in Identifying Learning-Disabled Writers: Two Case Studies." *JBW* 8 (Fall 1989): 72–86.

Illustrates the "complexity of recognizing and defining learning disabilities, and the need for a cooperative process of identification" by teachers and specialists.

1807. McCleary, Bill. "A Method to Determine Final Grades in Your Composition Class." *CompC* 2 (February 1989): 6–7.

Final grades should be determined by assigning different "weight points" to different papers.

1808. McCleary, Bill. "Using Evaluation Forms to Improve Grading Practices in Composition Classes." *CompC* 2 (September 1989): 8–9.

A pre-printed evaluation form helps students understand the criteria by which their papers are judged.

1809. McClure, Lisa Jane. "Response and Revision: Informing the Writer's Process." *DAI* 49 (June 1989): 3647A.

Examines how an instructor's comments on papers help students in their revisions.

1810. McConnell, Renee V. "The Impact of Information Processing Styles and Gender on Assessor Ratings of Competence in Interpersonal Communication." *DAI* 49 (January 1989): 1880A.

Examines the impact of information processing styles and gender on ratings of competence in interpersonal communication.

1811. McDuffie, Harriet E. "The Effect of Intelligence, Creativity, and Cognitive Style on Success in Composition." *DAI* 49 (January 1989): 1721A.

Describes the performance of 109 college English freshmen, using three tests to attain a composite portrait of a successful academic writer.

1812. McLeod, P. J. "Assessing the Value of Student Case Write-Ups and Write-Up Evaluations." *AM* 64 (May 1989): 273–274.

Argues that these exercises are valuable but that inter-rater reliability and individual standard setting can undermine their perceived usefulness.

1813. Moxley, Joseph M. "Responding to Student Writing: Goals, Methods, Alternatives." *FEN* 17 (Spring 1989): 3–11.

Notes the difficulty for writing instructors of meeting recommended kinds of responses to student papers and suggests using taped responses. Briefly reviews literature.

1814. Murray, Mary. "Measuring Insight in Student Writing." *DAI* 49 (March 1989): 2568A.

Studies how insight can be measured in student writing by measuring dissonance resolution and by analyzing students' awareness of writing progress.

1815. Murray, Mary. "A Scale for Identifying Insight in Student Writing." *Focuses* 2 (Fall 1989): 103–114.

Presents a "method of isolating and describing insight" that uses categories of dissonance for evaluating expressive writing.

1816. "New Code of Practices in Testing." *CompC* 2 (March 1989): 12.

Gives excerpts from the Code of Fair Testing Practices in Education applicable to composition.

1817. Peiffer, Ronald Aaron. "The Ability of Maryland English Teachers to Rate Holistically the Quality of Student Explanatory Writing." *DAI* 50 (October 1989): 929A.

Findings reveal 60 percent accuracy in scoring, with the number of words and syntactic errors serving as telling predictors of scores.

1818. Perry, William Shepard. "The Relationship of the Test of English as a Foreign Language and Other Critical Variables to the Academic Performance of International Graduate Students." *DAI* 50 (August 1989): 422A.

Presents the findings of two studies of the relationship between English language proficiency scores and the academic performance of international graduate students.

1819. Pickering, Miles. "Student Failure Is No Fun for the Faculty Either." *JCST* 19 (December 1989): 142–143.

Argues that teachers must "face the reality of failure" even though it is unpleasant to fail students.

1820. Roebuck, Deborah Britt. "An MBO Approach to Teaching Organizational Communication." *BABC* 52 (March 1989): 26–28.

Describes how the principles of management by objectives support a grading method in an organizational communication course.

1821. Rosser, Carl Frederick. "The Response of College Teachers to Undergraduate Foreign-Student Writing." *DAI* 50 (October 1989): 890A.

Results reveal tolerant and positive attitudes toward the writing, with content the major focus of evaluation.

1822. Russell, Raymond Scott. "Writing Tasks to Be Utilized as Criteria for the Evaluation of the Writing Competency of Secondary School Students in a Selected Public School District." *DAI* 50 (December 1989): 1550A.

Identifies written tasks to be used as criteria for evaluating writing competency in public schools.

1823. Ruth, Leo, and Sandra Murphy. *Designing Writing Tasks for the Assessment of Writing*. Advances in Writing Research. Edited by Marcia Farr. Norwood, N.J.: Ablex, 1988. 336 pages

Reports the results of a series of investigations of the properties of writing tasks, their author's intentions, and the responses that these tasks evoked in student writers and the teachers who rated them.

1824. Siskind, Theresa G. *The Basic Skills Assessment Program, Spring 1987*. Annual Report, no. 87–24. Charleston, S.C.: Charleston County School District Office of Evaluation and Research, 1987. ERIC ED 303 467. 189 pages

Presents comparative results from countywide tests, including writing tests for grades six and eight.

1825. Slattery, Patrick Joseph. "Writing from Sources: How Students Intellectually Approach Multiple Points of View." *DAI* 50 (November 1989): 1297A.

Suggests that students view their sources as "closed," "open," or "analytical."

1826. Smith, Ernest. " 'It Doesn't Bother Me, but Sometimes It's Discouraging': Students Respond to Teachers' Written Responses." *JTW* (Special Issue 1989): 255–266.

Analyzes students' responses to marginal comments, reader-response questions, marks correcting mechanics, praise, and clear responses.

1827. Soltis, Judith M., and Herbert J. Walberg. "Thirteen-Year-Olds' Writing Achievements: A Secondary Analysis of the Fourth National Assessment of Writing." *JEdR* 83 (September–October 1989): 22–29.

Findings indicate that interest in writing can be altered in educational settings and that writing performance appears tied to peer group, gender, and instruction.

1828. Sommers, Jeffrey. "The Effects of Tape-Recorded Commentary on Student Revision: A Case Study." *JTW* 8 (Fall-Winter 1989): 49–76.

Tape-recorded commentary is "more understandable to students" and "encourages individualized instruction." Instructors' comments alternate with quoted revisions in drafts.

1829. Strange, Marliss G. "Rx: Writing (II)." *AM* 64 (November 1989): 663–664.

Sees the MCAT essay as encouraging students to value communication skills, language awareness, and sound writing skills.

1830. Stroble, Elizabeth J. "A Look at Writers' Comments Shared on Computer Screens: Can Electronic Mail Facilitate Peer-Group Response?" Paper presented at the AERA, New Orleans, April 1988. ERIC ED 297 723. 44 pages

Concludes that electronic mail sessions may function best as a complement to

rather than a substitute for face-to-face sessions when peer groups respond to student writing.

1831. Tiedemann, Joachim. "Measures of Cognitive Styles: A Critical Review." *EdPsy* 24 (Summer 1989): 261–275.

Proposes several limitations among analyses of cognitive styles. Argues that measures of cognitive style are better interpreted as measures of cognitive ability.

1832. Tyndall, Belle P. "Assessing Maturity of Expression in the Written Compositions of Caribbean Secondary School Students." *DAI* 49 (June 1989): 3710A.

Finds little significant difference between compositions on basic proficiency examinations written by non-college-bound students and general proficiency English examinations written by college-bound students.

1833. Valcourt, Gladys. "Inviting Rewriting: How to Respond to a First Draft." *EngR* 40 (1989): 22–28.

Offers three techniques: written dialogues, conferences, and reader reactions in the form of summaries, questions, commentary, and recommendations.

1834. Valcourt, Gladys. "Inviting Rewriting: How to Respond to a First Draft." *IlEB* 76 (Winter 1989): 40–49.

Discusses inappropriate feedback from a teacher to student writers and presents ways of commenting more effectively on students' work.

1835. VanderMolen, Johanna A. "Peer Identified Writing Strategies: An Experiment in Peer Versus Teacher Deliveries." *DAI* 49 (April 1989): 2920A.

Identifies three components in peer response: compliments or praise, evaluation logic, and elaboration. Finds no significant differences in peer- versus teacher-directed groups.

1836. Van der Vleuten, C. P. M., S. J. Van Luyk, and H. J. M. Beckers. "A Written Test as an Alternative to Performance Testing." *MEd* 23 (1989): 97–107.

Describes the statistical validity of using written tests and suggests situations in which they can be used.

1837. Woods, Donald R. "Ideas about Learning Assessment." *JCST* 19 (September–October 1989): 46–47.

Summarizes articles on problem solving in *Assessment and Evaluation in Higher Education* 13 (1988).

See also 638, 945, 1124, 1275, 1697, 1847

5.2 EVALUATION OF TEACHERS

1838. Kessell, Gwen H. "A Study of the Effect of Training on Observer Agreement in the Interpretation of Teacher Observation Data." *DAI* 49 (April 1989): 2877A.

Concludes that providing for multiple observations and a feedback report along with training increases agreement among observers.

1839. Watkins, Beverly T. "Researcher Nears Climax of Four-Year Project to Evaluate Schoolteachers." *CHE* 35 (5 July 1989): A3.

Lee Shulman's $2.1 million study focuses on elementary and secondary teachers but also has implications for the college level.

See also 1069

5.3 EVALUATION OF PROGRAMS

1840. Bernhardt, Stephen A., Penny Edwards, and Patti Wojahn. "Teaching College Composition with Computers: A Program Evaluation Study." *WC* 6 (January 1989): 108–133.

An evaluative study of 24 freshman composition classes (12 using computers and 12 not) based on multiple quantitative mea-

sures. Generally, results favored using computers in composition classes.

1841. Carroll, Dennis G. "The Status of Advanced Placement English in North Carolina." *DAI* 49 (April 1989): 2908A.

Surveys 146 teachers of AP English.

1842. Deal, Nancy, and John F. Beaver. "The Missing Link: Internships in Professional Writing Programs." Paper presented at the Eastern Educational Research Association, Savannah, Ga., February 1989. ERIC ED 302 855. 12 pages

Describes an instrument that assesses attitudes towards the professional writing major by participants in an internship program.

1843. Elmore, Norma B. "A Study of Advanced Placement English in Alabama Secondary Schools." *DAI* 49 (February 1989): 2169A.

Describes the status of AP courses and criteria for selecting AP teachers.

1844. Fleming, John P., and Carolyn S. Hollman. "The Self-Study as Catalyst: Evaluating a College Business Communication Program." *BABC* 52 (September 1989): 10–15.

Describes a method for evaluating undergraduate business communication programs. Includes an evaluation planning schedule.

1845. Grimm, Joseph E. "An Analysis of Achievement Test Scores to Determine the Effectiveness of a Remedial English Program in a Small University." *DAI* 49 (April 1989): 2954A.

Studies the program at Sul Ross State University.

1846. Mickler, Mary Louise, and Ann C. Chapel. "Basic Skills in College: Academic Dilution or Solution?" *JDEd* 13 (Fall 1989): 2–4, 16.

Reflects past, discusses present, and projects future viewpoints on the continued debate over the effectiveness and need for college developmental education programs.

1847. Olson, Gary A., Elizabeth Metzger, and Evelyn Ashton-Jones, eds. *Advanced Placement English: Theory, Politics, and Pedagogy.* Portsmouth, N.H.: Heinemann, 1989. 216 pages

Eleven essays that focus on practical aspects of creating an AP program based on current composition research. Discusses program effectiveness, test bias, and the uses that colleges should make of AP test results.

1848. Otte, George. "What Do Writing Teachers Think?" *WPA* 12 (Spring 1989): 31–42.

Presents the results of a survey taken of instructors at Baruch College "to determine how well developmental instruction meshed with instruction in the composition core."

1849. Rowshan, Cyrus. "Student, Alumni, and Faculty Perceptions of Quality-Related Characteristics of the Ph.D. in English (Rhetoric and Linguistics) at IUP." *DAI* 50 (July 1989): 128A.

Assesses perceptions about the quality-related characteristics of the English Ph.D. program at Indiana University of Pennsylvania.

See also 1090, 1124, 1394

5.4   OTHER

1850. Baldwin, Janet. "Validating the Factor Structure of Ratings Assigned to Essays: A Confirmatory Factor Analytic Approach." Paper presented at the AERA, New Orleans, April 1988. ERIC ED 302 571. 20 pages

Uses confirmatory factor analysis to examine the dimensionality of writing skills measured by a direct writing test.

1851. Ferrara, Steven F. "Practical Considerations in Equating a Direct Writing Assessment for High School Graduation." Paper presented

at the AERA, Washington, D.C., April 1987. ERIC ED 302 572. 7 pages

Discusses the steps in statistically equating scores from the direct writing assessment of the Maryland Writing Test.

1852. Greenberg, Karen, and Ginny Slaughter, eds. *Notes from the National Testing Network in Writing, Vol. 8.* New York: City University of New York Office of Academic Affairs, 1988. ERIC ED 301 888. 34 pages

A newsletter dealing largely with assessment and evaluation methods. Contains 32 abstracts of presentations made at the 1988 National Testing Network in Writing Conference. Authors are not indexed separately in this volume.

1853. Greenberg, Karen L. "The National Testing Network in Writing." *CompC* 2 (February 1989): 5.

Describes the history and function of the organization.

1854. Hunter, John E., and Frank L. Schmidt. *Methods of Meta-Analysis: Correcting Error and Bias in Research Findings.* Newbury Park, Calif.: Sage, 1989. 460 pages

Explains methods that are useful in integrating research findings across studies.

1855. Huot, Brian A. "The Validity of Holistic Scoring: A Comparison of the Talk-Aloud Protocols of Expert and Novice Holistic Raters." *DAI* 49 (February 1989): 2188A.

Examines holistic scoring processes to determine whether the procedure is obtrusive to scorers' reading and rating texts.

1856. McKenna, Marian J. "The Development and Validation of a Model for Text Coherency." Paper presented at the National Reading Conference, Tucson, November 1988. ERIC ED 302 830. 18 pages

Correlates six scales—cohesion, context, focus, grammar, intent, and structure—with Bamberg's scale for coherency. Finds that intent was the strongest predictor.

1857. Patience, Wayne, and Joan Auchter. "Establishing and Maintaining Score Scale Stability and Reading Reliability." Paper presented at the National Testing Network in Writing, Minneapolis, April 1988. ERIC ED 301 592. 40 pages

Describes methods used by the GED Testing Service to ensure continuity and comparability in the holistic scoring of essays.

Subject Index
Name Index

Subject Index

Numbers in the righthand column refer to sections and subsections (see Contents). For example, entries containing information on achievement tests appear in Section 5, Subsection 5.1 (Evaluation of Students). When the righthand column contains only a section number, information on the subject appears in several subsections. Entries addressing assignments in the classroom, for example, appear in several subsections of Section 4, depending on the kind of course for which the assignments are appropriate.

Name Index

This index lists authors for anthologized essays as well as authors and editors for main entries.

Walczyk, Jeffrey J., 917
Wald, Patricia B., 597
Waldman, Robert H., 1099
Walker, Cynthia J., 1003
Walker, James E., 1728
Walker, Jeffrey, 292
Wall, Susan V., 1764
Wallace, David, 619
Wallace, Karl R., 84
Wallace, Ray, 1283, 1720
Wallace, W. A., 1039
Wallace, Wanda T., 200
Wallace, William A., 293
Wallat, Cynthia, 108
Waller, Preston L., 219
Walsleben, Marjorie C., 1721
Walter, Timothy L., 1188
Walter-Burnham, Molly L., 697
Walters, Joel, 699, 741
Waltman, John L., 1500
Walton, H. J., 1650
Walzer, Arthur E., 220, 1501
Wan-Tatah, Victor, 708
Warloe, Constance, 1485
Warner, John D., 826
Warnock, John, 157
Warnock, Tilly, 1801
Warren, Beth, 198
Watkins, Beverly T., 1122, 1201, 1722, 1839
Watkins-Goffman, Linda, 1677
Watson-Gegeo, Karen, 1321
Watters, Kathleen Brittamart, 367
Weade, Regina, 108
Weaver, William, 499
Webb, Sarah J., 221
Weber, David, 850
Weber, James R., 30
Weber, Robert L., 969
Webster, Janice Gohm, 1088
Weightman, John, 598
Weimer, Maryellen, 1077
Weinberger, Steven Howard, 827
Weingartner, Charles, 780
Weinstein, Rhona S., 108
Weintraub, Robin Lynn, 222
Weiss, Timothy, 1502
Welp, Mary, 1123
Welsh, Thomas J., 1459
Wenzel, Joseph W., 333
Wepner, Shelley B., 1761
Werner, Warren W., 1318, 1558, 1559
West, John D., 861
West, Peter, 923

West, Richard F., 693
Wetherell, M., 207
Wetzel, K., 1233
Wheeler, Samuel C., III, 975
Whisler, Jo Sue, 886
White, Aaronette Michelle, 918
White, C. Stephen, 622
White, Edward M., 780, 1124
White, William Howard, 828
Whitehouse, Kevin, 642
Whiteley, John, 1188
Whitlow, J. W., Jr., 698
Whitson, Steve, 223, 294
Whittenberger-Keith, Kari Elise, 295
Widdowson, H. G., 818
Wiegand, Richard, 1503
Wiener, Harvey, 1254
Wierzbicka, Anna, 829
Wigginton, Eliot, 936
Wike, Terry, 2
Wilde, Sara, 1761
Wildermuth, Mark E., 296
Wilds, Nancy G., 157
Wilhoit, Stephen, 224
Wilkerson, B. C., 668
Wilkerson, LuAnn, 1105
Wilkins, David, 719
Willett, Cynthia J., 989
William, David, 368
Williams, Bonnie A., 650
Williams, Daniel Lee, 369
Williams, David Cratis, 209
Williams, David L., 43, 1769
Williams, J. P., 668
Williams, James D., 1089
Williams, M. P., 814
Willis, Meredith Sue, 1083
Willis, Wayne, 1323
Wills, Claire, 544
Willumson, Glenn Gardner, 1040
Wilson, David Edward, 1090
Wilson, Elizabeth Anne, 599
Wilson, Martena G., 1324
Wilson, Robert Anton, 830
Wilson, Susan R., 600
Winchell, Mark Royden, 946
Winkler, Victoria M., 19
Winne, Philip H., 937
Winograd, Peter, 172, 649
Winsor, Dorothy A., 225
Winsor, Jerry L., 456
Winspur, Steven, 975
Winter, Eugene, 77

WITHDRAWN